Introduction 2014 Copyright © Jenny Thompson
ISBN: 978-0-9906574-0-8
Cover Photograph, Evanston, IL, c. 1890, Courtesy Evanston History Center

Includes introduction and notes.

Summary: A new edition of Frances E. Willard's history of Evanston, first published in 1891.
With a new introduction by Jenny Thompson.

A CLASSIC TOWN:
THE STORY of EVANSTON

Frances E. Willard

Originally Published 1891

Edited by Jenny Thompson

Introduction

American Evanston:
A Look at Frances Willard's *A Classic Town*

Evanston, the idyllic little village

-Frances Willard[1]

In 1858, Frances Willard moved with her family to Evanston, Illinois, a place she called a "human oasis." Born in Churchville, New York, Willard arrived in Evanston at the age of eighteen after having lived in Oberlin, Ohio, and, for most of her childhood, in Janesville, Wisconsin. Along with her father, Josiah; her mother, Mary; her brother, Oliver; and her sister, Mary, she settled into the family's first Evanston home known as "Swampscott." Later, for the vast majority of her time in Evanston, she lived in the family's second Evanston home, located on Chicago Avenue and lovingly known as "Rest Cottage," (now a National Historic Landmark and museum). Although Willard would be gone for long periods, Evanston would remain her home for the rest of her life.

In 1891, when she published *A Classic Town*, Frances Willard was a world-renowned figure, head of the Woman's Christian Temperance Union, and a highly influential public intellectual and reformer, particularly focused on matters relating to women's rights and education. She had sixteen years of teaching under her belt, having taught at eleven institutions, including the Pittsburgh Female College, the Kankakee Academy, the Genesee Wesleyan Seminary, and the Evanston College for Ladies (where she also served as college president); she had also notably served as professor and first dean of women at Northwestern University, and she had written several books. Clearly, Willard was an accomplished woman of the world. So why did she set her sights on writing an account of what can be fairly described as a "local" subject, when her professional life took her across the country and around the world, speaking, organizing, and extending her tremendous influence?

Although Willard's history of Evanston bears an air of propriety and formality, *A Classic Town* is almost surely a product of the nostalgia Willard must have felt as the final decade of the nineteenth century got underway. She was taking an accounting, as it were, of the place that had seen her grow from a young woman into a professional, respected

1 Frances E. Willard, *Nineteen Beautiful Years, or Sketches of a Girl's Life*. New York: Fleming H. Revell Company, 1864. Revised. 1889, 184.

international figure of tremendous accomplishment. "I speak as one of the earliest pioneers who yet survive in Evanston," Willard announces in her introduction. Having lived in Evanston since the "period of antiquity," as she states, Willard notes how different the town had become in the little more than three decades since she "cast in my lot for all the rest of the time with this Methodist Cambridge of the prairies." No Northwestern University or Garrett Biblical Institute building standing today, she observed in 1891, with one exception, was present when she had arrived in Evanston, and, she remembers, "traces of an Indian trail were noted by antiquarian eyes along the shore." (p.33)

Writing was something that seemed to come naturally to Willard, and throughout her life she turned to writing when mourning a loss. After her sister's tragic death from tuberculosis at the age of nineteen, Willard published a tribute to her, *Nineteen Beautiful Years*, and after her mother's death, she published *A Great Mother: Sketches of Madam Willard*.[2] In some respects, Willard's history of Evanston is also tinged with a sense of loss, and it was perhaps fuelled by a desire to grant a sense of permanence to a place that had undergone dramatic change.

Thus, Willard embarks on a retrospect of the subject of her "ain hometown," in the words of Sir Walter Scott. Her account is infused with a mixture of nostalgia and wonder at the changes she herself had witnessed in a relatively brief period. And thus she reveals the underpinnings of her historical approach, what historian J.B. Jackson described as an impulse to memorialize the past that is dependent upon the "necessity for ruins."[3] Jackson argues that the act of bringing history into focus only once the past (or place, specifically) has been lost or transformed by time's passage is a particular American tendency. It is only once "the ruins" exist that the past can be "resurrected" in full glory; what is lost can then be reassessed and, in essence, created, with contemporary meanings and values bestowed upon it. Willard here is engaged in such an act; calling herself an "old timer," she surveys "the ruins" of Evanston as she begins to chronicle its past, recording the stories that belong to a place that has, in some respects, already vanished.

This is not to say that Willard is constructing Evanston's history out of whole cloth; nor is she maudlin in her accounting. In fact, she is full of praise and forward-looking energy throughout *A Classic Town*. Blending history with biography, she renders Evanston as a contemporary product of a very noble past.

Willard's attitude toward both past and future reveals her to be

---

2 Chicago: Woman's Temperance Publishing Association, 1894.
3 J. B. Jackson, *The Necessity for Ruins, and Other Topics*. Amherst, MA: University of Massachusetts Press, 1980.

quite rightly a product of her own historical moment. A late-nineteenth century, modern, educated woman, she not only celebrates the classical empires (and their beautiful ruins), but she also maintains a faithful belief in what she calls the "inevitable order of evolution" (p. 34). Willard, and so many of her age, perceived the "long road of progress" (p. 35) as the positive trajectory that had shaped and molded Evanston. The ruins of the past are not, therefore, tragic remnants. They are symbols of an America on the just and proper path leading to an ever brighter and better future.

In fact, the pervasive idea of progress in Willard's time was something she wholeheartedly embraced. For her, progress was a personal issue, especially as it related to women and girls, and she viewed education and the attainment of rights as keys to moving forward. Willard's own education, so important to her both personally and as a matter of equality for women in general, although not begun in 1858 by any means, had been truly nurtured in Evanston. Her family had supported the (radical at the time) idea that girls should be educated, and both Frances and her younger sister Mary had been afforded the opportunity to attend college. In 1857, they attended the Milwaukee Female College, where their aunt, Sarah Hill, was a professor of history, and the next year, they enrolled in Northwestern Female College in Evanston, from which Frances would graduate in 1859.

As a student, Willard was both serious and dynamic, known for her many talents, but also for her approach to life—her insatiable hunger for knowledge. For her,

> [s]tudy did not end with the abandonment of the classroom, but, as she had planned, went on in new forms, and with the intent and intensity of original research. Her schoolmates when they visited her in her quiet little room, with its bright south and east windows brimming the cosy (sic) nook with warm sunshine, found her always at her desk with books, paper and pen, for with her independent mind, the thoughts and investigations of others were not properly her own until she had fixed them in the mold of personal judgment, and phrased them in the forceful language of her own opinions.[4]

Given her desire to think and investigate, it is no surprise that Willard did not remain static, despite her deep love for her family and her strong attachment to her home. Indeed, she moved several times, taking on a

---

4 Anna Adams Gordon, *The Beautiful Life of Frances E. Willard: A Memorial Volume*. Chicago: Woman's Temperance Publishing Association, 1898; 43.

variety of teaching posts in Illinois and New York. She also traveled, the first time in 1868 when she undertook a tour of "the continent" with her friend, Kate Jackson. But it was always to Evanston that she would return. There, she would remain deeply involved in the community of her church, the first Methodist Episcopal Church, of the university, and of the lives of the citizens who were, after all, her neighbors. Lucky for her, (and for Evanston), that the town itself was a place that was fairly enlightened in terms of the opportunities allowed to women. Although Evanston was quite conservative in terms of ideals of morality and fairly rigid in relation to the boundaries of social class, the moral and intellectual framework provided by the Methodist Episcopal Church (the basis for the town's two most important institutions: Northwestern University and the Garret Biblical Institute) provided a unique foundation for a strong, intelligent woman like Willard.

Deeply religious, Willard was a product of her church's community: she extolled the virtues of the Methodist lessons of mutual support and moral sanctity. To do well and to be well one needed not only one's God and church, but also one's community. Evanston, with its many churches and highly educated leaders, must have endlessly inspired Willard. That is not to say that she did not run up against a great deal of sexism as she attempted to wield her authority as dean of women at Northwestern. Indeed, looking at the lists of trustees and supporters of the various institutions where she taught, one remarks on the larger landscape she inhabited: Frances Willard's name on the rosters of these institutions usually stands out as that of the only woman so listed.

But whatever frustrations she endured (partially the reason she would quit academia altogether in 1874), she also found nourishment in her hometown. And thus, in many ways, with this history, Willard was doing more than recording the people and institutions of the place she called home. She was engaging in an act of civic pride. In the 1890s, the United States was in the midst of an era of accelerated industrialism. The effects of America's growth into a new, modern nation, formed in the post-bellum period, with its urban growth, increased immigration, labor demands, and a host of other political and cultural issues, were not lost even on the "sanctified" cultured town of Evanston and its roughly 12,000 citizens. It was a time when Progressive reformers would fervently tackle the issues facing the country in an effort to better the state of affairs of a rapidly growing nation. And Evanston, known for its attempts at cultivated high morality, civic virtue, and works of good will, was uniquely suited to act on the same reformist impulses.

Just outside of the vast metropolis of Chicago, Evanston was geographically the big city's suburb. But it was also a place quite unto itself. At the time of Willard's writing, the town of Evanston, which had been incorporated in 1863, was not yet thirty years old. In fact, it was still two towns: Evanston (which had absorbed the village of North Evanston in 1874) and South Evanston, which would exist as its own village until it was annexed in 1892 to become part of Evanston proper.

In the years since Evanston had been platted— after Northwestern University was chartered in 1851 and the university established in Evanston in 1853— the village had grown from a rural, swampy wilderness into a place of cultured institutions.

"Evanston differs from many suburbs — notably lake-shore suburbs—in respect to the manner in which it is laid out," Everett Chamberlin noted in his 1874 history of the region:

> Its streets run at right angles, and show no suspicion of a curve either to the right or left. In keeping with the sober character of the men who went into the speculation away back in 1838, the curved lines which form the distinguishing traits of some suburbs met with no approval. Evanston bears the stamp of its devoutly-inclined founders. Its garb is cut as squarely as though it were of "the cloth," and its morals are as strict as those of a New England village. By a wise calculation, the founders of the University inserted a provision in its charter providing that for a distance of four miles from the University building it should not be lawful to sell liquor of an intoxicating kind. The residents of Evanston are, therefore, compulsory teetotalers, so far as public drinking is concerned. The fact is to be commended — the law is strictly enforced, and apparently willingly obeyed.[5]

What Chamberlin describes, the "four mile rule," which made the sale of liquor illegal in the area surrounding Northwestern University, was not only why many outsiders would come to view Evanston as a "respectable, sober, prosperous town."[6] It was also, in fact, the manifestation of the founders' and civic leaders' intent: to engineer a village where the moral, intellectual, and religious could thrive. No wonder then that Willard, herself a fervent supporter of temperance, would view

---
5 Everett Chamberlin, *Chicago and Its Suburbs*. Chicago: T. A. Hungerford and Co., 1874, 381.
6 Ibid.

the success of Evanston's ban on alcohol as just one more reason for the town's trajectory on the road of "progress."

After the Chicago fire in 1871, Evanston had undergone a population boom. In particular, wealthy professionals and industrialists found its serene vistas and broad lake-front property too good to resist, and wishing to escape the city, they ensured that the town would burgeon in the years after the American Civil War, an event that provided Evanston with no little drama and patriotic fervor in its citizenry's support for the Union. (And the war, of course, is chronicled in Willard's volume.)

Historically, Willard's book is rooted in that same period of change after the Civil War: it is a record of the history of an American town at a time when America itself was fully acknowledging its own history. It was after the American Civil War, as historian John Franklin Jameson noted, that "the dominant impulse" of historical writing in the United States moved "toward a closer, and especially a broader, study of our own history."[7] American historians began to shift from focusing largely on Classical and European history to examining the American scene, a change that was owed in part to the sense that after the war, the United States had become a new, united nation. It was indeed "whole" in its truest form. At the same time, the shift was also simply the product of the passage of time. After a century, the American scene was long enough to be chronicled, and efforts to record and preserve its history multiplied. By 1891, just fifteen years had passed since America had celebrated its centennial, and that event would also spur more Americans to view their past as something to be honored.

Willard was one such American. As a witness to decades of "progress" unfolding in America, she saw in Evanston's history the country's story writ small. This was a town built by pioneering Americans, her history suggests. As she notes, many of Evanston's leading citizens hailed from Eastern states, such as Massachusetts, New York, or Ohio. Their move "west," as Illinois would be characterized well into the nineteenth century, meant that they were true pioneers. These were people who sought to better their lives, and many of them came to Evanston supported by the strong ties of the Methodist church with its broad network spanning out from New York and into the prairie. These new pioneers were not only out for their own betterment, but singularly focused on shaping their own wider community-- not very differently from the ways other communal groups attempted to shape their communities in places such as Oneida, New York; Brook Farm,

---

7 John Franklin Jameson, *The History of Historical Writing in America*, Cambridge, MA: The Riverside Press, 1891, 2.

Massachusetts; or Oberlin Colony, Ohio.[8]

Having built their schools and churches, crafted their laws, and literally laid out the shape of their town, Evanston's leaders wanted, by the 1890s, to ensure that their efforts would be chronicled and preserved. By the 1890s, Midwestern communities and towns were now founding their own historical societies, taking the lead from the East Coast, where historical societies had been established decades earlier. The Massachusetts Historical Society, founded in 1791, was the first of numerous societies founded throughout the early and mid nineteenth century. The "west" (Illinois) was much younger than its East Coast counterparts, and would take longer to recognize the need for the preservation of its history. Indeed, Willard's book would appear seven years before the Evanston Historical Society was founded in 1898.

A prolific writer, Willard thus put pen to paper to write and compile the material for *A Classic Town* out of a personal, but also practical need to do so. At the time, no other history of Evanston had been published. Evanston had been chronicled within larger histories of the region, such as Everett Chamberlin's 1874 *Chicago and Its Suburbs* and Alfred Theodore Andreas' 1884 *History of Cook County, Illinois: From the Earliest Period to the Present Time*.[9] These accounts were not shy in flattering Evanston's citizens. Chamberlin, in particular, offers a glowing description: "Some twelve miles northward from the city of Chicago, beautifully located on the lake shore, stands important, intellectual, ambitious, wealthy Evanston," Chamberlin wrote. "The most considerable in size and population of any of the suburbs that surround the city, Evanston, by reason of the enterprise of its inhabitants, and the eligibility of its location, seems determined to maintain in the future the proud position which it has secured in the past."[10]

Its past was, for Willard, one of Evanston's most important features, never mind that its history had not yet been officially recorded in its own full volume. Of course, those who lived in and built the city had engaged in a steady, if incomplete, recording of its history over the years, particularly in publications issued by Evanston's flagship institution, Northwestern University, but also in other more

8 In fact, the Willard family had originally come west from New York via Oberlin, Ohio, where both of Willard's parents attended Oberlin College. The family next moved to Janesville, Wisconsin, where the rural and idyllic life of the farmer was shored up by the nearby Methodist Church. Jane Robson Graham. 2008. *The Ideally Active: Frances Willard's Pedagogical Ministry*. PhD Dissertation, University of Kansas. Ann Arbor: ProQuest/UMI. (Publication No. AAT 3349895), 35.
9 Everett Chamberlin, *Chicago and Its Suburbs*. Chicago: T. A. Hungerford and Co., 1874. Alfred Theodore Andreas, *History of Cook County, Illinois: From the Earliest Period to the Present Time*. Chicago: A. T. Andreas, 1884.
10 Chamberlin, 378.

specialized publications. In 1887, photographer Alexander Hesler, who called Evanston home for several years, published a sort of visual love letter to Evanston in his *Photographic Views of Picturesque Evanston*.[11] Other more esoteric volumes related to Evanston include Charles S. Raddin's *Catalogue of the Phaenogamous Plants of Evanston and Vicinity, for 1883*,[12] and the utilitarian *Connorton's Evanston Directory*, published in various editions through the 1880s and into the 1890s, and which, the publisher noted, "embrac[es] a complete list of the residents and business houses, together with miscellaneous information about Evanston, South Evanston and Rogers Park."[13]

As the first full account of Evanston's history, *A Classic Town* combines aspects of all the above volumes; Willard's own love letter extols the town's virtues as she chronicles its history from its architecture to "personalia," from anecdotes to its very flora and fauna. In some respects, her history reads as a kind of directory itself, where the leaders of churches and educational institutions are described (and heralded). To this end, she opens her volume with a discussion of which Evanston citizens are deserving of streets named after them. Indeed, and of course, her biographies of the various people she chronicles contain no hint of criticism; they are pure acts of apotheosis. And, significantly, Willard also underscores the great and important contributions made by the town's female population. While some of the people she chronicles are her own closest friends and in some cases relatives, (her mother, sister, and sister-in-law are among those included in the book), she refrains from too much personal commentary, even in the case of listing the biography of her erstwhile fiancé, Charles H. Fowler. (Like some of the other accounts in the book, Fowler's biography is not written by Willard herself, but drawn from another source).

In drawing on the accounts and memories from a variety of Evanston citizens, Willard thus serves as a true local historian; she is compiler of history as much as she is a writer of history. Having solicited the letters and accounts that she includes in this volume, she brings together various parts of Evanston's past into a single volume. In her preface she notes that she has simply attempted "to preserve some dates, facts and personalities for the use of that staid and dignified individual who will in due season materialize, i.e., 'The Future Historian' " (p. 29)

11 Alexander Hesler, *Photographic Views of Picturesque Evanston*. Chicago: Hesler's Photo Art Gallery, 1887.
12 Charles S. Raddin, *Catalogue of the Phaenogamous Plants of Evanston and Vicinity, for 1883*. Evanston, IL: R. Vandercook, 1883.
13 *Connorton's Evanston Directory*. Chicago: J. W. Connerton and Co., 1880. One year after *A Classic Town* was published, a biography of one of the city's founders was issued: *Orrington Lunt: The Discoverer of Evanston*. Evanston, IL: Evanston Press, 1892.

That future historian is someone who might well pick up this volume today. What she or he will read on these pages may appear as a pure product of its time and its perspective may seem quite limited: where, after all, are the accounts of the Native American populations? While Willard notes that she is not reaching far back into the days of "Indians," she seems not concerned with the fact that in 1891, Native Americans were, of course, relevant to the history of Evanston. It had been just sixty years since the Treaty of Prairie Du Chien had relegated many Native Americans to areas outside of the land that became Evanston, and, at the time Willard wrote, the very land deals and the carving up of Evanston property were still playing out. Indeed, the town itself had been profoundly shaped by the relationship between the U.S. government (and Evanston residents) and the Native Americans who once called the land later named Evanston their home. Was this "progress"? For many, this unmentioned aspect of Evanston's history constitutes a shameful chapter of the American story.

Further, Willard's history is entirely focused on the prosperous, land-owing classes. No laborer or domestic servant is asked for his or her memories of the town. African-Americans, although a sizeable percentage of the town's population, are almost absent from *A Classic Town*, with only a few small exceptions. Willard mentions the Second Baptist Church of Evanston, which had an African-American congregation, and she also lists the society known as the "Willard WCTU," which was comprised of African-American women, and whom, she notes, had been "invited to belong to the original society, but preferred to form one by themselves" (p. 139).

History is a "dissecting process," as Willard asserts. And so it is. For those of us who turn to *A Classic Town* to dissect the story of the past, one finds in all its glorified accounts of great men and women, a clear sense of pride and a glowing regard for all that "progress" has achieved. But it is in the way that Willard has crafted this history—with its many uncomfortable absences—that *A Classic Town* can be seen as a truly American history; it is a story of the past that is a product of its time. It is not a full or entire history of a place. But in its selective focus, in its rhetoric, and in its intention, we, today, can peer into one version of the past, as it were. Like all histories, *A Classic Town* must be read and dissected by those future historians whom Willard imagined; it must be read and understood from our perspective today. American Evanston, I call this introduction, because *A Classic Town* is very much a product of its time and place; it is local history, through and through, but it is also shaped by the cultural mores of the nation at the time. It is a volume that is rooted in a particular period in the history of the United States and the very ways its tone, narrative, and attitude toward history are presented and constructed reveal something about the ways some Americans, and to be sure, some Evanstonians, have understood themselves and attempted to preserve themselves for the future. It is up to us, as readers today, to be discerning. After this volume is read, we can to turn to others, to broaden the story, and perhaps, we can even take up the pen ourselves and add our own accounts for those future historians to come.

    Jenny Thompson
    Evanston, Illinois, 2014

A Note on the Text

This new edition of *A Classic Town* presents Willard's original text from the volume published in 1891. The images and photographs included here are those that were included in that original volume. Willard made notes to the text, which are also included as endnotes in this volume. New notes to the material are also included. The original notes to the text made by Willard are identified by the use of her initiatls "F.E.W.," which she used in the original text.

CONTENTS.

Introduction, 7
Preface, 29
Dedication, 30
The Prohibitory Clause, 31
Introductory, 33
Evanston As It Is, 37
Earliest Memories, 40
Discovery and Purchase of Evanston, 44
Garrett Biblical Institute, 46
Origin of Northwestern University, 57
Preparatory Department, 66
Science Hall, 66
Dearborn Observatory, 68
Northwestern Female College And Its Evolutions, 69
Corporate Records, 75
Our Public Schools, 77
The Grove School, 81
The Methodist Women's Centenary Association, 83
Evanston's Churches, 86
Our Congregational Church, 87
Our Episcopal Church, 93
Our Presbyterian Church, 96
The German Evangelical Lutheran Church, 100
Our Methodist Church, 101
Our Baptist Church, Its Origin and Evolution, 116
Emmanuel M. E. Church, 118
Other Churches, 118
Evanston Township High School, 120
Our Literary People, 124
Evanston Societies, 125
Iota Omega, 125
Secret Societies, 130
Temperance Societies, 131
Literary Societies, 131
College Fraternities, 131
Miscellaneous, 131
Church Societies, 131
Evanston's Waterworks, 133
Evanston and Temperance, 135

Evanston in The War, 141
Evanston in Politics, 147
A Student's Point of View, 151
Letters From Deans Bancroft and Dean Sanford, 157
Our Libraries, 164
Northwestern University Library, 164
Free Public Library, 164
The Desplaines Camp Ground, 166
Personalia, 169
Orrington Lunt, 169
Dr. John Evans, 171
Major Edward H. Mulford, 173
L. I. Greenleaf, 176
Luella Clark, 179
Dr. John Dempster, 179
Rev. Dr. and Mrs. Kidder, 181
The Bannisters, 185
Rev. Dr. Henry Bannister, 187
Extracts, 191
Rev. Dr. Francis D. Hemenway, 193
Rev. Dr. Miner Raymond, 198
Bishop Simpson, 202
Henry Bascom Ridgaway, D.D., 206
Rev. Charles F. Bradley, 210
Rev. Milton S. Terry, 210
Rev. Dr. Charles W. Bennett, 211
Charles Horswell, 213
Nels E. Simonsen, 213
Clarke T. Hinman, 214
Bishop Foster, 215
Early Life of Bishop Foster, 216
Erastus O. Haven, 222
Charles H. Fowler, 223
Oliver Marcy, 224
Rev. Joseph Cummings, 224
Henry Wade Rogers, 231
Professors of the University, 234
Daniel Bonbright, 234
Julius F. Kellogg, 235
Herbert F. Fisk, 235
Robert Mclean Cumnock, 236

Robert Baird, 237
Charles W. Pearson, 237
Robert D. Sheppard, 238
Abram V. E. Young, 238
Charles S. Cook, 239
George Washington Hough, 239
James Taft Hatfield, 240
Eliakim H. Moore, 240
Deans of the Woman's College, 241
Other University People, 244
Bishop Thomson, 245
Bishop Harris in Evanston, 248
Edward Eggleston, 250
Father Wheadon, 254
William Deering, 256
William Frederick Poole, 257
Rev. Robert W. Patterson, 260
Orange Judd, 261
William S. Lord, 262
The Kirk Family, 263
James S. Kirk, 265
Bishop William Xavier Ninde, 266
John B. Finch, 268
Lorado Taft, Sculptor, 268
Some Former Evanstonians, 269
Some Women of Evanston, 270
Silhouettes, 277
C.G. Ayars, 277
Harry L. Belden, 277
General John L. Beveridge, 277
Professor H. L. Boltwood, 277
L. H. Boutell, 278
M. C. Bragdon, 278
A. J. Brown, 278
D. H. Burnham, 278
Alonzo Burroughs, 278
H. W. Chester, 279
E. H. Clapp, 279
E. P. Clapp, 279
W. P. Cragin, 279
F. P. Crandon, 279

James Currey, 279
Dr. N. S. Davis, 280
Simeon L. Farwell, 280
Julian R. Fitch, 280
Volney W. Foster, 281
General William Gamble, 281
C. J. Gilbert, 281
Mark Watroo Harrington, 284
C. G. Haskins, 284
Henry B. Hemenway, 284
Alexander Hesler, 285
Isaac R. Hitt, 285
Thomas C. Hoag, 285
Holmes Hoge, 286
George W. Hotchkiss, 286
Hon. Harvey B. Hurd, 286
Lewis Iott, 286
M. Bates Iott, 287
S. A. Kean, 287
J. H. Kedzie, 287
Mather D. Kimball, 287
Prof. H. H. Kingsley, 287
John B. Kirk, 288
Marshall M. Kirkman, 288
Oren E. Locke, 288
Thomas Lord, 288
Dr. O. H. Mann, 289
David S. McMullen, 289
O. H. Merwin, 289
George W. Muir, 289
C. R. Paul, 289
William B. Phillips, 290
Professor Charles Raymond, 290
C. H. Remy, 290
George F. Stone, 291
Allen Vane, 291
E. H. Webster, 291
Mr. T. K. Webster, 291
Col. E. S. Weeden, 291
The Natural History of Evanston, 292
Geology, 292

Botony, 293
Zoology, 293
University, 294
Copy of the First Subscriptions Made and Now Shown in the University Ledger, 295
The College Cottage, 296
Institute, 296
The Withington School, 297
Mary B. Willard Kindergarten, 297
Our Newspapers, 298
Authors and Journalists, 299
The Post Office, 302
The Business Men's Association, 303
The Citizens League, 303
Y.M.C.A., 304
G.A.R., 304
The Lighthouse, 304
The Life Saving Station, 305
The First Grace at Rosehill Cemetery, 306
South Evanston, 307
Notes, 312

FRANCES WILLARD

A CLASSIC TOWN:
THE STORY of EVANSTON

By "an Old Timer"

Frances E. Willard

"Breathes there a man with soul so dead
He never to himself said,
'This is my ain familiar town?'"

~Sir Walter Scott, "The Lay of the Last Mintrel," (1805)

PREFACE

The only satisfaction that I have in contemplating this desultory piece of work is that, as a loyal Evanstonian, and pioneer pilgrim to this human oasis, I have helped to preserve some dates, facts and personalities for the use of that staid and dignified individual who will in due season materialize, *i.e.,* "The Future Historian."

Finally, to "Evanston proper," Evanston South, North and West, Evanston as she was, and is, and is to be, let me offer the humble and earnest good wishes of her affectionate and loyal daughter,

Frances E. Willard,

Rest Cottage, 1891.

TO
ORRINGTON LUNT,
THE
DISCOVERER OF EVANSTON,
AND TO
EX-GOVERNOR JOHN EVANS WHOSE NAME OUR VILLAGE BEARS,
THIS HUMBLE RECORD OF ITS PAST
IS
DEDICATED

THIS HAS KEPT EVANSTON FREE FROM SALOONS
AND MOTEL BARS
FOR WELL-NIGH FORTY YEARS.

"No spirituous, vinous, or fermented liquors shall be sold under license or otherwise, within four miles of the location of said University, except for medicinal, mechanical, and sacramental purposes, under penalty of twenty-five dollars for each offense, to be recovered before any justice of the Peace of said County of Cook."

—From Charter of Northwestern University.

INTRODUCTORY.

Evanston is now the most popular as well as the most populous suburb of Chicago, and the literary center of the great Northwest. The date of its christening is February 3, 1854, and its thirty-seventh year has already ended. Four years after the village was named and platted, and when it numbered hardly more than five hundred inhabitants, my parents came here to live; here their three children were graduated, and from here three of the five who constituted our family have been laid to rest in Rosehill Cemetery.

But very likely it would never have occurred to me to try to put on record the history of the town that has been my home since I was eighteen years of age, had not Rev. Dr. Ridgaway, President of Garrett Biblical Institute,[1] asked me to speak to the students on the anniversary of Mrs. Garrett's (the founder's) birthday in 1886. For that occasion I wrote a familiar sort of "retrospect," and out of it has grown this more extended yet wholly informal account of the origin, history and present condition of our well-beloved town.

I speak as one of the earliest pioneers who yet survive in Evanston. No professor in Institute or University carries his experience of local chronology backward to a period of antiquity so remote as the spring of 1858, at which date I cast in my lot for all the rest of the time, with this Methodist Cambridge of the prairies. The University was but three years and a half old then, the Garrett Biblical Institute some six months older. Not a building now pertaining to either institution was visible save the preparatory department, which, shorn of half its present glories, stood, in glaring white, on the corner facing the home of Mr. T. C. Hoag, and was, in and of itself, "the university." The campus was bare of fences or buildings as the aborigines had left it, and traces of an Indian trail were noted by antiquarian eyes along the shore.

Several animate abridged editions of the rise and progress of Evanston are still accessible to the student of local history. All of it they have seen and part of it they have been. "On the ridge" they have lived anywhere between forty and fifty years, having at an early day drawn up their feet out of the swamps on either side, by which less hardy pioneers had been discouraged, and planted them upon the firm vantage ground of what later comers have developed into Evanston's most aristocratic street.

We will not try to penetrate the legendary period still more remote, when Indians skimmed the great lake in their skiffs, and wigwams wafted their smoke to the skies from among the trees that crown the college campus. After the Indian, came, in the inevitable order of evolution, the hunter and trapper, the soldier and trader; but all these periods, well accentuated as they are in Chicago's history, left small impress on the wilds of Evanston. It is the pioneer who built a home and tilled the peaceful acres his industry had won with whom all actual history begins.

Let us try to picture to ourselves that early day when there was no Evanston, but when the headland, now surmounted by our lighthouse, gave to the territory as far south as Graceland Cemetery the name "Grosse Point," and from the ridge to the lake was one truly "dismal swamp," without a road, and but faintly humanized here and there by the home-hearth of a log cabin.

The first road across the swamp was built at Rosehill by Mr. Samuel Reed,[2] who still dwells among us, the almost immemorial "pathfinder," or roadmaster of this region. A local chronicler gave to the public some time ago an account of the Reed family and its early experiences, which may fairly be taken as a type. Their log house was on the ridge, nearly opposite the present site of the South Evanston[3] railroad station. It was surrounded by water a good share of the time, and an old-fashioned cradle in which Mrs. Reed had rocked her first-born was used by her boys as a boat in which to go duck-shooting. In ranging over to the lake shore to look after his cattle, Mr. Reed was wont to wade through water up to his waist. Game was abundant and the enterprising housewife arranged a trap near by with a rope tied to her kitchen window from which it could be sprung. In this ingenious fashion she did her marketing almost as conveniently as modern matrons do by telephone; twenty-one prairie chickens at one fell swoop having become her prey. She used to see the agile deer go by in herds, and one day, by way of reprisal, a big wolf slipped into her barn-yard and before a gun could interrupt his mad career had snatched a squealing pig away. Mrs. Reed laughingly describes her little home with its loose board floor, and its roughly-chinked crevices through which the wind was wont to whistle, and tells of climbing the ladder to the loft on winter mornings and brushing the snow off her children's bed before she awakened them.

This enterprising woman planted an apple tree near her house over forty years ago that usually furnishes its thirty-bushel quota of choice fruit and is the only landmark of those good old times.

A picture like this shows at first glance how long is the road of progress that has been trod, with sometimes halting, sometimes striding steps, by our lovable old town. A few of these fast-fading daguerreotypes I hope to preserve in these pages, to be pointed out to visitors and future comers, along with the queer, gnarled oak and the bowlder with a history on the college campus, the university buildings and the Sheridan Road.

A CLASSIC TOWN

THE STORY of EVANSTON
BY "AN OLD TIMER."

EVANSTON AS IT IS.

History-writing is a dissecting process; therefore, before tearing apart the petals, let us mark for a moment the flower as a whole; let us have a glimpse of Evanston as the June sun finds it now. Of course the Evanston shore has its ice-bound days and its nights when thunderous waves beat ceaselessly. But the picture that is bright on memory's walls for those who no longer call Evanston their home, is not of these. It is of a quiet city that still prefers to call itself a village; kissed on one cheek by Michigan's waves, fanned from behind by prairie breezes, jeweled with happy homesteads set in waving green, and wreathed about with prairie wild flowers, a town as comely as a bride, even to strangers' eyes. The peculiar glory of the village is its trees—its long avenues bordered with wide-spreading elms and maples and grand old oaks, that stood proud sentinels over Indian wigwams in ages past. Broad streets bordered with parks and walks that run by unfenced velvet lawns, tell of freedom and peaceful security. A large fountain plays on the public square, and about a small park a block or two away are clustered three churches and a fine club house, while the stately Methodist spire is not far to seek. The college campus by the shore is still a grove of massive oaks amid which stand the noble buildings of the university. Winding along the beach, by the jaunty boat house and life-saving station, skirting the campus, runs the famous new driveway from Chicago— Sheridan Road—which, half a mile north of the college halls, passes the waterworks and lighthouse and leaves Evanston to pursue its winding way to Fort Sheridan. Count half a dozen blocks of stores, half a score of smaller churches, four spacious public school buildings and a fine high school, and fill in the rest with comfortable and often palatial homes for about twelve thousand people, and you have a faint outline of the picture which Evanstonians love.

Evanston; how wholly unexceptionable is this familiar designation! Suppose it had been *Evanstown,* as some profane ones have been known to write it, or *Evansville,* as my letters are not unfrequently addressed— the choiceness would be gone. Let us applaud the rare discernment that invented a name not then borne by any town on earth and since then by but one,—Evanston, Wyoming,—doubtless named in honor of our own. Consider, too, the wise adaptedness of the university's cognomen. It was then embodied prophecy; it is embodied history now. Men of more restricted vision planned a "Chicago" and a "Lake Forest" University, but our trustees looking with prescient gaze adown the future's mystic maze, saw "all the wonder that should be" in that "long result of time," of which we have seen nearly forty years, and wrote, not "Excelsior" but "Northwestern" on their banners. Mighty as the word was then, it is an hundredfold more mighty now. The old Northwest stopped with Minnesota, Iowa and Kansas; the new Northwest stretches to Puget Sound and the Pacific Sea. But iron links now tie those gigantic young commonwealths "where flows the Oregon" to the electric city beside Lake Michigan. Northwestern's vigorous sons and dauntless daughters are out yonder; I have found them as far away as my adventurous feet have wandered, and always they were preaching, teaching, toiling to lay broad and deep foundations for Christianity, for education and for the protection of the home.

Figure-heads have their value as character lessons, and enshrined history tells upon a town. When I visited Concord, Mass., it pleased and instructed me not a little to find its whole heroic story "writ large" on bowlder, tablet and emblazoned window, for the wayfaring man's especial benefit.

As a rule our college buildings have names that are significant. That noble pile called University Hall might well bear the name of some great light once with us, but now passed to holier regions, and the "Woman's College" will no doubt become "— Hall" some day;[4] while Science Hall should be called after him (or her) who built it, whenever that modest name shall be divulged.[5] Garrett Biblical Institute forever enshrines the memory of an earnest-hearted, Christian woman, Mrs. Elizabeth Garrett, whose husband was mayor of Chicago in 1843-46,[6] and who willed her fortune to the training of theological students in a day when our church lacked facilities in this regard more than in any other. Barbara Heck, "Founder of American Methodism," was honored by associating her name with Heck Hall in 1866, the one hundredth year after her "call" to Philip Embury, the neglectful young preacher in New York City, who had "fallen away" until her expostulations aroused his conscience.[7] Memorial Hall enshrines in the rich but chastened light of its great windows three of Evanston's most hallowed names:—Dempster, Bannister, and Hemenway, of the Institute, and two of our honored citizens, Queal and Button. The Dearborn Observatory, built by Hon. J. B. Hobbs, reminds us of a prince in our Israel, and I hope the name of L. I. Greenleaf, the past, and William Deering, the present Maecenas[8] of our town, may yet be associated with the institution they have done so much to build.

Significant figures rather than ciphers are good means by which to designate a street. Thus we have "Orrington Avenue," for the discoverer of Evanston, and our chief business thoroughfare is named for Dr. N. S. Davis, once a resident here, and for well nigh half a century the chief physician in the northwest. We have already Greenleaf Avenue; while Hinman Avenue enshrines the memory of our university's first president. I would we had Noyes Avenue, rather than street, for that great man who bore the brunt of battle as "acting president of the university" for many years, and laid his life upon its altar. Surely, too, the names of Bishops Simpson and Harris, Fowler, Thompson and Ninde, all of whom have been residents here, and all connected with our institutions, should be, as that of Bishop Foster already is, perpetually associated with our municipality, if not with our university nomenclature. Chicago Avenue, a name of small appropriateness, will, probably, one day be exchanged for some other that embalms more of local history, and it would be well if, in addition to Hamilton, Botsford and Brown, other honored names of Evanston's heroic fathers, including Judges Goodrich and Hurd, and those later but not less devoted trustees, the lamented Robert J. Queal and James S. Kirk, might be preserved perpetually here. I am glad there is a Judson Avenue, recalling that wise and witty chief, whose mind had the rare scintillant quality and whose manner the quaint originality that is so unforgettable and so refreshing. But Rev. Philo Judson, the man who at sixty-nine years of age had not a gray hair; whose constant cheer carried him so many years as a circuit rider through the wilds of Illinois, making hard work perpetual holiday; whose powers of observation were so keen that in his last agonizing illness, being unable to turn his head that he might look out of the window, he had a mirror brought that he might watch the falling snow—he merits a chapter by himself.

I am sincerely glad we have the "Haven School" in memory of Dr. Otis Haven, that bright and brotherly intelligence, beloved by all of us as few men are, who passed away in the glorious morning of his prime and left no voice behind that was not charmed to speak his praise.

For the rest we have Wesley Avenue and Wesley public school, as a town with Evanston's traditions could hardly be pardoned if it had not; and Asbury, for the first Methodist bishop in America.

For patriotism we have Washington, Lincoln and Colfax streets,—the last two furnishing indications altogether accurate concerning Evanston's prevailing politics!—while honored early settlers will be forever associated with our classic suburb by such streets as Mulford and Crain, Benson and McDaniel, Kedzie and Lyons.

EARLIEST MEMORIES.

The first schoolhouse and church of our little pioneer settlement was a log cabin of small dimensions which stood near where Mr. Charles Crain now lives, in South Evanston.[9] The school teachers were hired by individual subscriptions, the ministers were Methodist itinerants, and they all "boarded around." The first quarterly conference of the M. E. Church in Evanston was held in this house in July 1854. The preaching and teaching, the frolics and spelling bees that came off in that old log schoolhouse recall the frontier stories familiar to us all as among the most redeeming features of the olden time. Speaking of this historic cabin, Mrs. John L. Beveridge says:

"The first Sunday we went there to church [1854] the congregation numbered fourteen people, young and old, men and women. My mother, myself and Mrs. John A. Pearsons, I think, were the only women that had on bonnets such as ladies wear now; the rest had on large sun-bonnets and were dressed in primitive style. A Methodist minister who came through from Vermont, on his way to Minnesota, was appointed by the presiding elder as our pastor. His name was characteristic of everything about him—John G. Johnson. He was a tall, lank individual, dressed in dark blue cotton overalls, with large patches of new cloth on each knee, while the rest of the cloth had been washed until it was almost white. He always carried a big blue cotton umbrella, bulged in the center."

Mr. B. F. Hill,[10] now of Llewellyn Park, our newest suburb, has written a very interesting sketch of his residence in this locality, going back even so far as 1836. I must give some of his words just as he wrote them:

"Following the lake shore north as far as Mr. Westerfield's present residence,[11] we came to a tavern kept by Joel Stebbins. This building, I think, tumbled off into the lake about 1838. Mr. Stebbins afterward built a log house on the Ridge, or Green Bay road, as it was then called, a little north of Mr. Bailey's greenhouse. Traces of this house are still to be seen. Proceeding north from the Hathaway place, we came to the lake shore, a little south of the ravine which enters the lake just south of the Swedish theological school. This ravine was afterward known as Hazzard's Glen, taking its name from Captain Hazzard, who settled there, sailing summers and residing in his house winters. The old road along the lake shore has long since been washed away, and the more classic character of the present inhabitants is shown in the changed name of the old ravine, which students and professors now call 'the Rubicon.'

"Grosse Point was the name given to the point at the head of the Ridge more than a century ago, and it might properly be so called to-day out of respect to the Indians and pioneers. This was the burial place of the Indians—a sacred spot to them, where they were wont to meet annually from time immemorial, to mourn their departed. To this day I walk over this spot instinctively feeling that I tread on sacred ground. The land belonged to the Pottawatomies, though well known to the Chippewas who now inhabit the north of Michigan.

"From the Mulford place where the old Kirk homestead now stands up past Grosse Point to Stebbins' tavern, there were no houses, and the road was scarcely more than an Indian trail, though wagons did pass through. Three brothers of us, of whom I was the youngest, had occasion to go along this way. A little south of the spot where Mr. Bailey's house now stands, the body of an Indian had been deposited, sitting upright in a little pen about six feet long by four wide. His dog, gun and tomahawk were placed with him, it being expected that he would find abundant use for them upon his entrance into the happy hunting-grounds. As we neared this spot our pulses quickened, and we could not forbear glancing at the, to us, awful object. To our horror the flesh had crumbled from the face, leaving the teeth exposed. This proved too much for our bravery, and we broke into a dead run. It was a long time before I conquered my fears enough to go along this road any other way than on the run, always looking back, in the fear and expectation of being followed.

"When Mr. Stebbins had completed his new log house and got in a full supply of whisky, he was ready for business, and business began. All the 'claim meetings,' elections and meetings to transact public business were held here. I recall going many times with my father to these gatherings, and the impressions left upon my youthful mind by seeing the drinking and the conduct resulting therefrom were all the temperance lectures necessary for me."

At a meeting of the university trustees March 28, 1854, it was directed that the Chicago & Milwaukee railroad be requested to locate the station at Evanston on a line west of Davis Street, on the small ridge Carney farm. This land was bought of the Carneys October 7, 1853, by Messrs. Brown, Hurd and Benson. The plat of ground, showing the depot where it now stands, dated July 20, 1854, and recorded July 27, 1854, is still in existence. A. J. Brown deeded the depot grounds, and the right of way, consisting of about seven acres, was then staked out, April 15, 1854.

At that time Mr. John A. Pearsons occupied an old log house near where the Congregational church now stands, and he was one of the first to build a new house after the University had platted the village. In April 1854, Rev. Philo Judson bought a little house on the ridge, where Mr. B. F. Hill now lives,[12] and began to build a larger house beside it. During that summer he bought the lumber in Michigan for the building of Dempster Hall. Mrs. Governor Beveridge, Mr. Judson's daughter, gives this interesting reminiscence concerning the erection of that pioneer building —the beginning of Evanston's fame as a theological Mecca:

"My father came in one morning and said he had a propeller and a schooner both loaded with lumber lying off the point just above here. The lumber had all to be landed, and he had sent around to call out all the farmers and had succeeded in getting forty-five men together, who would want dinner. There were no markets near; but we sent out a boy with a horse, who bought up all the bread and early lettuce and a few radishes. We all went into the kitchen and fried and broiled and cooked all the morning, and at noon we got out the farm-wagon and filled two or three clothes-baskets with dishes and drove up to where old Dempster Hall afterward stood. Part of the cargo of wet timbers lay there on the knoll and the men stood in the lake, barefooted, some wet to their shoulders and some wet to their waists, getting that lumber ashore. We spread the plates along the timbers, and the men came out while we served their dinner. Then, gathering up the dishes, we went to the house and cooked again the whole afternoon. At six o'clock we were back to serve their supper. Those men worked for thirty-six hours without lying down, to get that lumber ashore and up the bank. This was the first picnic in Evanston.

"The Institute was soon begun, and not long afterward Mr. Danks' hotel, which has since grown to be the Avenue House;[13] my husband's house, on Chicago Avenue, was next. My father's house was the first built in Evanston, but his property was not then included in the village plat, though it now is, so that ours was the first residence built in the village plat. We got into our house early in December 1854. In the spring Mr. Pearsons moved into his new house. Then came the building of the railroad, which was in operation by the next year, and the opening of the hotel, and the moving in of several other families. A year or two afterwards the Willards made their home on the spot where Mr. William Deering has since built.[14] Next to my father's family and our own, came Judge Hurd, 'up on the ridge.' Then Dr. Evans followed, building by the shore, on the site where Mr. L. D. Norton's house[15] now stands.

"Dempster Hall[16] was, of course, full of students, and whenever there was a case of sickness, or any accident happened, it was the custom to send for Mrs. Pearsons or Mrs. Beveridge, for we were the only two women here who could go; and so it happened that our names were like household words to the first students of Evanston, who are now scattered all over the world as Methodist preachers.

"The first visit I paid in Evanston was to return a call that Mrs. Pearsons made on me, 'up on the ridge.' When I returned it, I came in a farm-wagon, with my feet laid across a board to keep them out of the water, so deep was it across the flat of land on which the depots are now built.

"Early in the winter of 1854, when the Institute building was completed and dedicated, our services were carried on there. Previous to this, the church had been moved from the old log schoolhouse into a little room over a store which had been built on Davis Street by my father. The building was known as Colvin's store, and stood on the corner now occupied by Mr. Garwood's drug store.[17] The identical building still stands a few hundred feet west, facing Orrington Avenue, and is used as a barber shop. My father had fixed the upper room tor a congregation of forty people, and gave the use of the room and furnishings to our little church, which had grown to fourteen or fifteen members."

DISCOVERY AND PURCHASE OF EVANSTON.

How did this particular site come to be selected for the University, and consequently for our university town? By way of answer, I give this curious narrative, from the lips of the discoverer, the Christophero Colombo of these classic shades, the man but for whom our village would have been located at Jefferson, where the county poorhouse is established; I refer to that indomitable "Father of Evanston," Orrington Lunt. He says:

"The executive committee were always favorably inclined to go north of the city, to some point on the lake shore, for a location. There was no railroad built at that time, but one was being surveyed—the Chicago & Milwaukee. The committee made several trips, as far north as Lake Forest, but all seemed too far from the city, excepting Winnetka, which was satisfactory; but on trying, we found the site could not be bought at any such price as we could afford, being owned by several parties. The present Rosehill was recommended by Hon. W. B. Ogden, but we found the same objection. It will be remembered that in going north, the travel was over what is now the Ridge road; between that and Chicago Avenue there was a wet, almost impassable slough or swamp, and so, in going north, we passed by the lake shore part, without knowing there was any suitable ground for our purpose.

"After several trips we gave up the idea of finding a suitable place on the lake shore at the price we could afford. The committee then went out to Jefferson, west of the city, where we obtained options for the purchase of John Gray's and other farms on the ridge, and were about to close the trade. But I had such a strong prejudice in favor of the lake shore, that I could hardly give it up. I one day embraced an opportunity to come again to this locality with a friend, and while he was engaged with his business, I took a stroll over to the shore, through the wet land; I well remember walking over logs or planks on a portion of it. In looking south, it was wet and swampy. Looking north, I noticed the large oak forest trees. The thought first struck me that here was where the high and dry ground began! I wanted to look at it, but it was so near night that I gave it up; but on the way back, I began to think possibly this might be the place we were seeking for. It continued in my dreams all that night, and I could not rid myself of the fairy visions constantly pressing themselves upon my thoughts,—fanciful, beauteous pictures of the gentle, waving lake, its pebbly shore and its beautiful bluffs. These impressions settled it in my mind that I would not vote to accept the options for Jefferson, until the committee should make another trip north. They were to meet that morning, to close the trade. In accordance with my request, the matter was laid over, and a number of the committee went to examine the property. It was a pleasant August day. We drove into what is the present campus, and it was, in its natural condition, just as beautiful as now. We were delighted and some of the brethren threw up their hats, shouting, 'This is the place!' "

Dr. J. H. Foster, the owner of this tract, was at first unwilling to sell on any terms, though he said the land was worth fifteen or twenty dollars an acre. He was finally induced to make a price, which was accepted and was as follows: twenty-five thousand dollars for the site (about seventy-one dollars an acre), one thousand dollars cash, balance in ten years, at six per cent interest, the trustees to execute their bond for the payments, secured by mortgage on the land, and guaranteed by the legal trustees present individually; any portion of the land to be released from mortgage from time to time, provided that one hundred dollars per acre should be paid for such release; all taxes and interests being paid. Mr. Lunt, in speaking of the transaction, recently remarked: "I well remember when I called on Dr. Foster and notified him of the acceptance of this proposition, that his countenance fell, showing that he was not really pleased with the transaction."

Orrington Lunt was a Maine man at the start and has been a Maine man ever since. I have often wondered if a love of the sea, which is the natural inheritance of those born, as he was, almost in sight of its billows, may not have confirmed in him, whose Chicago home was on the lake shore, the purpose to persist, as his associates did not, in the effort to discover a lake shore rather than an inland Evanston.

GARRETT BIBLICAL INSTITUTE.

Two important streams of influence united to form our theological seminary, each of which might be traced almost indefinitely by the curious historian. The most direct we shall follow back to March 5, 1805, when, near Newburg, N. Y., Eliza Clark was born. At the age of twenty she was married to Augustus Garrett and in 1834 came with her husband to reside in Chicago, then a small town of about 400 inhabitants. Mr. Garrett acquired quite a fortune and was one of the early mayors of the city. In the year 1839 under the pastorate of Rev. Peter R. Borein, there was a great religious revival in the First Methodist Episcopal Church. As a result of this many were received into the church, and among them Mr. and Mrs. Garrett. After her husband's death in 1848, Mrs. Garrett, a lady of beautiful character and earnest piety, desired to devote a large portion of her property to religious purposes, and consulted trusted advisers with this intent. Among those to whom she applied was her attorney, Hon. Grant Goodrich. When he suggested the founding of a theological school she said that "such a purpose had for some time been the subject of her thoughts." Rev. John Clark, her pastor, Rev. Dr. Daniel P. Kidder, and Rev. Hooper Crews, independently gave her the same counsel. A small book on Ministerial Education by Rev. Dr. Stephen M. Vail, also influenced her decision. In December 1853, her will was signed, as drawn up by Judge Goodrich, bequeathing the larger part of her property to found the Garrett Biblical Institute. The income of the estate being seriously impaired by financial fires and incumbrances, Mrs. Garrett would only accept $400 per year for her own support, that as much as possible might be applied to clear it.

Turning now to the other important source, we notice that among the missionaries sent by John Wesley to America was a Scotchman named James Dempster, who had been educated in the University of Edinburgh. To a son, born to him in Florida, N. Y., Jan. 2, 1794, he gave the name of John. Converted at the age of eighteen at a camp-meeting, John Dempster responded to a call to the ministry, and during the next thirty years experienced all the vicissitudes of a Methodist minister's life. He was a circuit rider in the Canadian wilderness, a pastor of important churches, a presiding elder, a missionary to Buenos Ayres and a popular preacher in New York City. Meanwhile he had always been a diligent student and had made himself familiar with Latin, Greek, Hebrew, philosophy and natural science. He would rise

Eliza Garrett
Founder of Garrett Biblical Institute
From a Painting

regularly at four o'clock in the morning for study. His observation, especially that as a presiding elder, wrought in him the profound conviction that the Methodist Church stood in pressing need of theological schools, and to the founding of these he resolved to devote all his powers. He was widely known in the church as an able preacher, a scholar of varied accomplishments, and particularly as a metaphysician.

With little encouragement and in the face of strong opposition Dr. Dempster began the work of the first theological seminary of the Methodist Episcopal church at Newbury, Vermont, in the year 1845. Closely associated with him in the new movement were Professors Osmon C. Baker, Charles Adams and Clark T. Hinman. In 1847 this Biblical Institute was transplanted to Concord, N. H., and ultimately became the School of Theology of the Boston University. To show the spirit of the man and the good fight he fought, I transcribe his own references to the conflict from a letter found among his manuscripts. It is dated June 27, 1856, and says: "For the last twelve years I have, from an overwhelming sense of duty, been occupied in an enterprise in the face of fierce and persistent opposition on the part of at least two-thirds of our entire ministry. Some of the highest dignitaries of the church have exerted official influence to embarrass and subvert the enterprise. Many friends of my tenderest remembrance forsook me for having allied myself to this cause, and even transferred their hostility from the cause to him who advocated it. To insure success to this persecuted enterprise I found such devotion to its interests indispensable as involved the almost total neglect of private friendships and the interchange of kindly courtesies."

Such was the history and spirit of the man who, seeing his first school well established at Concord, turned his face westward to found similar institutions in the Mississippi Valley and on the Pacific Coast. Filled with this purpose he accepted the presidency of the college at Bloomington, Ill. Upon coming west, however, he learned of Mrs. Garrett's generous provisions and was invited by those who represented her to co-operate in carrying out her plans.

The day after Christmas, 1835, a meeting was called of those favoring higher education for Methodist ministers, in the old Clark Street church, Chicago. Rev. Philo Judson presided, and Dr. Dempster, then on his way to Bloomington, addressed the meeting. The next day the organization of a Biblical Institute Association was effected, with five directors to act as trustees for a period of five years or until a charter for a permanent institution should be obtained. Two days later it was agreed between this directorate and Dr. Dempster that they were to provide a building at Evanston and $1,600 a year, and he was to serve as professor, secure two associates, and collect such additional funds as should be necessary for current expenses. A subscription was immediately taken.[18] In April of the next year a contract was let for the building, and in July the Revs. William Goodfellow and Wesley P. Wright were elected to professorships. In January 1855, the new building, known in later years as Dempster Hall, was formally dedicated. Mrs. Garrett was among those present. The Chicago friends drove out in sleighs. The term inaugurated began with four students and closed with sixteen.

The charter of the Garrett Biblical Institute is dated Feb. 15, 1855. The incorporators are Orrington Lunt, John Evans, Philo Judson, Grant Goodrich and Stephen P. Keyes. The first meeting of this board occurred June 22, 1855. Judge Grant Goodrich was elected president, and Mr. Orrington Lunt, secretary; the former retained his office until his recent decease, and Mr. Lunt continues to devote himself unsparingly to the arduous duties of secretary and treasurer.

The first term under the new organization opened Sept. 23, 1856.

Dr. Dempster was formally constituted professor of systematic theology; Dr. Daniel P. Kidder, professor of practical theology; Dr. Henry Bannister, professor of Greek, Hebrew and Sacred Literature, and Rev. John K. Johnston, principal of the preparatory department. Rev. Obadiah Huse was appointed house governor in charge of the school building.

Dr. Kidder, a graduate of the Wesleyan University, had been a missionary in Brazil, and also for twelve years corresponding secretary of the Sunday school Union and Tract Society of the M. E. church. Of his seven publications those on "Homiletics" and "The Christian Pastorate" are the most noteworthy.

Dr. Bannister was graduated at the Wesleyan University and the Auburn Theological Seminary, and had taught for eighteen years before coming to Evanston, chiefly in the Oneida Conference Seminary. Professor Johnston was a graduate of Dublin University.

The history of the thirty-seven years since this seminary opened its beneficent doors cannot be attempted here. Many references to it and especially to its trustees and faculty will be found in the following pages.

Tabulated lists of its trustees and professors have been formed from official sources, and will not only be convenient for reference, but prove suggestive to the older friends of the Institute.

TRUSTEES.

Hon. Grant Goodrich, 1855-1889.
Mr. Orrington Lunt, 1855-
Hon. John Evans, M.D., 1855-1859.
Rev. Philo Judson, 1855-1861.
Rev. Stephen P. Keyes, 1855-1865.
Rev. Luke Hitchcock, D.D., 1859-
Rev. Thomas M. Eddy, D.D., 1861-1869.
Rev. Hooper Crews, D.D., 1861-1871.
Rev. John V. Farwell, 1866-1871.
Rev. E.H. Gammon, 1869-
Rev. Charles H. Fowler, D.D., 1871-1879.
Mr. Albro E. Bishop, 1871-1880.
Rev. S. Hawley Adams, D.D., 1879-1884.
Mr. William Deering, 1880-
Rev. Robert D. Sheppard, D.D., 1884-
Hon. Oliver H. Horton, LL.D., 1889-

FACULTY.

Rev. John Dempster, D.D., 1854-1863.
Rev. William Goodfellow, A.M., 1854-1856.
Rev. Wesley P. Wright, A.M., 1854-1856,
Rev. Daniel P. Kidder, D.D., 1856-1871.
Rev. Henry Bannister, D.D., 1856-1883.
Rev. John K. Johnston, A.M., 1856-1857.
Rev. Francis D. Hemenway, D.D., 1857-1884.
Rev. Miner Raymond, D.D., LL.D., 1864-
Rev. William X. Ninde, D.D., 1873-1884.
Rev. Henry B. Ridgaway, D.D., LL.D., 1881-
Rev. Charles F. Bradley, D.D., 1883—
Rev. Milton S. Perry, D.D., 1884—
Rev. Charles W. Bennett, D.D., LL.D., 1884—
Robert L. Cumnock, A.M., 1884—

The bishops of the Methodist Episcopal Church constitute an official Board of Council and no professor can be elected without their approval.

Dr. John McClintock was elected to the chair of Ecclesiastical History in 1856, but did not accept it. From 1861 to 1865 Bishop Simpson was nominally president of the Institute, but his relation was not an active one. Professor Cumnock's connection with the Institute dates back to 1869, from which year he served as instructor until his election to a professorship in 1884. The Revs. Moses S. Cross, B. D., Milton S. Vail, A. M. and Charles Horswell, B. D.,[19] have been regularly appointed instructors in Elementary Greek and Hebrew. From 1879 to 1884 Dr. Ninde occupied the President's chair most acceptably. Since that time the position has been ably and successfully filled by Dr. Henry B. Ridgaway.

Heck Hall, a substantial and commodious dormitory costing sixty thousand dollars, was built in 1866-67, when Rev. Dr. James S. Smart was financial agent, and his efforts were nobly seconded by the Ladies' Centenary Association, of which Mrs. Bishop Hamline was president, and Miss Frances E. Willard corresponding secretary. I think Miss Willard regards this work as her introduction to public life. It is not unfitting here to make grateful acknowledgment of the large part women have borne in the support of the Institute. Its founder is the first of a noble succession. Mrs. Cornelia A. Miller's generous endowment of the chair of Practical Theology by the gift of thirty thousand dollars has linked her name forever with that of Mrs. Garrett. It was appropriate that the new hall built so largely by the efforts of the ladies should bear the heroic name of Barbara Heck. Another revered name, that of Mrs. Sarah Stewart, has been, by the liberal gift of her sons, assured of perpetual remembrance among those of the school's benefactors. Other names, which cannot yet be recorded, will soon prove their claim to a place in this goodly list.

All the liberal friends who have contributed to the prosperity of the seminary can not be mentioned here; but the constant devotion of "the trustees and their wise administration commands the admiration and gratitude of all concerned. It is fitting to make special mention of Judge Grant Goodrich, who for thirty-five years devoted unremitting attention to its welfare; and to Mr. Orrington Lunt, who throughout the same period, as secretary and treasurer, has made the interests of the Institute of equal importance with those of his own family. A worthy successor to Judge Goodrich in the presidency of the board has been found in Mr. William Deering.

We quote from a historical sketch by Judge Goodrich some interesting facts concerning the finances of the school.

> "The financial history of the Institute has been one of marked vicissitude, but under the unremitting labors and skillful management of the trustees, the generous liberality of the church, and the blessing of God, it has been

one of marvelous success. The endowment left by Mrs. Garrett was in real estate, most of it in the business part of Chicago. When it passed from the executors of Mrs. Garrett to the trustees it was mostly unproductive. The trustees put as much of it as possible under ground rents, in which they were satisfactorily successful, but the financial embarrassments of 1857 compelled the lessee of the most valuable part to give up his lease in the succeeding year. In 1860 the Wigwam in which Mr. Lincoln was nominated, was erected upon it at a comparatively nominal rent. This building was afterwards purchased and converted into business tenements, but was burned in 1867. In 1870, a block of brick stores was built upon it at a cost of $65,000, which with $25,000 assumed in the erection of Heck Hall, and $2,000 paid on the purchase of the Wigwam, constituted an indebtedness of $92,000. This building, with two other brick stores, was swept away in the great fire of October, 1871, leaving most of the property not only unproductive, but incumbered with the whole debt of $92,000. This great calamity left the financial affairs of the institution in a most deplorable condition; but by the generous liberality of the entire church in its contributions for the relief of the suffering brethren of Chicago, the Institute realized as its share $62,500, and the trustees, as the only means of paying the debt and securing the support of the school, erected in 1872 a larger building at a cost of $110,000. For the ensuing year the property yielded an income of $25,000, but the panic of 1873 so bankrupted lessees and depressed rents that in 1878 we had run behind $1,500, and the estimated deficiency for the ensuing year was $5,000. The trustees called the faculty together, and having submitted the financial condition, informed them that they had resolved to sell none of the property and contract no liabilities for the current expenses of the school; that the only way it could be continued was by an appeal to the church for relief, and if that failed, the school must be closed until its endowment could be relieved of incumbrance. A meeting of the friends of the institution was then called, and it was resolved to make an appeal to the church to cancel the indebtedness and increase the endowment. The faculty generously contributed one-fourth of their salaries, but little progress was made until, by appointment of the Rock River Conference in 1879, the services of the Rev. W. C. Dandy, D.D., were procured. He entered upon the work with a thorough appreciation of its importance, and prosecuted it with an intelligent zeal, an earnest but kind persistency, which gave him a wonderful success, not only in obtaining pecuniary relief, but in awakening an interest in behalf of ministerial education in the church at large. Among the numerous gifts obtained during this period was the noble benefaction of Mrs. Cornelia A. Miller, of Joliet, of thirty thousand dollars for the endowment of the chair of Practical Theology. Through Dr. Dandy's labors and the fortunate sale of some riparian rights, we are able to make the gratifying announcement to the church that all the debts of Garrett Biblical Institute have been paid. Reliable progress is also being made towards a handsome increase of the endowment, and the income will be adequate to meet all current expenses, unless an unforeseen depreciation in rents should occur. It is earnestly hoped that as the wants of the school are constantly increasing, the worthy example of Mrs. Miller will be followed by others, that thus the Institute may be placed fully abreast with all the requirements of the age."

The history of the beautiful Memorial Hall is officially given as follows: "The building originated with the Centennial year of the Methodist Episcopal Church, 1884, as Heck Hall had with the Centenary of American Methodism, 1866.

"Three of the professors, feeling the need of such a structure, pledged themselves to the amount of eight hundred dollars when it should be undertaken. There was no further movement until the sr. ring of 1885. The President, Dr. Ridgaway, received from Rev. E. H. Gammon, a member of the Board of Trustees, the generous pledge of five thousand dollars toward the object. Soon after, at the annual May meeting of the trustees, Mr. Wm. Deering, another member of the Board, pledged an additional five thousand dollars; whereupon the trustees, in their corporate capacity, promised six thousand dollars, or one-fifth of the cost, provided it should not exceed thirty thousand dollars. With these subscriptions for a beginning, the work of raising subscriptions was steadily prosecuted, until, in the spring of 1886, it was thought the amount of subscriptions justified contracting for the building.

"The contract was accordingly made after plans and specifications by W. W. Boynton, Esq., of Chicago. These plans were worked out from drawings by Prof. Charles F. Bradley, who had embodied the result of observations in some of the halls in the east.

"Ground was broken for the foundation by the venerable Judge Goodrich, president of the Board of Trustees, on Thursday, May 13, in the presence of the trustees, official visitors, members of the faculty and a large number of friends.

"The building is made of red pressed brick with a foundation of gray limestone, and with trimmings in buff Bedford stone and red terra cotta; the whole length, including apse, is one hundred and fifteen feet, and average width, sixty feet. It stands facing the south, with the entrance by the base of a tall tower, in the open belfry of which at some time it is purposed to place a bell or chime of bells. The architecture is peculiar, but might be called Romanesque in its general outline."

"It was dedicated with appropriate services on May 10, 1887, Bishop C. D. Foss, D. D., LL. D., preaching the sermon, and Bishop S. M. Merrill, D. D., LL. D., performing the dedicatory services.

"It contains fine large lecture rooms, library, reading-room and chapel, besides offices for the president and professors. The spacious and beautiful chapel contains rich memorial windows of exquisite coloring and appropriate designs. The plans for these are mostly due to the painstaking care and critical taste of Prof. C. W. Bennett. They commemorate the deceased professors, Doctors Dempster, Bannister and Hemenway, Bishops Simpson and Wiley, the Reverends Hooper, Crews, A. G. Button, and S. G. Lathrop, Judge Goodrich and Mr. Robert F. Queal. The donors of these windows were the Alumni, the First Methodist Episcopal church of Evanston, the Cincinnati and Rock River Conferences, Mrs. A. G. Button, and Messrs. H. N. Higinbotham and Wm. H. Craig."

Biographical sketches of the presidents and professors will be found elsewhere in this volume with an account of the important contributions made by several of them to theological literature. It is worthy of notice that most of the bishops and leading men of the church have been brought to Evanston to lecture before the students of the Institute, and that the annual lecture course is greatly enjoyed by many of our citizens.

In all, up to 1891, five hundred and twenty-four have been regularly graduated from the Institute, but over twelve hundred have received instruction during these thirty-seven years. The Alumni are ministering in all parts of the church, about thirty having gone into foreign mission fields. Thirty-four have received the degree of Doctor of Divinity. Among those who have been appointed to official position are Bishop Charles H. Fowler; the General Conference Secretaries, Doctors James S. Chadwick, William A. Spencer, and Joseph C. Hartzell; the college presidents, Wm. H. H. Adams, Thomas F. Berry, Edmund M. Holmes, Thomas Van Scoy, Horace N. Herrick and Joseph H. Sparling; the professors, F. Wm. Heidner, J. Riley Weaver, John Poucher, Henry J. Crist, Benton H. Badley, Robert D. Sheppard, Nathan Burwash, Melville C. Wire, Eli McClish, George E. Ackerman, Charles F. Bradley, George T. Newcomb, Edward L. Parks, John J. Garvin, Edward Thomson, Nels E. Simonsen, George H. Horswell, William H. Crawford, Charles Horswell, Gerhardt C. Mars and William Rollins. It is significant, as showing the radiating influence of the seminary, that twelve of the above are teaching in some department of theology. Our journalists are Oliver A. Willard, [20] William S. Harrington, Charles H. Zimmerman and Charles M. Stuart. The preachers and pastors sent out, constitute a noble army, whose work is of the utmost importance, but it seems impossible to name any without making unfair distinctions. The distinguished need no record here.

The founding of the Norwegian-Danish Theological Seminary and its affiliation with the Institute as a department, has been accomplished under the wise administration of Principal Nels E. Simonsen. It has an excellent building and an encouraging attendance, and is doing admirable work.

The growth of the past ten years has been rapid and gratifying, and the standard of instruction has been steadily advanced. The attendance for the year 1889-90 was one hundred and eighty-six, including twenty in the Norwegian-Danish department. With twenty-six students in the Swedish theological seminary, our neighboring school, the total of two hundred and twelve places Evanston as a theological centre in the front rank. Together with the four other Protestant theological seminaries of Chicago, a strength in numbers of over five hundred students and an aggregate of ability in theological instruction is secured, such as would surprise those who know Chicago only as a commercial city, and gives assurance of immeasurable Christian and educational influence.

The material equipment of our Evanston theological school in buildings, library and endowment is generous if not wholly adequate. Its faculty includes men of ability, learning, and distinguished reputation. Its alumni are exerting a wide and extending influence in the Methodist Church in all lands. Its history, location and present prosperity justify large expectations for its future.[21]

REV. HENRY BANNISTER, D. D.

REV. JOHN DEMPSTER, D. D.

REV. DANIEL KIDDER, D. D.

REV. F. D. HEMENWAY, D. D.

ORIGIN OF NORTHWESTERN UNIVERSITY.

Our great institution, the University, always the central figure of Evanston's lengthening and varied panorama, has had a growth notably slow and sure. The men who laid its strong foundations and imparted to it their own exact and masterful character, were in no hurry to have it become famous. They had studied the institutions of the Old World and knew that a century is of small account in the growth of a great seat of learning. The banyan tree is perhaps its truest emblem—sending its roots deeply into the soil, spreading them out far and wide, while its broadening canopy does not outgrow its hidden basis of supply, and when its life force warrants the new venture, not before, sending out strong arms, which, striking downward, take fresh root and hold in gigantic steadfastness the whole, great tree. A strong financial groundwork has always been beneath the gradually growing structure that gives to Evanston its fame, and is, as it will always be, its chief determinative force.

In the order of evolution, University and Theological School preceded Evanston and gave it being.

Were this not true, our little burg could not boast of fourteen Doctors of Divinity! But Evanston began in a prayer-meeting, and I can prove it. On the 31st of May 1850, half a dozen earnest Christian men met by appointment, in the law office of Hon. Grant Goodrich in the city of Chicago. Their object, often talked and prayed about before, was the founding of a university that should be a fountain of Christian scholarship for the northwest. Rev. Zadoc Hall, pastor of Indiana Street M. E. Church, led in prayer, and if others did not pray audibly I know that Richard Haney, pastor of Clark Street M E. Church, and Rev, R. H. Blanchard, pastor of Canal Street M. E. Church, were lifting up their hearts to God as they knelt there together, and I am equally sure that this was true of Judge Goodrich, Orrington Lunt, John Evans, J. K. Botsford, Henry W. Clarke and Andrew J. Brown, the chief laymen with whom Chicago was then blessed in the M. E. Church. So, as I said before, our town began in a prayer-meeting, and that fact prophesied its beautiful career.

Mr. Lunt gives the following statement in relation to this first meeting and other preliminary steps in this great movement:

> "Grant Goodrich was called to the chair, and Andrew J. Brown appointed secretary. Addresses were made by Rev. Richard Haney and Dr. Evans, after which the following preamble and resolutions were offered, and

REV. C. T. HINMAN,
First Prest. of N. W. U.

PROF. H. S. NOYES.

REV. E. O. HAVEN, D. D.

REV. C. H. FOWLER, D. D.

unanimously adopted:

"WHEREAS, The interests of sanctified learning require the immediate establishing of a university in the northwest, under the patronage of the Methodist Episcopal Church; be it

"*Resolved,* That a committee of five be appointed to prepare a draft of a charter, to incorporate a Literary University, to be located at Chicago, to be under the control and patronage of the Methodist Episcopal Church, to be submitted to the next General Assembly of the State of Illinois.

"*Resolved,* That said committee memorialize the Rock River, Wisconsin, Michigan, and Northern Indiana Conferences of the Methodist Episcopal Church, to mutually take part in the government and patronage of said university.

"*Resolved,* That a committee of three be appointed to ascertain what amount can be obtained for the erection and endowment of said Institution.

"At the next meeting, Dr. Evans, on the part of the committee, reported a draft of a charter, which, on examination, was adopted. It was substantially the same as the present charter.

"Pursuant to public notice for the purpose of organizing the Northwestern University, a meeting was held at the Clark Street Church, in the city of Chicago, on the 14th day of June, 1851. To fill the place of Eri Reynolds, Dr. N. S. Davis was elected. A ballot for officers resulted as follows: John Evans, president; A. S. Sherman, vice-president; Andrew J. Brown, secretary; J. K. Botsford, treasurer. The Presidency of the Institution was established, with a salary of one thousand two hundred dollars; the person occupying the Presidency was also to be professor of moral philosophy and belles-lettres. A Professorship of Mathematics, one of Natural Sciences, and another of Ancient and Modern Languages, were established.

"It was resolved at that meeting that a Preparatory Department should be established; it was to be located in Chicago, and the executive committee was given power to purchase a site for the same. This committee opened negotiations with the Universalist Church of Chicago, for the purchase of eighty feet on Washington Street, but the offer of four thousand eight hundred dollars for both lot and church was not accepted; they wanted five thousand five hundred dollars."[22]

There were no schools to prepare for college or university at that time in the city of Chicago, no high schools or anything of that kind; and it was thought best to commence with an academy or preparatory school in Chicago. John Evans and O. Lunt were appointed committee

University Hall

to search for a site for a preparatory building. They finally hit upon the block now occupied by the Grand Pacific hotel.[23] The owner, Mr. P. F. W. Peck, asked eight thousand dollars for it—one thousand dollars cash and the rest on two years' time. The trustees had no money as yet, so to raise the one thousand dollars cash the following men showed their loyalty to the cause by subscribing the money: O. Lunt, two hundred and fifty dollars; Dr. John Evans, two hundred and fifty dollars; J. K. Botsford, two hundred dollars; A. S. Sherman, two hundred dollars; Grant Goodrich, one hundred dollars; George F. Foster, one hundred dollars; A. J. Brown, fifty dollars; Dr. N. S. Davis, twenty-five dollars.

The trade was closed by Dr. Evans, who took a deed of the land in his own name, and gave Mr. Peck a mortgage, and the trustees became personally responsible. This property is still in the possession of the University. Mr. Lunt recently remarked:

This was the smartest thing we ever did. There was nothing particularly smart in the purchasing, but the smart thing was in the keeping of it, for it is now worth about a million dollars.

At the next annual meeting the plan of having a preparatory school in Chicago was abandoned, so that the land was never used for a university building.

Soon after this purchase, a subscription paper was circulated, to raise funds for the university, and to erect a preparatory building. That subscription amounted to about twenty thousand dollars; the names and exact amounts will be found in the appendix at the end of this book.

At a meeting held October 1, 1852, Rev. Philo Judson was appointed agent for the university, to solicit funds. At the third annual meeting, June 22, 1853, Rev. Clark T. Hinman, trustee from the Michigan Conference, was elected president of the university. He was decidedly in favor of beginning a university proper, instead of a preparatory, in Chicago. At the next annual meeting he was formally elected professor of moral philosophy and logic. Rev. Dr. Abel Stevens was elected professor of rhetoric and English literature, but did not accept. Rev. Dr. Wm. D. Godman was made professor of Greek, and Henry S. Noyes, of mathematics. At the latter meeting the agent reported the estimated valuation of the university property at $191,000, with liabilities of $32,000. Perpetual scholarships had been sold to the amount of $90,000, but this amount was never all collected.

At a meeting of the executive committee, held March 15, 1855, a committee of five, consisting of Dr. N. S. Davis, John Evans, O. Lunt, Grant Goodrich and Philo Judson, were appointed to correspond and make preliminary arrangements for the election of a president at the

Top, Heck Hall. Middle, Memorial Hall.
Bottom, University Gymnasium.

approaching annual meeting of the Board, Dr. Hinman having died.

It was resolved that the university be opened on the first day of the following November, and the committee was appointed to procure plans and estimates for the building, and report at the next meeting of the Board.

It was in the fall of 1869 that the preparatory[24] was first opened to ladies. There were less than twenty the first year, but the experiment finally resulted as favorably as its warmest advocates could wish. In the fall of 1871, owing to the large increase of lady students through the connection of the Evanston College for Ladies with the university, the first lady teacher was employed. Mrs. Lizzie Winslow was the person upon whom the honor was conferred. In 1889 we had three—Miss Harriet Kimball, Miss Leila Crandon and Miss Ada Townsend; and the young lady students in the department numbered 161, young men, 436.

During the summer of 1871 the preparatory building was moved to its present site,[25] and greatly enlarged and refitted to meet the new demands, for which, as it was, it was entirely inadequate.

In 1873 Prof, (now Dr.) Herbert F. Fisk succeeded Rev. Mr. Winslow, and the subsequent years of prosperity bear everywhere the impress of his strong personality and hard work.

The University museum, a monument to the devoted labors of Dr. Oliver Marcy, deserves more than a passing mention, but must be seen to be understood and appreciated. From the time of its origin, under Robert Kennicott, in 1857, to the present hour, it has been steadily growing, mostly through the contributions of graduates, who delight thus to show their love for their *alma mater* and for the revered doctor who has lavished his days and years upon the great collection.

In 1873 it was thought wise to erect the first permanent building of the noble group that makes our otherwise commonplace village a "classic town." The best models on both sides of the water had been studied; Chicago's then chief architect, G. P. Randall, was chosen to superintend the work, but it is well known that Dr. Bonbright was the good genius of the building that elder Evanston was wont to call "a poem in stone," but which technically bears the proud designation of "University Hall."[26] If there is anywhere a fairer or more noble single structure, devoted to scholastic purposes, "old timers" would be glad to have it pointed out. Already the university had rejoiced and sorrowed over the gain and loss of three great presidents, Drs. Hinman, Foster and Cummings, sketches of whose lives will be found among the Personalia. The former died after having been at the head of affairs but a brief period; the latter, great and gifted, resigned in 1860 and returned universally bemoaned, to New York city, whence he had come. Thereafter for nine years (1860 to 1869), Prof. Henry S. Noyes had the title of "Acting President," and during his incumbency the beautiful new hall aforesaid was built and dedicated, a number of distinguished men participating in the exercises.

Prof. Noyes had the department of mathematics, in which his acquirements reached the height of genius, and, unlike most men of that stamp, he was equally good in mathematics applied to everyday affairs. Nobody better understood the potential value of real estate, or planned more wisely for building up the finances of the university, which was beloved by him as if it were his child. During his period of management the Snyder farm[27] was added to the real estate basis of the enterprise. He attended to the leasing of property, opened new streets, collected debts; indeed, looked after every detail with the scrupulous exactness which was one of his most pronounced characteristics; conciliated everybody with whom he dealt, so that to this day I have never heard a harsh word spoken of him; went to the city to endless executive committee meetings, for the institution had then no office here save in his study, and no quorum of its trustees nearer than the office of Judge Goodrich. Few sights were more familiar on our streets than the bay horse and light covered buggy, in which at all hours and in all weathers, that indefatigable man fulfilled the duties of business factotum to the university. Beside these he carried his full complement of heavy college classes, attending to the ceaseless hospitalities incumbent upon the president, maintaining discipline, pronouncing baccalaureate addresses that were gems of classic thought and diction, presenting the diplomas in sonorous Latin, greeting everybody with a brother's hand of kindness at the levee, and never missing a church prayer-meeting in all those crowded years. If his mental processes had not been lightning-like, his temper perfect and his physique phenomenal in power, this remarkable man could never thus have wrought. What wonder that under such pressure his health began to break! I met him in Paris in the spring of 1870, whither he came with Mrs. Noyes and their only daughter, Maggie, hoping for recuperation. But disease had gone too far, and on May 24, 1872, the whole town sorrowfully followed him to his rest in Rosehill Cemetery. No one ever connected with the institution has placed upon it a more skillful hand or at a time when it was more plastic to his touch. "To the last syllable of recorded time "that honored name should be associated with Northwestern, and doubtless it will some day be permanently connected with some building of the growing group upon the college campus.

Rev. Dr. E. O. Haven, later known still more widely as Bishop Haven, was elected to succeed Prof. Noyes, in 1869, and resigned in 1872.

Rev. Dr. Charles H. Fowler, now a bishop of the Methodist Church, was elected president of the university in 1872 and resigned in 1876, after which Dr. Oliver Marcy, professor of natural history, was acting president until 1881. From that time until May 7, 1890, Rev. Dr. Joseph Cummings ruled in love and wisdom over this now great institution, and impressed upon it his strong personality; lavishing in its interest the best thoughts and unsparing labor of his days and nights. Short personal sketches of these noble men will be found in the chapter devoted to those salient Evanston personalities which circumstances have brought within my individual ken.

When we consider the grain of mustard-seed planted in that Chicago lawyer's office forty years ago, the old timer looks with a feeling very like admiration on statements like this, which recently appeared in a leading newspaper:

"Northwestern University now has an endowment of nearly $3,000,000, largely productive, and a total attendance of 1,692 students, with 112 professors and instructors. It has a large equipment of buildings and implements of instruction, with its departments of letters and theology situated directly upon the shore of the lake, in an ideal campus of fifty acres, chiefly grove land of ancient white oak. Its standards of admission are high, and yet they are advanced almost annually. It admits women to all departments, and they do good work. Its several colleges are liberal arts, law, medicine, theology, dentistry, pharmacy, fine arts, music and oratory. Its founders bought farm lands, platted the village, now of 10,000 people, and secured in its legislative charter two remarkable benefits: (1) that no property it might acquire should ever be taxed; (2) that no intoxicating liquor should ever be sold as a beverage within four miles. In both cases prohibition has prohibited."

THE PREPARATORY DEPARTMENT.

At the annual meeting of the trustees in 1857 it was voted that the use of a portion of the university building be granted for an academic institution, such as should meet the approval of the faculty of the university. This was the beginning of the preparatory school which now overcrowds the whole of the building which was then the 'University,' and whose 671 students in 1891 are a convincing argument for new and larger quarters in the near future.

For nine years the college and preparatory school were under the same faculty. But in 1866, Prof. Kistler made out separate courses of study for the preparatory, and in the fall of that year it started in its new life. Both departments continued in the old building until the university moved into its present quarters, in 1873. Prof. Kistler, in addition to his work in the university, had charge of the preparatory and continued his work there for two years, achieving a grand success in getting the department fairly on its feet. At the end of that period, finding the double work too hard, he resigned his position in the preparatory school, and Dr. D. H. Wheeler, acting president of the university, was put in charge. Almost at the commencement of this school year the management of the department was left to Rev. Geo. H. Winslow, who had been an instructor in the department since its organization, and at the close of the year, on Dr. Wheeler's recommendation, he was elected principal. This position Mr. Winslow held for four years, during which time the attendance more than doubled. (1869-73.)

SCIENCE HALL.

Science Hall[28] as a feature of the university, had its inception in the recognition on the part of the faculty and trustees that the most pressing need of the institution was for proper facilities for laboratory instruction in physics and chemistry, in order that these departments might be brought up to the standard demanded of higher institutions for scientific education. The next step, a very important one, was taken by the energetic agent, who bestirred himself and found a liberal friend of the institution to make the gift of forty-five thousand dollars to be devoted to this specific purpose. The building, especially designed from the start for the accommodation of these departments, was begun in the spring of 1886. It was first used for class work in April of the following year. At the present time it provides for each of the two departments a lecture room, apparatus room and professor's room; in addition for

Top, Science Hall. Middle, Observatory.
Bottom, Preparatory School.

physics, a general laboratory, five smaller rooms for special work, and a workshop; for chemistry two laboratories, an assistant's room and store rooms. The two laboratories contain together fifty-eight individual work tables. This provision, three years ago, was considered a liberal one. At the present time it is not equal to the demand.

DEARBORN OBSERVATORY.

In June 1889, the telescope and other astronomical apparatus belonging to the Chicago Astronomical Society were permanently remounted in the elegant new observatory building which stands on the north campus of the university, a monument to the generosity of Hon. James B. Hobbs. This apparatus had been in use by the Chicago University since 1864, but when that institution lost its realty by the foreclosure of a mortgage, the Astronomical Society found it necessary to find new quarters, and the dome on our campus is the result of liberal offers from our university and of a generous gift by Mr. Hobbs.

From 1877 to 1882, Mr. S. W. Burnham,[29] now at Lick Observatory, used the great equatorial a portion of the time, for double star observation. During this period he discovered more than four hundred new double stars, and made micrometrical measurements of about thirteen hundred double stars previously known.

Since 1879, the genial and devoted astronomer, Prof. Geo. W. Hough, has been director of the Dearborn Observatory, and the present almost perfect building was constructed under his supervision. His special work with the great equatorial has been a continuous and systematic study of the planet Jupiter, and the observation and discovery of difficult double stars, of which he has discovered about three hundred.

THE NORTHWESTERN FEMALE COLLEGE
AND ITS EVOLUTIONS.

The "higher education of women" is now so much a matter of course that when a "university girl" leads her class in Greek or mathematics or wins the prize in an oratorical competition it surprises no one; but it was a new idea in 1855. A woman's college course equal to that arranged for young men was unheard-of, except at Oberlin and Antioch, Ohio. Vassar was unknown, and the Harvard annex[30] would have been looked upon as an impiety. The founders of our university, although they were keen-sighted beyond their contemporaries among Chicago's Christian men, had not perceived what Goethe's prescient eye had seen so long before, that "the ever-feminine draweth on," and no provision had been made for women in their far-reaching plans. Even good Mrs. Garrett, while she made mention in her will of doing something for women's education, conditioned this upon a contingency so remote that it is practically certain never to arrive.[31] Yet Evanston was to be the classic suburb of Chicago, the western Athens, with its face to the future and its keynote caught by college towns along the opening ways of civilization. How much it meant then, that at the very beginning of the active educational movement here, even on October 29, 1855, the "Northwestern Female College" quietly took its place as one among a trio of schools, founded in the name of Christian education, and having the whole northwest as their territory of supply! Evanston has thus been, from its first hour, a paradise for women. Here they began to study Homer and Horace while the Indian's trail was yet visible along the shore; here they wrought out intricate problems in calculus when Greenwood Avenue was an unexplored morass. With no forceful business men back of the enterprise; no real estate basis; no distinguished names adorned with "lunar fardels"[32] to lend prestige to the movement, it moved all the same; it came, not welcome over-much, and came to stay.

Mrs. John L. Beveridge, in a bright reminiscent letter, has mentioned that in 1854 she began to gather a few children in a school, when a young man whom she had met at Rock River Seminary, Mt. Morris, asked her to let him undertake the tiny enterprise, and opened a preparatory department in that room over Colvin's store where the early church assembled; from this nucleus rapidly developed a college for women. This young man's views were met with disgust and scorn by many good, influential and wealthy men. They said that academies and seminaries for girls were very well, but to associate the sacred name

Northwestern Female College

Woman's College
(Later renamed Willard Hall, ed.)

of "college" with the unscholarly name of woman was to cheapen and degrade an appellation pertaining always and only to institutions for the education of men. Besides, it was a foregone conclusion that girls had not the intellect to grasp live mathematics and dead languages. Had not the young educator been gifted with a rarely resolute and liberal mind, he would not, at twenty-three years of age, have begun speaking here in Illinois, on Sunday evenings, whenever the pastor would permit, upon that unpopular theme, the higher education of women; he would not have gone, as he finally did, before the ever wide-awake Rock River Conference with his plans. Several of the ministers fell in with his views, urged him to "go up to Evanston," and promised influence and pupils. Beyond this he did not ask for aid, believing that while it is desirable to have educational institutions under the patronage of the church, they should be self-supporting. The young man came to Evanston, and was taken by Rev. Philo Judson to see the fine block on Chicago Avenue, between Lake and Greenwood streets, which he selected and bought.

When the trustees were chosen from Rock River Conference and from good men in Chicago, a difficulty arose as to the selection of a name. Northwestern Female College was the young founder's choice, even he not having then perceived the absurdity of the word "female" as involving a generalization whimsically indeterminate.

This young man's name was William P. Jones, and of the three buildings that climbed above the aboriginal groves of Evanston thirty-five years ago, or thereabouts, the most expensive and ambitious was the one built by him. He had no money, but his generous brother, Col. J. Wesley Jones, who loved and believed in this courageous educational pioneer with a chivalric devotion beautiful to see, came to the front with the necessary funds. Bishop Simpson, a lifelong friend of the young founder, and a noted champion of women's rights, dedicated the "Female College." Special trains were run from Chicago to the new village on this occasion, three hundred friends of the infant enterprise thus testifying their faith in its success,—among them John L. Scripps, then editor of the Chicago *Tribune,* Chas. L. Wilson, of the Chicago *Journal,* many pastors, and earnest-hearted women not a few. This was on December 20, 1855, several months after the school began.

One year from the day of moving into the new college came the burning of the building, caused by defective heating apparatus. The insurance also was lost, as repairs on the furnace had been made only a week before, and the insurance companies were not satisfied in regard to them. To add to these troubles, Professor Jones was taken violently ill with inflammatory rheumatism caused by exposure in his heroic efforts to save the building. The school continued, however, temporary rooms having been kindly offered by the university professors, and the teachers cheerfully doing additional work. When the term closed, the "Buckeye," a tavern building on the ridge, was secured, where the pupils boarded, and the school was opened February 25, 1857.

On the first of May Professor Jones went to Chicago for the first time after his long illness to engage materials for the new building. He was thin and pale, but full of enthusiasm and hope. Two weeks after the fire, a committee had waited upon him, bringing a proposition to start another college on the ridge, but it was a movement not in reality friendly to him. They said: "You are very ill. It is probable you cannot live. You have lost everything in the fire. Your plans must be given up." He replied: "It is true I may die, but I do not expect to; I fully intend to rebuild, and *I will not give up my plans.*" He then sent for his brother Wesley, who went immediately to Springfield and secured a charter from the legislature then in session. The other scheme was abandoned, and the "old original" college went on, its founder and his friends working with so much vigor that he moved into the second building,[33] five stories high and fitted up as both home and college for the pupils, nine months after the first one burned. The term opened with a large attendance, in September 1857, and the enterprise continually prospered. In the winter of 1862 came a second attack of inflammatory rheumatism, involving the heart, and Professor Jones, was ordered abroad for a year. Then came the same good brother to his aid, and, through influential friends, secured for him from President Lincoln the appointment of consul to Macao, China. Thither he sailed, with his wife and two babies, October 25, 1862.

During the interregnum Mrs. Lizzie Mace McFarland became lady principal of the Female College. Miss Luella Clark was teacher of "Belles-lettres," and I led the young women in what Oliver Wendell Holmes calls "barn-door flights" of natural science, while Rev. and Mrs. Jones, parents of the college proprietor, conducted home affairs. After two years Rev. Dr. L. H. Bugbee came, in 1865, and was president until 1868; building up the institution into prominence and power.

In 1868 Professor Jones returned, and continued at the helm until 1871, having with him as associate principal and acting president, Prof. A. F. Nightingale, an educator of the first rank, under whom the institution went prosperously forward.

But, meanwhile, the arrest of thought had come to many women's minds in Evanston. They knew that Mrs. Eliza Garrett had hoped the fortune left by her might some day warrant the founding of a college for women; they knew this was not likely to occur, as the theological school rightly demanded all the money given by that elect lady of Methodism, and needed much more. Their work in building Heck Hall had given them knowledge of their own powers, and Mrs. Mary F. Haskin, always one of our most public-spirited women, was led to speak out the purpose she had long cherished: "The next work of this kind that we do will be for girls." She did not fail to recognize the invaluable pioneer work done by Professor Jones, but felt that no private enterprise could measure up to the occasion. Mrs. Haskin went first to Mrs. Bishop Hamline, of blessed memory, who pledged her interest and co-operation. Rev. Dr. Bannister, president of the Board of Trustees of the Northwestern Female College, was the next one visited, and he said in his hearty tones, "It is just the thing to do." So a meeting was called in September 1868. Mrs. Hamline presided, and an "Educational Association" was formed, of which Mrs. Haskin was made president. In 1869 this society petitioned the town authorities to set apart as a site for the new college one of the chief parks of Evanston, which was generously done by the village board. A charter granting the power of conferring diplomas and degrees was secured from the legislature in 1869 through the efforts of Hon. Edward S. Taylor, and fifteen ladies were chosen trustees.[34]

On Feb. 13, 1870, (soon after my return from two years and a half of foreign study and travel), I was elected president of the new college, for these women had the courage of their convictions and believed a woman had as good right to be president as they had to be trustees of an educational institution of high grade. Its name was "Evanston College for Ladies," and through the influence of Rev. Dr. Haven, the new president of the university, Professor Jones consented to merge the old school in the new, surrendering his charter to the ladies' board, who in return agreed to perpetuate the history of the Northwestern Female College, and to adopt its alumnae as their own. On the day of the 16th annual commencement (June, 1870), the work of the old college ended and the transfer was completed. The new college was opened with 236 pupils, in the buildings of the old, in September 1871. On June 3d of that year the ground was broken for the Evanston College for Ladies, and on "the women's Fourth of July" its corner stone was laid. That "Fourth" was one of the most memorable days in the annals of our village. Ten thousand persons came up from the city to witness the Zouave drill, regatta, base-ball match, and other entertainments provided by the ladies, also to hear the address of United States Senator Doolittle, and witness the laying of the corner stone. About thirty thousand dollars were subscribed that day, Governor Evans, who had come from Colorado, leading off with a gift of ten thousand dollars. Rev. Obadiah Huse and L. L. Greenleaf had already subscribed like sums. But on October 9, 1871, the greatest fire of modern times devastated Chicago, and shriveled the subscriptions of Chicago men. Still the college went on, a self-supporting institution, in the old buildings, established its own departments, of art, of music, a preparatory school, and adopted a Kindergarten founded by Edward Eggleston during his sojourn in Evanston. From the first the older students of the college paid tuition and recited in the university, which, since 1869, has been open to women, Dr. Haven making this a condition of accepting the call to become its president.

In 1872 the first and only commencement exercises were held in the M. E. church, and diplomas given to a graduating class of six; and the degree of A. M. was bestowed on Mrs. J. F. Willing.

June 25, 1873, by an agreement between the two boards of trustees, the Evanston College for Ladies became the Woman's College of Northwestern University; four of its trustees being added to the University board,[35] and its president becoming Dean of the Woman's College. An Aid Association had been organized by the ladies, Rev. Obadiah Huse having suggested the plan and given the first money for carrying it out. College Cottage[36] was built, and is not only a benevolent but a self-supporting institution, in which some of the best scholars that Evanston has produced have had their home. Dr. D. K. Pearsons and Isaac R. Hitt have helped on this enterprise, and the committee of ladies has had, throughout the years, no more steadfast central figure than Mrs. John A. Pearsons.

The Conservatory of Music has been, since 1877, under the management of Prof. Oren E. Locke. Previous to his coming it existed chiefly on paper. He established four courses of study for pianists, vocalists, organists and performers on orchestral instruments. The largest number of pupils thus far has been 200, from almost every state in the Union.

The art school, which also finds its home in the Woman's College, was long under the care of Miss Catharine Beal; but this talented lady has resigned, and Miss Eva Hutchison, who has already made a name for herself, will hereafter be at the head of this important department.

The following ladies have been deans of the Woman's College: Miss Willard, Miss Eilen M. Soulé (now Mrs. Prof. Carhart, of Ann Arbor), Mrs. A. E. Sanford (of Bloomington, Ill.), Miss Jane M. Bancroft (now Mrs. George Robinson, of Detroit), and the present dean, beloved by all her great household of girls, Miss Rena M. Michaels. The number of ladies in the college increases yearly, and at present is about seventy-two.

CORPORATE RECORDS.

Away back in 1850 they had a town hereabouts called "Ridgeville," mustering at the first election, on the second of April in that year, ninety-three votes, Edwin Murphy being the first supervisor. The post office of this now mythical center was "down to Major Mulford's," he being also a tavern keeper and justice of the peace. At a special meeting the new city fathers voted down a proposition that one hundred and seventy-five dollars must be raised to meet township expenses that year. Later on they seem to have thought better of it and voted two hundred dollars for general expenses and a survey of the "Ridge Road." The first recorded township assessment was in 1853, at which time its taxable property was estimated at six thousand dollars. We find familiar names on the old tax list: George Huntoon, Eli Garfield, William Foster, Paul Pratt, Mrs. Pratt, O. A. Crain, Charles Crain, and others. In view of the "peace and good neighborhood" for which Evanston has been remarkable, such a form of oath as was required a generation ago strikes us oddly enough:

> "Peter Smith, having been elected clerk of the town of Ridgeville, made the following affidavit before E. Bennett, J. P., on the 9th day of April, 1853: 'I do solemnly swear that I have not fought a duel, nor sent or accepted a challenge to fight a duel, the probable issue of which might have been the death of either party, nor in any manner aided or assisted in such duel, nor been knowingly the bearer of such challenge or acceptance since the adoption of the constitution, ... nor will I be during my continuance in office; so help me God.' "

The village of Evanston, was laid out and platted in the winter of 1853-54, under the superintendence of Rev. Philo Judson, the university agent, who did very effective work in church and state. The plat was dated July 20, 1854, and recorded July 27, 1854. The streets were laid out during the winter and spring, and the agent was authorized to sell lots one-fifth down, and the balance in five annual payments.

Our town of Evanston, as distinct from the village aforesaid, was not organized until 1857. George Reynolds was the first supervisor, holding that office until 1863. He built our first hotel, the Reynolds House,[37] which was to the primitive Evanston what the Avenue House or French

House is to the elegant Evanston of to-day. He built "Swampscot,"[38] as we used to call it, my own early home that once stood where William Deering's beautiful residence stands now. Edwin Haskin was the next supervisor, George F. Foster, Edward S. Taylor, E. Haskin again, George Reynolds again, E. H. Gage, H. A. Grover, H. Humphrey, James Curry, George Huntoon, Jr., Max Hahn and James McMahon having severally filled the office.

Brother J. B. Colvin, who was the first "storekeeper" of whom I have cognizance, and whose anything-and-everything shop stood where Garwood's drug store[39] now gleams resplendent, was our first town clerk. The others were J. W. Clough, L. Clifford, Edwin A. Clifford, Captain J. R. Fitch, H. M. Walker, George Ide, and Harry Belden, who is the present incumbent.

Not until December 29, 1863, was the village incorporated. The first trustees were chosen January 6, 1864; Mr. H. B. Hurd, president of the board. Brother John Fussey, the good and quaint-speaking class leader, whom old settlers thought so much of, was commissioner of streets, and reported in the following August the expenditure of ninety-seven dollars and twenty-five cents, the first record of a corporate effort to ameliorate our lot—or lots! The total valuation of property was then one hundred and twenty-five thousand four hundred and eighty dollars. The presidents of the board from that day until the village organization was completed were E. Haskin, J. F. Willard, Eli Gage, E. R. Paul, J. L. Beveridge, H. G. Powers, and C. J. Gilbert.

Our wise men decided to evolute once more, and a village organization was voted April 5, 1873. C. J. Gilbert was made first president, and the other members of the new board were H. G. Powers, Lyman Gage, William Blanchard, Wilson Phelps, and Oliver A. Willard; with Charles K. Bannister, clerk. Other presidents were O. Huse, Dr. N. S. Davis, J. M. Williams, Thomas J. Frost, T. A. Cosgrove, J. J. Parkhurst, C. H. Remy, M. W. Kirk, James Ayars, H. H. C. Miller and Dr. O. H. Mann, the present incumbent of that office. Mr. Miller was the first president elected by the people, the others having been chosen by the members of the board. Mr. Miller served three terms.

OUR PUBLIC SCHOOLS.

It will doubtless be a matter of surprise to the boys and girls in the Evanston schools of to-day to learn that some of their fathers and mothers took their first steps in knowledge in a cemetery. Long before the town of Evanston was organized, a school had been in operation in an old log schoolhouse which stood on the east side of the Ridge road, as it was then called, and just south of the present Crain Street. This lot, an acre in area, had been deeded to the town by Henry Clark, grandfather of our townsman, F. W. Clark, for the rather incongruous use of educational and burial purposes. As such it was held in trust by the township trustees; and the school treasurer, in addition to paying the teacher's salary, had, as his official business, the further duty of selling lots in the cemetery. This schoolhouse did service for many years. It was not an uncommon thing in wet seasons for children to have to be carried on horseback from the east side of the town to the schoolhouse, as the region lying along Benson and Maple avenues was frequently under water.

Soon after the town of Evanston was projected, about 1855, District No. 1 was organized. As the old log house fell outside of the district, a new building had to be provided. Accordingly a one-story building was constructed about on the site of J. F. Tait's wagon shop,[40] just beyond the Haven school on Church Street. This building still stands, though removed and enlarged. At present it is located on Orrington Avenue, just north of the police station, and is occupied by a laundry. It is a pleasant thought, and one that should encourage the promoters of educational facilities among us, that this structure, the first nursery, in our district, of the young plant that has since attained such vigorous growth, has thus never been diverted from its original lofty purpose—that of elevating and purifying the community of Evanston. Our district was growing then as now, and better educational accommodations had to be provided. Accordingly, the Benson Avenue building was erected about 1860, was located in the precise geographical center of the district, and in its construction the district first contracted a bonded debt. The building consisted at first of the main upright. Afterwards a wing was added to the rear, and in 1870 the north and south wings were added at an expense of about three thousand seven hundred dollars. During the same year the district bought the lots on which the Hinman Avenue building and the north ridge school now stand.[41] Of the buildings originally erected, the north ridge school remains, while the Hinman Avenue building was removed in 1881 to make place for the more commodious structure which now ornaments that lot. The old building after its removal stood on Benson Avenue and was used as the Second Baptist church until its destruction by fire on the 14th of September 1889.

About 1879 as more room was needed, some people of the village advocated the plan of building all the schools of the district in one locality. The ground whose purchase was contemplated, is the block-just south of the Baptist church, known as the Lakeside property, and formerly a beautiful park, in the midst of which stood the Northwestern Female college. A special election was called for the purpose of deciding the question of purchase. The opponents of the plan carried the day, urging as an objection the danger to children of the west side arising from their crossing the railroad track, and a further objection to buildings of two or more stories, which would have to be erected. Upon the rejection of this plan, almost immediately measures were instituted for the construction of the Hinman Avenue and Wesley Avenue buildings, which were erected respectively in 1881 and 1882. These buildings are models of convenience and excellence, and will stand for years to come as monuments of the wisdom and good taste of the board under whose direction they were built.

The Benson Avenue building[42] served its day and generation well, till the omnivorous railroad forced its removal, and in 1888, our elegant Haven school, a noble building, named after a noble man, was built in the anticipation that it would furnish sufficient room for years to come, but it may be worthy of mention that such has been the phenomenal increase in our school population that our buildings to-day are hardly capable of containing the pupils in actual attendance. So much for our buildings. Evanston seems to have furnished little or nothing in the line of anecdote or personal reminiscence among her teachers. Mr. and Mrs. W. L. S. Bayley and Mrs. Wilbur were the most notable, of earlier annals; Frances E. Willard and Mary Bannister Willard, carried on the school in 1862, and Mary E. Willard, of "Nineteen Beautiful years,"[43] "supplied" for Mrs. Wilbur a few weeks. The names of Jenny L. Wells (now Mrs. Thomas Craven) and Miss Mary Woodford (now Mrs. Merrill) should also be included, with affectionate memory, in the enumeration of Evanston's earlier public school teachers. Among our later principals and superintendents may be mentioned Mr. Hanford, who was shot some years ago in Chicago by Alexander Sullivan. Mr. Charles Raymond was superintendent from 1869 to 1873. He was succeeded by Mr. Otis E. Haven, under whose nine years' administration the schools were brought to their utmost efficiency. Superintendent Haven was a born teacher, and to rare executive ability united an earnestness and conscientiousness which never flagged, and personal qualities which endeared him alike to associates and pupils. The high school was organized by Professor Haven, and, in lieu of other accommodations, was held in Lyons Hall. The high school was a great success, and did very efficient work, maintaining so high a standard as to prepare pupils for many of the Western colleges. Among Professor Haven's associates in this school may be mentioned Professor E. J. James, at present of the University of Pennsylvania, a young man who is rapidly gaining a national reputation as a political economist. On the organization of the Evanston township high school, in 1883, our village high school was merged in that, and thus surrendered up its individual being. The history of our present high school under the efficient management of Professor H. E. Boltwood is too well known to need comment. In 1882 Professor Haven gave up school work to enter upon the study and practice of medicine, which he had long had in contemplation as his life work. He was succeeded by Mr. George S. Baker, under whose supervision there was no lack of earnest work, and during his four years of superintendence our schools enjoyed a period of great prosperity and usefulness. In 1886 Mr. Baker resigned, and took up the practice of law, since which time the superintendence of schools has been in the very efficient hands of Mr. H. H. Kingsley, who is universally esteemed. There are twenty-five teachers in the public schools, all, with the exception of Superintendent Kingsley being ladies. A list of their names will be found in the appendix. The number of pupils in the schools, by the last report, is 1,111 of whom 589 are boys and 522 girls.

As to the financial management of our schools, much might be said both of commendation and otherwise. While there may be no charge of mismanagement, there are certain indications that great lethargy and "masterly inactivity" must have prevailed at some time. All the records of the district previous to 1872 were burned in the Chicago fire. Since that time, however, the records have been kept in perfect shape. When the board of education came together in 1879, they found eight thousand dollars in bonds due in 1880. Of these bonds there was no record of when, why, or how they were issued. It was not even known whether or not they were legal. All that could be learned about them was traditional, and the only satisfactory explanation of their existence was that they must have been the old Benson Avenue school bonds, issued back in 1860, and that, when they became due in 1870 they were called in and new issue made to cover the old. Their legality, however, was not disputed. Messrs. A. N. Young and

Simeon Farwell were then on the board, and it is due to their clearheaded financial management that the matter was promptly and satisfactorily settled. Under the direction of these men a tax of four thousand dollars was spread on the district. As to the other four thousand dollar bonds, arrangements were made with Preston, Kean & Co., to take them up and carry them for one year, Messrs. Young and Farwell giving their personal guarantee to secure the bankers against loss. They made no mistake in their faith in the people of the district, and in 1881 a further tax of four thousand dollars was levied, which wiped out the balance of the debt. Since 1880, the board have displayed great discretion and energy in the management of school matters. There are no bonds on the market that command a higher premium among bankers than those of District No. 1, Evanston, and the credit for this excellent financial standing is cheerfully conceded by his colleagues on the board to be due to Mr. A. N. Young, whose sound judgment in matters of finance has always dictated a wise and vigorous policy of management, and whose energy and ability have been untiringly devoted to the best interests of the schools during his ten years' service on the board.

Evanston has been blest in her board of education in the fact that good men have always been obtainable and willing to give their best service to the people. No man, actuated by selfish motives, has ever gained a position on this board. It has always been nonpartisan, and a policy of concession, peace, and harmony has prevailed. The list of its members includes many of our best known and most influential citizens.

It will doubtless be of interest to our taxpayers to know a bit of unwritten history. By the famous "Ordinance of 1787," organizing the Northwest Territory, provision was made to foster the cause of education by a grant to each township of one quarter of section 16 in that township, to be held in perpetuity for a school fund. By an act of May 20, 1826, in case any section 16 were not available, an equivalent amount might be set off from some other section. In Evanston township, section 16 lies in Lake Michigan. Accordingly there was assigned to Evanston, in lieu of the submerged section, the east half of the southwest quarter and the south half of the southeast quarter of section 12—a total of 153 48-100 acres. The act confirming this grant was approved July 28, 1845. For some unaccountable reason, whoever had the administration of this property sold it in 1846 at the munificent rate of *one dollar and twenty-five cents an acre,* realizing from the sale a total of one hundred and ninety-one dollars and sixty-eight cents. This amount was held in trust by the school treasurer for several years as a school fund, but was lost sight of along with all the other funds of the township, on the occasion, too fresh in our minds, when one of our treasurers suddenly disappeared, leaving no clew as to his whereabouts or future movements, and "*Ilium fuit*"[44] occupied its place in the treasurer's safe. Nothing could be more condemnatory than the short-sighted policy which dictated the sale of the property. By its disposition Evanston lost what would now be a magnificent school fund. The land referred to lies in the northwestern part of our village and at a moderate estimate is worth a thousand-fold its original selling price, and the income from its rental would serve very materially to decrease our taxes. Perhaps, after all, the loss of this fund has been a means of grace to us. The state of our union which has the most generous school fund, is notorious as having the poorest schools. People appreciate most what costs them most, and doubtless the Evanston schools would not be enjoying their present high standing and the cordial support and sympathy of the people of the village, were it not for the very generous taxes which they have been called upon to contribute, and to the call for which they have responded with such unfailing liberality.[45]

THE GROVE SCHOOL.

Among the unique institutions of historical Evanston was the "Grove School," where no grove now remains. The building dedicated to its use still stands on Hinman Avenue, just around the corner from the home of Rev. Dr. Raymond.

January 6, 1864, is the date of its beginning, and my cousin, Miss Minerva Brace (later Mrs. Norton, associated with the Woman's College), was its first principal. Her assistant was Miss Susan Warner, long a missionary in Mexico. They systematized the school, arranged the course of study, and made things easy for their successors, who were, in later years, Misses Kate Kidder, Kate Jackson, Anna Fisk, Emma B. White, and myself. We had the children of the well-to-do class for our pupils, the school having been founded by Edwin Haskin, Esq., for the good of his own six young folks, his neighbors sharing its advantages.

A letter from Mrs. Norton adds the following points:

> "In the autumn of 1863, besides the University and Female College, the educational facilities of Evanston were confined to two small rooms on the first floor of the old public school building, on Benson Avenue, each presided over by a young lady, without opportunity for the proper grading of the pupils, and with little or nothing in the way of apparatus and teaching helps. Mr. Haskin then owned and occupied the dwelling which

was formerly the home of Bishop Simpson, and south of which Hinman Avenue was undeveloped. Great forest trees stood on the northeast and southeast corners of Davis Street and Hinman Avenue, reaching to the end of the sand belt south of the point where now stands the elegant home of Mr. Stockton.[46]

"Mr. Haskin determined to found a school which should afford to his own and other children the advantages lie desired for them. Some of those monarchs of the forest had to be cut down to clear a site for the building, but others remained, giving the name to the 'Grove School.' Here the new school was opened early in January 1864. Rev. Dr. Bannister, Mr. John Chough and Mr. Haskin were the directors."

Fred. D. Raymond, one of my pupils in those days, adds fact and spice to this effect:

"There were two rooms in the building, one upstairs and one down. The older scholars were above, the younger below. There is not much difference in the ages of those of us who are here, alive, to-day, but a year or two then meant the difference of a flight of stairs. Among those upstairs were Ella Bannister, Lizzie White, Alice Judson, Rebecca Hoag, Annie Marcy, Charlie and Walter Haskin, Addison DeCoudres, George Bragdon, Henry Ten Eyck White, Will Somers, and Frank Denison, who was killed by the cars one evening on his way home from school. I was admitted to the upstairs grade. Among those downstairs were Frank and Lewis Haskin, Will Evans, Joe Somers, Evarts and Harry Boutell, Lou Bannister, Eda Hurd and Delia Ladd; and I must pause here long enough to say that if the artistic work of the last two girls were still on the blackboards, Mrs. Cayzer, the present occupant of the house, would leave the wall-paper off that its beauties might be seen . . . . . Questions were written on the board by the scholars in turn for the teacher to answer. I remember wondering at Lizzie White's daring, when one day she wrote on the board for Miss Kate Kidder to answer, 'What makes dimples?' but Miss Kate's dimples were only a little deeper and her eyes a little brighter, if possible, as she good-naturedly said that she really didn't know.

"The boys had their special friends and the girls had their secrets, and generally I suppose we behaved twenty-five years ago just about as our children behave to-day. None of the other houses on the block had then been built, so that our playground extended as far north as Davis Street, and as far east as Judson Avenue. The same peculiarly deformed tree is still standing in Mr. Boutell's back yard,[47] which formed the favorite roosting place for the girls during recess, while the boys indulged in more boisterous pastimes. A sort of rivalry, not any too generous, perhaps, existed between our boys and the public school boys, and once we all went over there to give them battle with snowballs. Ad DeCoudres, who was our biggest boy, was our leader, and as he was almost as big as he was good-natured, he had no great difficulty in inducing the rest of us to go on to victory under his protection.

"At the end of one year I left and went into the Preparatory School. I do not remember that the Grove school long survived my departure."

After about four years of successful work this school fulfilled its mission and in the interest of the public schools was peaceably and permanently closed.

THE METHODIST WOMEN'S CENTENARY ASSOCIATION.

In 1865 appeared upon the scene in Evanston a striking personality. Tall, and of large, strong frame, furnishing a symmetrical pedestal for his massive head, cliff-like brow with eager eye, aggressive nose and kindly, smiling lips, the Rev. James S. Smart, of Michigan, was somebody to notice as one passed by. Garrett Biblical Institute was still housed, after ten years of vigorous life, in the plain, wooden structure on the lake shore, later known as "Dempster Hall," burned down in 1879, and now succeeded by the Swedish Theological Seminary. Brother Smart, as we called him, (now Rev. Dr.,) had been made financial agent of Garrett Biblical Institute in the hope that his immense energy might lift and his rare ingenuity coax the enterprise out of the financial ruts into which it had fallen. Dike the sensible man he is, it forthwith occurred to Brother Smart to call the women to his aid. He took account of the fact that 1866 was to be the centennial year of Methodism. He proclaimed the discovery that Barbara Heck, that earnest-hearted Irish woman, went to Philip Embury, the first Methodist preacher on our shores, when he had proved recreant to his duty and was playing cards with a group of reckless comrades in New York city, and saying to him, "You must preach to us lest we all go to hell together," gave him his effectual call and became what Dr. Abel Stevens calls her, the "Foundress of American Methodism." He declared that in honor of this intrepid woman, faithful among the faithless a hundred years before, the contemplated building should lift its walls upon our well beloved university campus, and in September, 1865, in the old Clark Street church, Chicago, he convened us loyal Methodist sisters to listen to his plan and plea. Suffice it that our enthusiasm was equal to the good man's hopes. Such women as Mrs. Bishop Hamline (then newly arrived among us), Mrs. Governor Evans, Mrs. Dr. Kidder, Mrs. George C. Cook, Mrs. J. K. Botsford, Mrs. William Wheeler and a score of their associates, said," Let us arise and build." They associated themselves under the name of " The American Methodist Ladies' Centenary Association," and looked about for a feminine factotum of the new enterprise. It has always been my private opinion that Brother Smart desired to import from the wilds of his ever-favorite Michigan that elect lady of so much good work, Miss S. A. Rulison, but in this he was promptly overruled by valiant friends of a young woman who was at that time teaching in the Grove school, and whose defenders declared that " come what would or wouldn't, Frank Willard should have that place; she was a home institution, and no alien need apply." Brother Smart, though disappointed in the selection, was most considerate and kind toward the wholly inexperienced corresponding secretary with which his new enterprise was provided," the executive committee standing as follows: Mrs. Bishop Hamline, president; Mrs. Rev. Dr. C. H. Fowler,[48] recording secretary; Frances E. Willard, corresponding secretary; Mrs. E. Haskin, treasurer; besides Mrs. Dr. Tiffany, Mrs. Dr. Raymond, Mrs. George C. Cook and Mrs. William Wheeler. Our first move was to prepare an appeal, couched in all the eloquence that we could muster, which was sent with a personal letter from the " Corresponding Secretary" to the wives of the eight thousand Methodist ministers then included in our Zion — though we "hypothecated the bonds" in many instances, as the humorous replies of the young dominies revealed. Articles by scores were sent to the white-winged *Advocate* family throughout the nation, all of which were most courteously printed, and every paper published by our church was sent me gratuitously, for which collection my good father arranged a unique framework of a file, taking a great interest in the arrangement of my first visible "office." He it was who kept my books and looked after my financial responsibilities, else I am sure I should have fallen into speedy disgrace, never having had a head for figures, except figures of speech. Our honored townsfolk, Mr. and Mrs. Simeon Farwell, had recently removed to Evanston, living just across the street from our new M. E. church, and with these generous friends I spent the winter of 1866, our own home, one block east, having been sold soon after my sister Mary left us, and Rest Cottage not being yet sufficiently settled for so large an enterprise as our "Cen-*ten*-ary," as gainsaying friends were wont to call it. Many a "bee" we made at the Farwell house, my church friends and

Grove school pupils gathering to help me and trundling off packages to the post office by the wheelbarrow load. Dr. Abel Stevens, our famous church historian, wrote a delightful book, at the request of our association, which he entitled," Women of Methodism," and dedicated to Mrs. Bishop Hamline and me. Brother Smart had a certificate prepared for all our members, donors, etc., in which was inserted the amount given, certified by Mrs. Hamline and the corresponding secretary, Miss Kate Kidder acting in this capacity when, in the autumn of 1866, I went to Lima, N. Y., as preceptress of Genesee Wesleyan Seminary. This certificate I come upon occasionally in these days .in Methodist homes, and smile to note what Brother Smart regarded as a *chef d'oeuvre,* representing a library adorned with portraits of Wesley and Francis Asbury wherein Eliza Garrett presents a lengthy roll containing his gospel commission to a mild-looking young man of slight figure and noticeably ample brow. We had no visions in those benighted days of lovely Rev. Mary Phillips, the first lady graduate of the generous Institute, nor of Rev. Eliza Frye and other ladies who have held their own so nobly as theological students in these broader years. Our efforts to collect money were measurably successful, but as Brother Smart could put no patent on his new idea, every separate educational enterprise of Methodism seemed suddenly possessed to enlist the efforts of women, hence our territory steadily decreased, and though kept in countenance by the great " Centennial Committee," it also and equally countenanced all the other sets of women, therefore we were somewhat put to confusion, although we were particularly careful not to say so. In all the philanthropic tintinnabulation of that year we kept trying to be heard, and in the din we literally "drummed up" about thirty thousand dollars. Heck Hall was built, the cornerstone being laid by Bishop Thompson, who delivered one of his classical addresses on the occasion, and Brother Smart read the paper prepared by me, as corresponding secretary, while I stood by in modest meekness, for woman's hour of utterance was not yet come. The dedication occurred in 1867, Rev. Dr. Eddy and Gen. Clinton B. Fisk participating, and the "American Methodist Ladies' Centenary Association "passed out of sight and out of mind. But I have often thought that through the widespread organizations of women in that memorable year of 1866, tens of thousands first learned their power in organized and widespread movements.

EVANSTON'S CHURCHES.

It was a very interesting and curious thing to see the various branches of Zion begin to sprout as our village increased. For many a happy year we had said: " Behold how good and how pleasant it is for brethren to dwell together in unity," and rejoiced in the catholicity of spirit that set Episcopalian and Quaker side by side in a Methodist meetinghouse. To be sure, in all this halcyon period, distinctive doctrinal features were so wisely held in abeyance that no one could feel himself estranged or his own tenets criticised. All of us alike believed in " the faith that works by love and purifies the heart; " all believed in God, in duty, in rewards for right living, and punishments for wrong, not based on favoritism or on vengeance, but as the inevitable outcome of the laws written in our members and our minds and reflected on the shining mirror of the Bible's open page; and all believed in One who came to show us what God's heart is like, the Ideal Man, the Incarnate Deity, the World's Redeemer. But for questions of method, then, we might have stayed together, and while we did stay, we were most kindly affectioned one toward another, and when any went it was with the blessing of those who remained and a building lot from the Methodist university, and help from the Methodist brethren to begin their new enterprise. For we all recognized the fact that one church will not yet contain all who accept Christ's gospel, though I think we almost all believed the broader generalization of divine truth that is yet to be universally accepted and will bring humanity to the blessed estate of "one fold and one Shepherd."

Each of the denominations stands out like an individual, or, better, each typifies a temperament. To my imagination handsome Pope Pius IX, as I have seen him, robed in his dazzling pontificals and celebrating mass at the high altar of St. Peter's, incarnated the Catholic church; conservative Dr. John Hall, erect and noble, in the stately pulpit of his million dollar church in New York city, incarnated the Presbyterian; cultured Dr. Phillips Brooks, at Trinity church, Boston, the Episcopal; clear-cut, scholarly and eloquent Dr. Richard S. Storrs, in his plainer Brooklyn church, the Congregational; Spurgeon, in the great people's tabernacle in London, the Baptist; and Bishop Simpson, before the Ecumenical Council of his church, the Methodist. Very likely the most loyal members of these different communions would accept the characterization thus suggested. As to temperaments, let us say that the Methodist stands for the sanguine; Congregational for the nervous (in a good sense, of course); Presbyterian for the bilious (still in a good sense); Baptist for the sanguine-bilious; Catholic and Episcopalian for the aesthetic. Far be it from me to adopt the profane but witty *bon mot* of an English reviewer, who characterized the High, Broad and Low church parties of that realm as Attitudinarians, Latitudinarians and Platitudinarians. It seems to me the jubilee singers showed a better appreciation of the eternal fitness of things when they vociferated

Methodis' and Baptis' jus' gone along,

for these two churches are pre-eminently fraternal, and, in one sense or another, both are dedicated to cold water. The natural affiliations of the Congregational and Presbyterian faith and practice were clearly illustrated when the two set up housekeeping together in Evanston.

OUR CONGREGATIONAL CHURCH.

The first thing I can recall about this favored branch of the church universal, probably the most thoroughly *American* in its genius and methods of any that can be named, is that Rev. Dr. S. C. Bartlett was advertised, sometime in 1859, to speak in the university chapel on Sunday afternoon. Though Dr. Foster's morning lecture, the regular church service, and Sunday-school at two o'clock, had been already an ample portion for a young student who carried eight solid studies on five days of the week and was devoted to the work of the "Minerva" Literary society of her college, I nevertheless went to hear this already celebrated man. Even had he been less well known, the "leanings" of my nature would have carried me to this first service of the Congregationalists, for during the five years that they were students at Oberlin, Ohio, my parents had belonged to Rev. Dr. Charles G. Finney's church; he was the first minister to whom I, as a child, had ever listened; my mother had joined the Congregationalists of Janesville, Wis., under the pastorate of Rev. Henry Foote, and in 1857 with my sister I had been a student of Milwaukee Female college, where we attended Plymouth church, Rev. Z. M. Humphrey, pastor, and rejoiced in the Bible class instructions of his gifted wife, who, had she lived in a more enlightened age, would have been a preacher like her husband; indeed she is in these last days.

On this first Congregational day in Evanston an observant school girl, "watching out" to learn all that she could, and especially fascinated by individualties pronounced and noble, saw standing up in the little pine pulpit of our small university chapel, with a group of thoughtful

First Congregational Church

folks before him, Dr. Bartlett, now and for many years president of Dartmouth college.

A more thorough New England type was never transplanted to the west; he was pure nerve, with just enough muscle to serve as insulator. That mountainous brow, thatched with brown hair; that eagle-beak nose; those thin, mobile lips; blue eyes, flashing like electric lights—made up a human galvanic battery the shock of whose thought was a stimulus to the intellect such as across the wide space of thirty years must remain with all who then received it.

Dr. Bartlett never spoke after that day without crowding the chapel with students; for, unlike most ministers, he *spoke*, although at the same time he read his manuscript. But the vibrant vigor of his tones; the quick, yet graceful, action; the intense countenance; the martial music of his balanced periods; all held us as closely to his thought as if no film of a paper intermediary intruded between his mind and ours.

Sometimes Rev. Dr. Fisk, who, like Dr. Bartlett, was a professor in the Congregational Theological Seminary, at Chicago, came out to preach; and him we also liked—another typical New Englander with its iron in his blood and its granite in his backbone— though he was not an orator so striking as his *confrere*. Rev. Fred Beecher came, and to him we young Methodists were also attracted by his youth, his mingled culture, and offhandedness;—besides, he was "Henry Ward's" nephew, and who was quite so *magnifique* in all America as that great and brotherly soul?

It stood to reason, then, that we were glad our Congregational friends had set up housekeeping by themselves among us, for the advent of their men of power gave an added intellectual impetus to our ways of thinking on religion, and was thus in line with the splendid teachings of our own Simpson, Dempster, Foster, and the rest.

The records say that on the eighth of December 1859, an ecclesiastical council met and organized the First Congregational church of Evanston. At this meeting Rev. Dr. Wolcott preached the sermon, and Rev. Dr. W. W. Patton offered prayer. Eight women and three men made up the church, and their names were as follows: Mrs. M. T. Earle, Mr. and Mrs. Isaac D. Guyer, Miss Charlotte A. Kellogg, Mrs. Hannah L. Porter, A. G. Sherman (clerk), Mrs. S. A. Sherwood, Mrs. William G. White, Silas S. Whitney, Anna C. Winfield, Harriet C. Wood. Just here would naturally come in the letter of Mrs. Judge Stacy (née Kellogg), once teacher of music in the Northwestern Female College, in which she tells me of her "charter membership," and reveals the fact that she was the first organist of this new church. Miss Hattie Wood was a student at the college and classmate of my sister and myself. Mrs. Porter was our Professor Godman's mother-in-law. I wonder if Mrs. Earle was not the wife of Parker Earle, the temperance lecturer, who then lived in a modest cottage about where Mr. Francis Bradley and family have so long had their beautiful home.

It seems curious that all of this pioneer eleven should have moved away within a few months after the formation of the church, from a town that had hardly more than five hundred inhabitants, but so it was. No pastor had been settled, and there was an interregnum of six years or more until the Bradley family appeared upon the scene, in 1865, in whose house the first weekly prayer-meeting of the new church was held November 6, of that year. Several other families soon joined them, and by April 1 of 1866, it was decided to hold meetings in the university chapel. Sunday services began June 1, 1866. An independent church was formed, and the Rev. James B. Duncan, of the Canada Presbyterian persuasion, was invited to become its pastor at a salary of two thousand dollars per year. He accepted the call and began his labors in July 1866. The church was formally organized on the first of August following, the services taking place in the Baptist church, then located at the northeast corner of Hinman Avenue and Church Street. Rev. Mr. Duncan was, on the same evening, installed pastor. A Sunday-school was organized on the nineteenth of the same month. The society purchased a lot on the southeast corner of Chicago Avenue and Lake Street and erected a church edifice, aided liberally in the enterprise by the people of the town and by the Northwestern University. This church was styled the Lake Avenue church, from its location.

But this enterprise had been carried on by Presbyterians as well as Congregationalists, and in 1868, the latter swarmed into a separate church, whose edifice was begun in November of that year, and within about two years it was completed and had a fine organ, the total expense being nearly twenty-five thousand dollars. The beautiful site on Hinman Avenue was intended for a village park but was given by the university to this new church.

The trustees of the church were Francis Bradley, John M. Williams, Heman G. Powers, Julius White, and Samuel Greene. On September 19, 1869, public services began in the new lecture room, and a Sunday school was organized. Prof. F. D. Hemenway, D.D., of Garrett Biblical Institute, supplied the pulpit for a few months before a pastor was settled. Rev. Edward N. Packard, of Brunswick, Maine, a graduate of Bowdoin college, assumed this relation January 1, 1870, and the church was dedicated January 9. Rev. Dr. Bartlett preached the sermon, and President E. O. Haven made an appeal for the removal of the floating debt, which resulted in clearing it away by raising five thousand dollars. The installation occurred January 13, when Rev. Dr. Fisk preached the sermon, Rev. Dr. Patton gave the pastor's "charge," Rev. E. F. Williams and Rev. Dr. L. T. Chamberlan gave the "right hand of fellowship to church and pastor respectively," and Rev. Dr. J. E. Roy the address to the people.

The nine years' pastorate of Rev. Mr. Packard is most pleasantly remembered by Evanstonians, not only by reason of that scholarly and genial man's own sturdy hard work in his church and his brotherly interest in every good thing for which the villagers were striving, but because of the noble, gracious presence of Mrs. Packard, a strong, clear-headed woman, who did not a little to help forward the interests of church and community in general. We all bemoaned their going, but they thought it best to accept the invitation to Dorchester, Mass., and went there in response to the earnest call of the historic old "Second Congregational church," in the spring of 1879.

The next pastor was Rev. A. J. Scott, a brilliant young graduate of our university, who had been a Methodist minister and came at first as a supply, but was installed November 6, 1879, and remained for about six years and a half, resigning the pastorate June 28, 1886. Meanwhile, in 1883, the church was enlarged, repaired, and its seating capacity increased one-third at a cost of thirty-two hundred dollars; but on the night of November 23, 1884, it was destroyed by fire. The zeal and wealth of the people combined to rebuild promptly; December 6, 1885, worship was commenced in the basement of the present handsome edifice, and April 11, 1886, the new church was dedicated, its cost, with the organ, being about fifty thousand dollars.

On the thirty-first day of March 1887, the church and society voted unanimously to invite Rev. Nathan H. Whittlesey, of Creston, Iowa, to become their pastor, and he was installed June 7, 1887. Brother Whittlesey is a man of exact thought, ready expression, and outspoken opinion, and has the record of a hero on the temperance question during Iowa's great prohibitory campaign and harder battles for the enforcement of her law.

Two experiences of my life especially endear this church to me. Returning from Europe in the autumn of 1870, the very first invitation to make use of what I had there learned came from my earnest sisters here. They asked me to speak of my observations on missionary countries: Greece, Turkey, Asia Minor, Egypt and Palestine. So I prepared a little address entitled "The New Crusade," and stood up before them in an afternoon meeting to make the first speech of my life outside of a student's and teacher's exercise, —the paper shaking in my hands so that I had no small ado to read it. Soon after, my Methodist friends in Chicago invited me to give the same address before the local Woman's Foreign Missionary society of Centenary church, and other church societies went on doing so until (usually in the pleasant company of Mrs. Mary H. B. Hitt, and sharing the exercises with her) I had repeated the operation about thirty times. Albro E. Bishop, then its leading member, having heard me at Centenary M. E. church in the spring of 1871, generously came to Evanston to see me, urged me to go upon the platform, and introduced me there under most favorable circumstances, and from that time dates my public work.

The other meeting was soon after my election as president of the Evanston College for Ladies (February 14, 1871), when Mrs. Mary F. Haskin presided, and Dr. Haven and I sang the praises of the new venture in women's education, which was so thoroughly undenominational that our Congregational sisters were foremost in its every good word and work.

The membership of this grand church in Evanston is three hundred and fifty; Sunday-school, three hundred and six; its officers are all men, the present trustees being J. H. Kedzie, J. M. Larimer, Nelson DeGolyer, W. H. Brown, and Frank Gould. Its Sunday-school officers are also men, as shown by the following complete list of superintendents since its beginning:

Mr. Francis Bradley, Mr. L. H. Boutell, Mr. Charles Dutton, Rev. E. N. Packard, Mr. George F. Stone, Mr. H. W. Chester, Rev. A. J. Scott, Mr. E. D. Redington, Hon. Burton C. Cook, Mr. A. K. Brown. But among its teachers twenty are women and nine men. Its work is chiefly done by women, as the "Directory of Societies" abundantly illustrates, in which, among the five societies enumerated, Christian Endeavor, Home Missionary, Foreign Missionary, Young People's Missionary and Light Bearers, there are twenty-five names, all but four being the names of women. Some day, in this and all other churches, the proportion will be more equitably maintained between labor and power. A noble beginning in this direction has been made recently by the Congregational Theological Seminary in Hartford, Conn., which publicly announces that all its privileges are henceforth open to women. Heaven bless the church of the Puritans in Evanston. Its *morale* is excellent, its spirit progressive; long may it liberate!

OUR EPISCOPAL CHURCH.

As everybody knows, John Wesley never left the Church of England, and did his best to have no schism. He went to the Bishop of London and asked him to send out a "shepherd and bishop" to the struggling groups of gospel Christians organized in America, and not until that prelate somewhat loftily declined, did the Father of Methodism authorize Thomas Coke to go over and ordain Francis Asbury, the first Methodist bishop. Naturally enough, with antecedents of this sort, there is much in common between the two communions.

My father was one of the most pronounced and loyal Methodists I ever knew, but when, in the old days of our life in Wisconsin, the circuit preacher had an appointment elsewhere, we children went with him to Trinity church, Janesville, of which that gracious old saint, Rev. Dr. Ruger, was rector so long. There I first learned to repeat the Apostles' Creed, to revere the litany and to love the music of the organ.

Our Episcopal friends remained with us here in Evanston until the spring of 1864, when the Rev. John Wilkinson, chaplain to Bishop Whitehouse, gave notice in the chapel of the university that a church would be organized in the M. E. church building on April 20. The same gentleman conducted the first service in the same building on the third Sunday in May. At the preceding meeting a constitution had been adopted and signed by the following persons: A. G. Wilder, John A. Lighthall, H. B. Hurd, D. J. Crocker, John Lyman, J. H. Kedzie, F. M. Weller, P. G. Siller, H. C. Cone, J. S. Haywood, William C. Comstock. Charles Comstock was elected senior warden, and D. J. Crocker, junior warden.

Concerning this infant church, a lady who has been devoted to its fortunes from the beginning writes me as follows in response to an earnest request for facts:

"I remember that the Methodist church was very kindly offered to us and accepted at least twice for special services, many of the students and others joining with us in the responses. Our first regular services were held in the university chapel. I remember the little melodeon we used was carried every week to and from the Avenue House, where our lady organist boarded, and that Will Comstock acted the part of sexton and chorister combined. The Comstock carriage was in request to gather up the singers for Saturday night rehearsal. Those were certainly the days of small beginnings. I think there were only three or four families who were really our people when the parish was organized.

"Rev. Mr. Holcombe was minister in charge. In the spring he

accepted a call to Wisconsin and left us. We had no further services until the following August. In the meantime our church was built and paid for, and in August 1885, was consecrated. Our diocesan convention was then in session in Chicago. The convention adjourned, and with Bishop Whitehouse all the members came up to the consecration of our little church. There was also a very pleasant reception given for them on the grounds of one of our members. Our first rector, Rev. John Buckmaster, had just come to us. He remained two years. Afterwards we had Rev. Mr. Lyle, Rev. Mr. Barrow, and Rev. Mr. Abbot, the latter remaining four years. Rev. Dr. Justin, to whom you refer, was a very kindly, genial and excellent man, and most interesting in his accounts of his travels in Scandinavia and elsewhere, but he was not our rector, only minister in charge for a short time; a great worker, too, yet I hardly think his work left much lasting trace upon the church. The one who, it seems to me, did the most to raise the whole tone of church life and worship, was Rev. J. Stewart Smith, who was our rector from 1876 to 1880. One advance made then, I for one regret we have lost. The seats in our church were for a few years free. Perhaps it was the coming into the parish afterwards of so many who had always been used to the pew system which made the other, and as I think better, seem impracticable to some. After Mr. Smith, came Rev. Dr. Jewell and Rev. Mr. Hayward, for both of whom I have a high regard, and both of whom, I think, did much good and lasting work in the church, especially in the work of instruction and churchly life. Now we feel ourselves so happy and blessed in our present rector, Rev. Arthur W. Little, that we can hardly be thankful enough. And I can not but feel that we have come to a new era of real growth and prosperity when our church life, sending its roots deep down into the eternal verities, will, I hope, bear not fair flowers only, the external features of a noble and reverent worship (and they are a part of God's plan), but also abundant fruit of good works which shall be a beneficent influence through time and beyond.

"The Woman's Guild, which is at the same time the parish aid society and a branch of the Woman's Auxiliary, our general missionary organization, has done faithful and excellent work, as have also, at times, the Men's Guild and the St. Andrew's Society. Recently the young girls have united under the name of St. Margaret's Guild, and are doing their share in the work of the Master."

The original church building on Davis Street between Ridge and Oak avenues was erected in 1865, the lot having been given by the university. The consecration occurred in September 1865, when Rev. John W. Buckmaster became the first rector. The first confirmation was administered by the assistant bishop of Indiana to ten persons, March 26, 1866. The second rector was Rev. Thomas Lyle, of Philadelphia, who took charge of the parish May 26, 1867, Mr. Buckmaster having resigned April 1, 1867. The second Episcopal visitation was made April 19, 1868, by Bishop Henry J. Whitehouse, of Illinois, who confirmed four persons. During the summer of 1868 the church building was enlarged, the belfry added, and a bell procured. During the years 1868 and 1869 the parish more than doubled its membership. The rectors in succession after Dr. Lyle have been as follows:

June 7, 1869, Rev. A.J. Barrows.
September, 1870, Rev. J. P. Justin.
April, 1872, Rev. C. D. Abbott.
February, 1876, Rev. J. Stewart Smith.
May, 1880, Rev. Dr. Fredericks. Jewell.
February, 1886, Rev. Richard Hayward.
November, 1888, Rev. Arthur W. Little, the present rector.

Rev. James Stewart Smith, B. D., deacon, for some time assistant to Rev. Edward William McLaren, D. D., rector of Trinity parish, Cleveland, O., and after the elevation of the latter to the episcopate, minister in charge of that parish, was advanced to the priesthood to enter upon his labors as rector of St. Mark's parish, Evanston.

This was the beginning of a new order of things wherein was a striking contrast to the old. The change was a marked advance in catholic teaching and practice, and the work thus earnestly begun has been faithfully increased and widened by Mr. Smith's successors. The trend of this movement has steadily been in harmony with that of the catholic revivalists of the Anglican Church, and St. Mark's has been highly favored in the men who have been her pilots in this reform. The enthusiasm and tact with which Rev. Stewart Smith inaugurated and planned, were confirmed and strengthened by the scholarly eloquence and firmly-guiding hand of Dr. Jewell, and these talents are now combined in one whose foresight and energy augur well for the future of the parish,—Rev. Arthur Little.

This church, very small at first, has been enlarged four times, once by lengthening toward the street, once by adding the bell tower, then the east side or aisle, and lastly the west side or aisle and the organ loft with the organ.

And now, as a sequel to all this, comes the white building of stone which stands in its completed majesty on the corner of Ridge Avenue and Lake Street. The lot was purchased some time ago by the church, and the edifice itself cost forty-five thousand dollars, and was formally opened for public worship on Easter Sunday of 1891, which was the greatest day ever yet seen in Evanston for this branch of the universal household of faith.

All hail to the leisurely graces of our Episcopal church; long may it live; long may it lucubrate![49]

OUR PRESBYTERIAN CHURCH.

It was in the year 1866 that the Evanston Congregationalists and Presbyterians together launched their ship and added one more to the glorious fleet that sails under the cross as an ensign. After two years of peaceable companionship, the Presbyterians went their way, the sister denomination paying them for one-half of their joint property. In this case, as heretofore, the university gave a building lot; this was exchanged for one occupying the corner of Chicago Avenue and Lake Street, where the present commodious church edifice of the Presbyterians is located. During the period of union, Rev. James B. Duncan, of the Canadian Presbyterian church, was pastor, serving acceptably. On July 27, 1868, the First Presbyterian church of Evanston was organized in the building erected by the two societies, by the help of both university and town, as in all other cases. Thirty-eight persons, twenty-four of them women, would afterward become the welcome and happy home of himself and his family—numbered thirty-eight members.

"Since the organization of the Congregational church in 1869 there have been seven other churches organized within the village. Twenty years ago there were five, and I believe only five, in the whole town, and not in the village of Evanston alone. Now there are twenty-one, of which eight are Methodist, so this denomination maintains, though not in such a degree as formerly, its ascendency.

"In 1870 we enlarged our own church edifice, adding a hundred sittings to the main audience room, and a pleasant lecture room. This building, with all its contents, was destroyed by fire in the early Sabbath morning of May 2, 1875. The work of rebuilding on the same site was begun almost immediately, so that we were able to hold our first service in the lecture room—a Christmas service—on December 26 of the same year. On July 26, 1876, the nation's centennial year, this house was dedicated to the worship of Almighty God. The cost of the edifice was about twenty-five thousand dollars, including all its appointments,

First Presbyterian Church

but not including the lot.

"In the interval between the destruction of the old and our entering the new house of worship, the homeless flock, though generally offered hospitality by all our sister churches, yet found it best suited to their convenience to meet in Lyon's hall. Those were days of peril, and days, too, of trial. At the time the necessity was laid upon us to build, the whole community was suffering, and our people not less than others, from severe and protracted financial depression. The prevailing tone in business circles was one of despondency. The devastating Chicago fire, by which some of our people were financially ruined and all of them crippled, had occurred only three and a half years before, and none of them had recovered from that fearful blow. But harmony in council, unity in effort, brave hearts and self-sacrificing spirits, with the rich blessing of God crowning all, brought us safely through. We were obliged for a time to carry a burden of debt, which, however, was entirely canceled in 1883.

"During these twenty years it has been my privilege to welcome to the communion of this church six hundred and eighteen persons by letter and three hundred and forty-five on confession; making a total of nine hundred and sixty-three. If we had suffered no losses by removal and death in all these years, our membership would now amount to one thousand and one. The average annual addition has been a little more than forty-eight, while the average annual addition on confession has been seventeen and one-fourth. The great joy has been mine to place the sacramental sign and seal of the covenant upon the brow of one hundred and forty-five children. Twenty-seven have come into the church, seventy-eight are still too young to come, leaving twenty-two whose parents have moved elsewhere with them, unaccounted-for. During these years seventy-five couples have stood before me to take upon themselves the sacred and inviolable vows of marriage. A group of one hundred and fifty newly wedded people, if they could all be brought together, ought to be surely a very happy company.

"Passing now to speak of our contributions for benevolent objects and for the support of our own church work, I am sorry that I have not the full record of what we have done. I can only present the figures from 1883, when we first adopted the plan of systematic giving, to 1887, inclusive. During this period of five years our contributions to the boards and other benevolent objects aggregate twenty-three thousand one hundred and thirteen dollars, or a yearly average of four thousand six hundred and sixty-two dollars; and for our church support an aggregate of forty-one thousand five hundred and thirty-eight dollars, including the payment of a debt of seven thousand dollars. All our contributions for the past five years not including the year now closing, amount to sixty-four thousand six hundred and fifty-one dollars, or a yearly average of twelve thousand nine hundred and thirty dollars. Before the adoption of the plan of systematic giving, our annual contributions were not nearly so large as they have since been. Probably the aggregate of all our contributions for the fifteen years not included in the statement just made would amount to one hundred and ten thousand dollars, making for the whole twenty years a grand total of one hundred and seventy-four thousand dollars, or a yearly average of eight thousand two hundred dollars. How much outside this sum individual members of the congregation have given to all good causes and objects, only He knows who ever watches what is done and all that is done by everyone in his or her ministrations to the persons and causes which are needy and worthy.

"A delightful spirit of peace and harmony has so prevailed among us that it has never been once broken or interrupted. We began with thirty-eight members and we have now somewhere from four hundred and fifty to five hundred, and have besides a goodly, proper and prosperous child of our love in the South Evanston Presbyterian church, organized with fifty members three years ago the 28th of last June, and numbering now nearly or quite three times as many. In our Sabbath-school, larger now than ever before, we are well officered and well equipped for doing more faithful work than at any time in the past; the same is true of our Bethel school, which offers an enlarging field for missionary work, and where many of our young people are doing a faithful service that is worthy of all praise; our Young People's Society of Christian Endeavor, which is stronger than ever; our woman's missionary societies and Young Ladies' Society and Children's Mission Band—all working by little and little to carry the blessed gospel to those who have it not; our Ladies' Church Association, diligent as Dorcas in providing garments for the poor missionaries and their families; and our kitchen garden, where, yesterday forenoon in the lecture room below, were gathered, as they will be every Saturday, eighty-four poor girls who are taught how to sew and make their own garments, while, in addition, twenty-four of this number are taught to do kitchen and housework; in all these organized, and in manifold private and unobserved ways, we are trying to do the work which belongs to us as a church of Jesus Christ."

With the month of April, 1890, came the young and devoted pastor, who is to be the Elisha succeeding this ascended Elijah,—Rev. N. D. Hillis. He brings with him an accomplished wife, who is no less consecrated to the work of the Lord.

The church manual gives the name of H. E. C. Daniels as Sunday-school superintendent, a name that is fragrant with the love of the young people and children, to whom he is like a second pastor, and of Mrs. Bancroft, who has the infant class, and of whom it is said "nobody in the church is a greater success than she; to lose her would be nothing short of a calamity." The present ruling elders of the church are: Thomas Lord, H. C. Hunt, O. L. Baskin, A. B. Hull, William H. Lewis and H. J. Wallingford.

Probably the most distinguished name ever on the church list is that of the late Mrs. Jane C. Hoge, of Chicago, who shares with Mrs. Mary A. Livermore the distinction of having stood at the head of all those "women of the war," whose record in caring for the wounded is as glorious as that of our soldiers on the field.

Our Presbyterian church has now five hundred members, and four hundred and fifty-five in its Sunday-school. Its church property is valued at twenty-five thousand dollars. Born of a heroic epoch in church history; nurtured in classic halls; and sturdy in the faith, may this magnificent denomination broaden out to the full meaning of the words "there is neither male nor female in Christ Jesus," so that in its household of faith there shall be no official service which women shall not be called upon to share. Heaven bless that branch of the great Presbyterian church with whose presence our town is favored. Long may it live and love and learn, and learned be!

THE GERMAN EVANGELICAL LUTHERAN CHURCH.

The German Evangelical Lutheran Church was founded in 1874 by Rev. Edward Doering, pastor of the Lutheran church at Glencoe, Ill. In June, 1872, Rev. Dr. Reinke, pastor of one of the Lutheran churches of Chicago, began preaching to a small number of Germans who assembled in little cottages about once in four weeks. Most of the Germans who came to Evanston were from Mecklenburg, a rich country it is true, but at that time still subject to the oppressions of landlordism. Poverty and ignorance were the natural consequences. Many could not even write their own names. How difficult the religious work was among such people, how difficult to gain their confidence and elevate them to a higher plane, may be imagined. Dr. Reinke, however, succeeded in awakening the dormant soul of a small number, who finally organized in a small room of a little cottage, somewhere in the neighborhood of the present gas works. In 1874 Rev. Mr. Doering, who had been sent to take charge of the Lutheran church at Glencoe, began preaching here every two weeks. After a few years of his ministry the little congregation, mostly poor people, built a small chapel on Florence Street, on-the very verge of the prairie. Those principally interested in the church work then, were Wm. E. Suhr, Aug. P. Handke, G. Glaser, Martin Becker, C. Randt and Henry Witt. The work progressed slowly, when, in August 1881, Rev. J. A. Detzer was called as pastor of this church and of that at Glencoe, which place Rev. Mr. Doering had vacated to go to Portland, Oregon. There were only twenty-three members enrolled here at the time. Mr. Detzer immediately established a German school with less than a dozen children, in the attic of a little cottage at the foot of Greenwood Street. His work having increased greatly, he gave the school in charge of Mr. H. Fenchter in 1885. In 1886 Mr. Martin Bittner was called, and is still the teacher.

In 1884 the church purchased a lot on the corner of Greenwood Street and Wesley Avenue, upon which they built a neat little schoolhouse, which was also to serve as a dwelling for their pastor. The school prospered, and with it the congregation, so that in the course of another year the old chapel began to be too small and a new church became indispensable. It seemed a great undertaking and promised a hard struggle, but with the help of God they were able to dedicate their new church on the 21st of November 1886. The building is quite a handsome structure, and has a capacity of about five hundred. The congregation now numbers over seventy voting members, and over two hundred and fifty communicants, and the school seventy-four pupils. These good friends have seen many dark and stormy days, but God has been with them, and is prospering them both externally and internally. May the time not be distant when women will vote within its sacred walls.

OUR METHODIST CHURCH.

Our Methodist church virtually began with that kneeling group of ministers and laymen who met in Judge Goodrich's office May 31, 1850, to take the initial steps toward founding the Northwestern University. But the first quarterly conference for Evanston was not held until July 13, 1854, at the log schoolhouse in the town of Ridgeville, eighteen years after Mr. Hill's family first appeared upon the scene and a still longer period after Major Mulford and his family spied out the land. Those present at this church conference were Reverends Philo

First M.E. Church

Judson and J. G. Johnson, traveling preachers; George W. Huntoon, class leader; James B. Colvin, John L. Beveridge, and A. Danks, elected stewards; Abraham Wigelsworth, Sunday-school superintendent. This school was represented as having eighty-four children, thirteen officers and teachers, and one conversion.

The second conference was held Jan. 24, 1855, Rev. P. W. Wright, then a teacher in Garrett Biblical Institute, was appointed by the elder as preacher in charge.

The church now met in a comfortable room over Colvin's store, and Mr. Judson, the owner of the building, made no charge for rent. Garwood's drug store now stands on the same site, and the original building is behind Garwood's, on Orrington Avenue, and is occupied by a barber shop.[50] Its general form and appearance remain unchanged.

No record of gifts for benevolent purposes occurs until the fourth quarterly conference held by the church. It then took a creditable position by sending nine hundred and twenty dollars for missions, and three hundred and twenty dollars for tracts, and raising four hundred and seventy-four dollars for the support of preachers.

Having vitality enough to give, it had enough to *live,* and not at a "poor, dying rate," either, but to ask for a regular pastor, who was appointed December 22, 1855, in the person of that genial soul, "Father Sinclair." He was one of the pioneers of the west,—a model specimen of the Methodist preacher, tall, of dignified bearing, well dressed, and always wearing the spotless white tie now quite generally forsworn by all but bishops. His iron gray hair, smooth-shaven face and genial smile were good to see. Accosted on the train by a stranger, with the words, "Are you a professor in the new Methodist Heavenston?" he dryly answered, "Yes—professor of religion."

His "official board" was as follows: Rev. Philo Judson, Rev. Dr. Dempster, Professor Wright, J. McNulty and F. B. Harris, local preachers; Meander Clifford, J. W. Klapp, exhorters; Professor Noyes, James B. Colvin, John L. Beveridge and A. Danks, stewards; S. R. Cook, local elder.

The next spring a church edifice was reared on the north side of Church Street, between Chicago and Orrington avenues, and it was dedicated July 27, 1856, the sermon being preached by Dr. Dempster, while Professor Godman and Rev. John Sinclair, pastor, assisted in the services. The next fall (1857), Rev. A. D. Cooper, of Vermont conference, a student in our theological school, and an amiable and excellent man, was appointed pastor. He was followed in the autumn of 1858, by Rev. C. P. Bragdon, of Rock River conference. The coming of Brother Bragdon and his family was a notable event in the history of early

Evanston. Our new pastor and all belonging to him were greatly beloved. To him some of us young people are glad to remember that we gave our names as " members on probation." He served us faithfully and was a blessed presence in our homes during the two years that he remained with us, but consumption, the disease against which he had battled long and bravely, overcame him in the winter of 1861 (January 8), and he left us with the wonderful legacy of his spotless life and the memorable words in life's last hour, "*Christ is my Malakoff.*"

Brother Bragdon's ministry was followed by that of Rev. R. K. Bibbins in 1860. Rev. J. R. Goodrich came in 1861, and was especially endeared to us by the Christian courage with which he received the awful tidings that his only son had been instantly killed in battle.

In 1862 came Rev. Dr. Tiffany, whose pastorate stands out clearly by reason of his culture, elegance, and eloquence, and his wife's genius for geniality. The doctor was esthetic; flowers on the pulpit were a joy to him; and I remember the pleasure it was to me to gather the prettiest ones from our garden, which Mr. William Deering's rare conservatory has replaced, and to take them to the church on Sabbath mornings. One day, however, our tasteful pastor came to select them for himself, and made a bouquet so much finer than I had ever seen evolved from such raw material as we could furnish, that I quite lost heart in my endeavors. The doctor could not put up with the bareness of our "old church," as we called it, which was accordingly enlarged by means of a transept, and decorated within, according to his wishes. The present parsonage was also built during his stay, Rev. O. Huse and my father being the prime movers in that enterprise, if I rightly remember. The church had one hundred and seventy-five members at this time, and by the addition of the transept, accommodated six hundred persons,—that is, it could seat almost all the village, and had need to do so, as there was no other public assembly room for miles around.

Rev. Dr. Miner Raymond, who had lately come among us as the successor of Rev. Dr. Dempster in the chair of systematic theology, became our pastor when Dr. Tiffany went east in 1865. This man, great in the perfect simplicity and sincerity of his character and universally endeared to church and world's people alike, it would be presumptuous to sketch in the small space at my command. He is probably the most childlike and philosophical nature among us.

Of our prayer meetings Dr. Raymond has been a central figure ever since he was our pastor. His benign presence, earnest tones, and clear putting of the truth from philosophic, psychologic and theologic points of view, have been especially helpful to persons of speculative quality of mind, and many a time have lifted them aloft, where, above the clouds of interrogation, shines the bright sun of faith.

As an instance of the intense loyalty during the war, of this now intensely Republican church, take from its records the following extract:

"Thomas Morris Green, recommended from the church south, was examined by the quarterly conference on his profession of loyalty to the government, and his belief of the antislavery doctrines of the M. E. church, and also assenting to all the doctrines and usages of the M. E. church, this conference voted unanimously to give him license as a local preacher."

Our next pastor (1868) was Rev. Dr. Dandy, a clear-cut reasoner and admirable man of business, under whose supervision the present handsome brick church was projected, the corner stone being laid July 4, 1870, at which time Dr. Dandy was presiding elder and Rev. Dr. James Baume, pastor. This man of apostolic demeanor, sweet spirit, and lofty Christian faith, after many years in India, remained in the pastorate at home for many more, then returned to India, and is still a successful missionary there.

The old wooden building, after about sixteen years of service that had hallowed it in the eyes of those who had gone in and out at its portals, was deserted for the larger structure which is now our church home. Later it was moved to the corner of Sherman Avenue and Church Street, where, with the legend, "Norsk-Dansk Kirke,"[51] above its doors, it still echoes, though in a foreign tongue, the same sweet songs and old, old story. Dr. Kidder and William H. Lunt were prime movers in selecting the site and helping forward the building of our present church, which was dedicated on a memorable Sabbath, by that famous debt-extinguisher, Rev. Dr. B. I. Ives. Time would fail me to tell of all the notable gatherings within its hospitable walls, or the great and good men and women whose kind voices have been heard there.

In 1872, Rev. Dr. M. C. Briggs came to us from a leading church in Cincinnati, and it was during his stay that we dedicated the auditorium of the new church, after three years passed in the basement. In Dr. Briggs we had a pronounced character. He was an "out-and-outer," and had the mental ability to back up his positions. We have never had before or since a pastor so strictly Methodistic. He turned not only to the law and the testimony, but to the discipline, and gave but little peace to the easygoing violators of rules they had solemnly covenanted to obey. The doctor was an admirable preacher to children, and usually reserved especially for them the first five minutes of each morning sermon. He was a strict constructionist of Sabbath law, and ceased not to admonish and reprove from the pulpit, in a wise and impersonal way, until I believe there were fewer Sunday papers taken by our members than at any period before or since. He was a strong, determined man, physically, as well as mentally and morally. Of him it might be justly said," he stands four square to every wind that blows." Erect, vigorous, wearing a single breasted coat of clerical cut, yet a real" fighting parson" (in a good sense), nobody expected to control his utterances. Happily he was not ambitious, and being somewhat lethargic in mood, he kept, as still he keeps, the even tenor of his way, being now and for many years past, a California preacher, greatly respected and widely useful.

In 1875 Rev. Dr. J. B. Wentworth became our pastor,—that man of mind so logical and method so judicial that, had he been a lawyer at the bar, or a judge upon the bench, he would have made a mark as deep and clear as he has made in the pulpit. Everything moved on like clock-work under his firm guidance and keen gaze, his quiet urbanity of manner and solid qualities of thought and character securing the sincere esteem of all concerned.

Next came Rev. Dr. Robert Hatfield, from 1875 to 1878. His reputation introduced him to us in a louder voice than had that of any predecessor. For many years we had been reading his spicy letters in the New York *Independent;* we knew his record in Brooklyn as a valiant anti-slavery preacher and devoted adherent of the party and the army that together saved the Union. We knew his fearless assaults upon the theater-going and other popular customs of Chicago, the Paris of the West. We knew him as a radical indeed, in whom was no guile, but a great deal of grace.

In the autumn of 1880 Rev. A. W. Patten became our pastor. It was the first time that an alumnus of our institutions had been called to preside over the church to which all his former teachers belonged, but this young man proved himself equal to his difficult task. He had none of Dr. Briggs' downrightness, or Dr. Hatfield's touch-and-go directness. He was quiet, kindly, unexceptionable. He did the right thing, at the right time, in the right way. Without salient traits of character, he was rarely symmetrical in word and deed, preached thoughtful, scholarly sermons, built up the church and had the universal good will. Of him one may justly quote the famous line, "And thus he bore without abuse the grand old name of *gentleman.*" On a certain bright summer day our people gathered by invitation, in the beautiful church, and down the aisle to the marriage altar walked our immaculate young pastor with Miss Ella Prindle, our prima donna of the choir and unexcelled graduate of the university, on his arm, whereupon we all thought him tenfold wiser and more admirable than he had ever been before!

A dozen years ago our church had what we used to call "an everlasting debt," and people verily believed it would have been sold under the hammer but for the heroic work of its women, led by Mrs. Dr. Marcy, who was for three years a figure no less familiar than pastor or sexton. As she sat at the receipt of custom, in the upstairs vestibule, on Sunday mornings, all who had a heart to do so left their contributions in her hands. She began this work in June of 1876 and ended it in June of 1879, having in this interval raised about ten thousand dollars. This remarkable woman, full of originality in thought and expression, and known throughout Methodism as a writer in verse and prose, and as a speaker who can make even a prosy theme poetic, is now raising ten thousand dollars for the Bohemian mission in Chicago, under the auspices of the Woman's Home Missionary Society. Bishop Harris introduced Mrs. Marcy to a group at one of the sessions of Rock River conference with these words:

"There's the woman who sat three years in the vestibule of Evanston M. E. Church, and wouldn't let any of us in unless we paid." Although the large sum named was mostly made up by these pledges, the committee of women, of whom Mrs. Marcy was chairman, and Dr. Raymond's sister, Mrs. Peck, was financial secretary, raised a considerable fraction thereof by festivals, harvest homes, concerts, and a Fourth of July restaurant in the university grove. Other leading women in these enterprises were: Mrs. Dr. Bannister, Mrs. Dr. Hatfield, Mrs. T. C. Hoag. Lyman J. Gage, the celebrated Chicago banker, then a member of our church, named Mrs. Marcy as chairman of the committee on our "Church Debt," and he with Dr. N. S. Davis, J. B. Kirk and others of like spirit, stood by her nobly from first to last. But the women helped to pay that debt, and yet these devoted and valiant daughters of the church have not one word to say, when the " powers that be" decide whom we shall have for a preacher, what his salary shall be, and other like questions of vital moment to the church enterprise we have in hand.

The debt on our church was as follows: mortgage debt, eighteen thousand dollars; floating debt, ten thousand dollars. The trustees cleared off the former, Mrs. Marcy's committee, the latter. For the marked improvement by which the auditorium has been renovated and the spire completed, we must thank our next pastor, Rev. Dr. S. F. Jones.

It was over eighteen years from the laying of the corner stone to the completion of the spire,—a fact suggesting the slow growth of European cathedrals,— but in 1888 we had a church complete and also incumbrance-free. Who that recalls the impressive appeals of Dr.

Benoni J. Ives, that matchless "dedicator" and debt raiser, would have dreamed that we should so long wander in the wilderness? That man would draw tears from the frescoes and tiling of an unpaid-for church. On dedication day he did, to my certain knowledge, lead many an impecunious soul to the very verge of bankruptcy by his impassioned appeals. My own case is one in point. Without a cent in my pocket or the least idea where I could get one, I pledged one hundred dollars, to the consternation of all whom I held dear. But the very next week came my first invitation to lecture for that amount (at Pittsburgh, Pa.). A member of our official board got me a pass there and back, and my check for the amount was in the treasurer's hands in less than ten days from the time the pledge was given! In 1882 all our church debts were cleared away, and may they ever thus remain.

Our next pastor (October 1883) was Rev. (now Dr.) Lewis Curts. He found the church with a membership of over six hundred and holding property worth about seventy thousand dollars. Brother Curts was a man in his early prime, of fine, robust physique, clear, cheery countenance with truth-telling eye, complexion pure as a child's, and a voice strong and sweet as a silver trumpet. Sturdiness of mind and purpose were his salient traits and he was one of the upright in heart that did us good and not evil in all the days of his somewhat difficult pilgrimage. His wife was a help who proved herself meet for the occasion,—an individualized woman of strong character and pronounced, but most considerately uttered views.

Following him in this distinguished procession, came Rev. Dr. Sylvester F. Jones, in 1885.

The fact that his politics were in accord with those of the majority, whereas those of Dr. Curts were not,—the latter being a political prohibitionist,—was a point in Dr. Jones' favor from the first; bat it was something far deeper than politics that held him in the universal esteem and favor of his congregation through five years,—the longest period allowed even under the new itineracy rules. He, too, in his more conservative way, is a friend to the temperance, woman and labor movements,—that splendid trinity of reforms in which the cause of Christ and of humanity are so palpably enshrined in these days of rapid transit in opinions as well as in avoirdupois. Brother Jones is a man of remarkably fine fiber, physically as well as mentally and in heart. Of refined and attractive personal appearance, cultivated tones, rare polish in style and in delivery, a close student and an earnest Christian, he is a preacher much sought after and a pastor much beloved. When there is a bereavement in the home, this tender and sympathetic nature fills the ideal of his sacred office beyond almost any one else that can be named.

Mrs. Jones is a woman of unusual native powers and rare accomplishments,—her husband's true correlative.

In the long interval between October 1884, when Brother Curts left us, and March, 1885, when Brother Jones arrived, we had as our pastor Rev. Dr. Henry B. Ridgaway. This new president of famous old "Garrett" had come to Evanston in 1882 from such leading city churches as St. Paul's in Cincinnati and St. Paul's in New York; had made the Oriental as well as European tour, and written an admirable book. A Baltimorean by birth and breeding, a graduate of that most historic among Methodist colleges, —Dickinson, at Carlisle, Pa.,—Dr. Ridgaway came into his own when he came to the Athens of his church. We had all known him long, not only through the church press, but through the family of his aunt, Mrs. Sarah W. C. Bragdon, and the reputation of Professor Merritt Caldwell, of Dickinson, his father-in-law, who, dying in the zenith of his gracious fame, left a long twilight of tender memories.

Our present pastor (1891) is Rev. Dr. W. S. Studley, who comes to us from Ann Arbor, Detroit, Brooklyn, Boston and "all along shore,"—a gifted, scholarly and way-wise pastor and a genuine brother-man, already dear to us. He and his wife have seemed like "our own folks from the first day." Evanston is always pre-eminently loyal to her ministers and their families,—that is one of our best traits!

Our Methodist church has always been remarkable for the continuous presence and work of its regularly appointed pastors, supplies being almost unknown. This fact is the more notable because the current church directory gives the names of thirteen doctors of divinity, besides three other ministers, all of them abundantly able to supply the pastor's place should circumstances render this necessary.

Since the foundation of our church in 1854 we have had fourteen regular pastors; and a recent enumeration showed seven hundred and forty-two members, besides thirty-three on probation, five hundred and thirty in the Sunday-school, forty of whom are teachers. The church property is valued at seventy-five thousand dollars. We have had six Sunday-school superintendents,—F. H. Benson, Warren Taplin, E. S. Taylor, Edward Eggleston, H. F. Fisk, Harvey B. Hurd, John F. Miller, William T. Shepherd, and F. P. Crandon. We have had two women as assistant superintendents,—Mrs. Dr. Marcy and Mrs. Dr. Raymond. The position of infant class teacher—probably the most influential office in the whole list—was filled for many years in a remarkably successful manner by that beloved and lamented pastor of the juveniles,—Mrs. Kate E. Queal. Her chief predecessors were Mrs. Benson, and Miss

Wells (afterwards Mrs. Thomas Craven).

Our choristers' list begins with the honored name of John A. Pearsons (who raised the tune with a fork at that remote period of antiquity when "our choir" occupied the right hand amen corner of the old church among the trees; and I was alto singer!). O. H. Merwin held the position longest. His engagement ran from 1869 to 1884. He had a chorus choir, the number varying from twenty-five to sixty. The organists during that time were H. A. Cooper, M. S. Cross, and W. H. Cutler, the present incumbent. Many attractive entertainments were given by the chorus, such as the concert in 1878, at which Annie Louise Carey (Raymond) was the chief attraction, and the oratorio of the " Messiah" given in the following year, with Myron W. Whitney as the bass. Professors O. E. Locke and W. H. Cutler succeeded to the management of the choir, both being accomplished organists.

Of class leaders we have rejoiced in a rich variety. Among the pleasant pictures of the past, I cherish, in common with scores besides, that of the fragile figure, silver hair, blue eyes, and smiling mouth of Mrs. Melinda Hamline. I may not, in these brief pages, name the consecrated faces that rise before memory's eye when I think of those groups of earnest young girls and boys and thoughtful men and women clustering about the leader in the quiet, restful atmosphere of those dear old rooms, while we each testified to the power of the indwelling Christ or sang Charles Wesley's hymn:

> *Refining fire go through my heart.*
> *Illuminate my soul;*
> *Scatter thy life through every part*
> *And sanctify the whole.*

No Methodist can be a stalwart who neglects the formative force of the class meeting upon his character, especially in early years. All class leaders are, by virtue of their office, part and parcel of the "Official Board" and the "Quarterly Conference," and I am told that it has not been unusual to see women in both here in our Evanston Methodist Episcopal church. But those two meetings are the units of power out of which go forth all church authority. The "lay delegates" to our great General Conference are chosen by the delegates sent from quarterly conferences to an electoral conference; women are members of the quarterly conferences; their vote at many an electoral conference determines who shall go to General Conference, but, when duly elected and certified as delegates to the General Conference, women are turned from its door. O tempora! O mores!

Of noteworthy events, our church has witnessed many. Commencement exercises were held in the white, green-blinded church in the grove, when young hearts beat pit-a-pat as the long procession in white muslin moved up the aisle, with Professor Jones at its head, and slowly climbed to the great, pleasant platform, redolent of evergreen branches, festoons and arches of greenery, brightened by flowers. There I "took my diploma" by proxy of my sister Mary, being very ill at home, and opening it nervously when she brought it to me, tossed it out of the window because it was " in blank," my teachers being too busy to sign their names till later on. There the first man of national distinction I ever saw, Benjamin F. Taylor, that heavenly-minded poet, lectured in the spring of 1858. His subject was "Words," and his words were to my fancy like a river of gems with flowers between. Edward Eggleston walked into that same church one evening, before a large audience, introducing his friend, Theodore Tilton, editor of the New York *Independent,* whose lecture on equal suffrage convinced everybody whom I ever heard speak of it, and made thoughtful circles to become what they have ever since been here,—so solid " for that great reform" that I heard a new pastor wittily remark that "he did not know, until he got acquainted, that woman's ballot was sacred as an article of faith to the women of Evanston."

The only commencement exercises ever held by the Evanston college for ladies before it was merged in the university, had the basement of our unfinished new church as their arena and took place in June, 1872. Our board of women trustees was on the platform; Mrs. J. F. Willing preached the baccalaureate. We gave her the degree of A. M., and it fell to me as president to present diplomas to our five "sweet girl graduates."

The first exercises in our new church (lecture room) came off just as soon as it was finished, August, 1871, and consisted of a farewell to Dr. Kidder and family who then left us to go to Madison, New Jersey, where the doctor had been elected professor in Drew Theological Seminary. Our chief citizen, Mr. L,. L. Greenleaf, presided and made the presentation speech,— for there were handsome gifts, contributed to by high and low so as to represent the entire village,—and Dr. Kidder responded in his usual polished style. Here lectured Emily Huntington Miller, and here I gave my first Evanston temperance talk.

In the great church above, the Rock River conference, presided over by Bishop Merrill, met in 1886. There the general executive committee of the W. F. M. S. was held in 1885: there Francis Murphy held one of his pledge-signing campaigns in 1884, and the W. C. T. U. and Citizens'

League have had great mass meetings; there the grand commencement exercises of later years have been held; the concerts, "children's days," and lectures by a long list of distinguished men and women have been held in lecture room and church. I recall those of Wendell Phillips, Anna E. Dickinson, John B. Gough, Henry Ward Beecher, Edward Everett Hale, Gilbert Haven, Joseph Cook, Richard Proctor, Gen. Lew Wallace, James Whitcomb Riley, Mary A. Livermore, George Kennan, Albion W. Tourgée, Henry M. Stanley, and the notable Shakspeare-Bacon controversy between Hon. Ignatius Donnelly and our own Prof. Charles Pearsons, in which we think the Evanstonian came out ahead.

As the largest auditorium in Evanston, our church was in request for the recent Washington centennial exercises, and in its character of "the mother of churches," as Mrs. Dr. Marcy very properly says, all our people feel at home within its ample and hospitable walls. Many a bright speech has that same lady made here and many a delightful hymn of hers have we sung,—also of Mrs. Emily J. Bugbee's (now Mrs. Johnson).

Probably no officer, and few men, have been connected with our church so long as T. C. Hoag, who became church treasurer in the fall of 1858, and has held that office continuously since then, and has been a member of the board of stewards during that time,— a period of about thirty-three years.

In earlier times our "church sociable" was the most representative gathering of the kind that the village could furnish; rich and poor, students and townspeople, met here on common ground, these gatherings being held in the houses of our church members.

They were most informal and generally most agreeable, though the students sometimes complained that by reason of their numbers they were apt to be relegated to the rank of "wallflower." My merry sister Mary came home one night and said, "That solemn ' Bib'[52] named --- haunted me half the evening with this theological conundrum: 'Miss Mary, what, in your judgment, is the exact dividing line that separates sin from holiness?" She said that at another sociable an unlettered old member whispered dryly, as he saw her for a moment sitting alone, "Yer losin' time!" Some mischievous maidens I wot of in families of the professors made bouquets of a deceiving nature, having a pin concealed, thorn-like, among the flowers, and offering certain unsophisticated theologues a chance to smell the winsome posies, playfully administered to each proboscis a prick of the unseen pin. We used to promenade in the open air in pleasant summer weather;— that was an enjoyable feature of the sociable to the young folks; —and we used to take up a collection out of which much fun was had. As to refreshments, I do not remember whether we had them or no, but our feasts of reason—they never failed.

The Sunday-school of those days was so primitive, compared withthe full-blown glories of Brother Crandon's establishment, that I am abashed by my comparative study of the same. The first real "gospel song" book I ever saw was introduced under Mr. Benson's superintendency, and in it I first learned "Sweet Hour of Prayer." The "International Lessons" were unheard-of;—indeed, we old-timers still claim that our Edward Eggleston, who introduced into Evanston the first kindergarten of which we ever heard, also suggested the International method;— I think it was at a Sunday-school convention in Indianapolis.

We had Christmas festivities; and people brought their own home gifts and hung them on the tree, which wasn't a good plan. The modern method of giving rather than receiving, on the part of those called "well-to-do," is much the best, but when Edward Bellamy's "brotherhood" idea comes in, which is simply Christianity applied, we shall, according to my notion, have a far higher evolution of the Day of days! Who that saw it will forget the Christmas-tree in the old church, when, as we all sat silent and expectant, Santa Claus dashed in, encased in buffalo robes and behung with sleighbells, to take the place by storm,—said Santa Claus being no other than handsome Charlie Bannister, of auld lang syne.

What "watch nights" were those when we began at seven and closed at twelve, with thrilling sermons, tender testimonials, and everybody kneeling in confession and consecration as the bell tolled the midnight hour! One's spirit grew at those seasons faster than corn in July.

Three notable revivals, conducted by three women evangelists, and three conducted by men, stand out in bold relief upon the records of our church. In 1865 Mrs. Phoebe Palmer, assisted by her husband, held meetings for several weeks that proved to be of lifelong benefit to some of us. Mrs. Maggie Van Cott, of New York city, in the winter of 1872, during the pastorate of Rev. James Baume, did a noble work here. To memory she stands there still, upon the vestry room platform, with glowing face, upturned, inspired, and beautiful. A third figure comes to view, "in my mind's eye, Horatio," standing on the same platform of the dear old lecture room, under the odd little chandelier,—Mrs. L. O. Robinson, who, one Sabbath, preached in the large auditorium a sermon so full of pentecostal power that everyone knew those walls had seldom resounded to the tones of a voice so potent or to a plea the tenderness of which was so prevailing. It was like the magnanimity of Dr. Ridgaway, in introducing the woman-preacher on that morning, to say, "listen to her with grateful hearts that God has raised her up to

REV. N. H. WHITTLESEY, D. D.,
Congregational Church.

REV. M. DONOHUE,
St. Mary's Catholic Church.

REV. N. D. HILLIS,
Presbyterian Church.

REV. H. A. DELANO, D. D.
First Baptist Church.

REV. ARTHUR W. LITTLE, St. Mark's Episcopal Church.
REV. W. S. STUDLEY, D. D., First M. E. Church.
REV. S. F. JONES, D. D., Emmanuel M. E. Church.

A GROUP OF EVANSTON PASTORS.

speak while we men keep silent on the principle that 'the *poor* ye have always with you!' "

What other church has developed such a woman as she and Mary T. Lathrap, Jennie F. Willing and other preachers that we might name? "By their fruits ye shall know them," and the gospel movement that radiated forth from Susanna Wesley's son John and was sung by her son Charles, has by its fruits fulfilled that broadest declaration of the universal church: "There is neither male nor female in Christ Jesus." Other remarkable figures of women have lent an added sanctity to this typical church, by us so much beloved. Sarah Smiley came in 1873, that mystic-natured saint "whose soul is like a star and dwells apart." Mrs. S. M. I. Henry, national evangelist of the W. C. T. U., Mrs. Jennie F. Willing, Miss Belle Leonard, Mrs. Stroud-Smith, of England, Mrs. Hannah Whitall Smith, whose book, "The Christian's Secret of a Happy Life," has been translated into twelve languages, Mother Stewart, of Ohio, Rev. Anna Shaw and Miss Mattie Gordon, of Tennessee, have all expounded God's Word in the First Methodist Church, Evanston. Probably not another in America has echoed so many of the voices that help to fulfill Isaiah's prophecy, "The Lord gave the word, the women that publish the tidings are a great host."

Three other evangelists, Rev. Charles Uzzell, Mr. Yatman and Rev. B. Fay Mills, have also labored here. The former is held in affectionate and grateful remembrance by reason of the rare results that yet remain. Mr. Yatman I have never seen, but hear him everywhere spoken of with high regard for his earnest and remarkably successful efforts to enlist church members and unbelievers alike, in the study of God's word. Brother Mills, that brother indeed, is undoubtedly the greatest evangelist who ever blessed our village and our homes in the Redeemer's name. His were "union meetings" in the broadest and best sense of those words, bringing a harvest of souls into all the fraternizing churches of Evanston.

In the foregoing sketch I have not meant to be invidious, only to give an outline of what I know about my own church home since girlhood days. Because it grew up with the university it is the chief church of Evanston, hence, perhaps, entitled to more space, but the reason first stated may sufficiently excuse the length of this account, viz., I *know* about its history. *God bless the M. E. Church of Evanston—long may it lead!*

OUR BAPTIST CHURCH—ITS ORIGIN AND EVOLUTION.

Our Baptist friends were on a vantage ground from the beginning, and were the first to swarm from the old hive. This they did April 24, 1858, about four years after the first Quarterly Conference of the Methodist Episcopal church was held (July 13, 1854, at the log schoolhouse in the town of Ridgeville, later called Oakton).

The chapel of our university was the place in which they organized and where they worshiped "off and on" for nearly ten years, their church being dedicated Feb. 16, 1865. At that first meeting six persons were received as members, viz.: Major and Mrs. Mulford, Mrs. Iglehart, Mrs. Julia Burroughs (now at more than ninety, our oldest resident), Mrs. Westerfield and Moses Dandy.

The moderator at this meeting was Major E. H. Mulford, the most prominent figure that looms up in the early history of this neighborhood, he having be come a resident of Chicago in 1825, and pre-empted two sections of land from the United States government at one dollar per acre, and having been the first justice of the peace in Cook county. Until his death the major was a deacon of this church. Its first trustees were N. P. Iglehart, E. H. Mulford, Joseph Ludlam, Moses Dandy and Mr. Trumbull.

Near the old Mulford place (now the Kirk homestead) at Oakton, the Iglehart family had erected a building on their lot, known as "Oakton chapel," and there a Sunday-school was conducted with Mrs. Iglehart as superintendent. Indeed, this noble Christian matron was justly known as the " Mother of the Baptist church," and in the handsome edifice that has long been its home, a marble tablet attests the veneration and gratitude that glorify her sacred memory.

Though the Fox River association had received this brave little church into full membership in the first year of its history, its fortunes and pastorates were varied, and its small life barque rode the uncertain waves with a vigor and a vim best explained by its Baptist birth and destiny. Once for a few months (in 1863, when war's alarum dulled " the sound of the church-going bell"), its twinkling taper was extinguished as far.as public services were concerned, but meetings for prayer were resumed the next spring and a revival breeze sprang up that wafted it along more swiftly than before. A new church edifice was dedicated by Rev. Dr. Everts, then Chicago's Baptist Boanarges, Feb. 16, 1865. It stood about where our present President of the Council Miller's pleasant home now stands, and was removed afterward to serve as the chapel of the elegant new church, dedicated ten years later, Nov. 21, 1875.

In all the early years, the baptismal services of this denomination gathered our entire village on lake shore and pier. I remember standing there to watch the solemn scene in reverent mood, remembering the baptism of my brother Oliver in Rock river at Janesville, Wis., many years before,—for it was in my blood to believe this was the true and only way, my grandfather Willard having been forty years pastor of one Baptist church at Dublin (near Keene), N. H., and both my parents having sacredly observed the rite after this manner. Indeed, it took a winter's study of the Bible and Rev. Dr. Hibbard's (Methodist) treatise on baptism to make me conclude that not the method but its spirit was the essential quantity, and to be contented to be "sprinkled," as our Baptist brethren say.

In the thirty years of its history our Baptist church has had this list of pastors regularly installed: Rev. Ira F. Kinney, Rev. I. S. Mahan, Rev. W. J. Leonard, Rev. M. G. Clark, Rev. F. L. Chapell, Rev. G. R. Pierce, Rev. Fred Clatworthy.

All these have been good men and true, but it is not, perhaps, invidious to say that the last-named pastor held not only his own people but the wide constituency of church-going Evanstonians with the grip of that one inexorable power called Love. He was a radical, and yet was never dubbed a "crank"; he was an enthusiast, and yet was never named "fanatic" because he held his blessed hobbies well in hand and gave to every other rider his right of way. In speaking of him and his admirable wife, it seems to me we should pay the deserved compliment of accenting their name on the last syllables.

In the regrettable departure of this gifted man, our Baptist church is to be congratulated on securing his friend and classmate, Rev. H. A. Delano, of South Norwalk, Conn., who is among the foremost young men of that communion in pulpit power. The church has almost doubled in strength, in missionary enterprise, and in all its departments of work; has had an accession of one hundred members, and has raised, since the present pastorate, of a year and a half, over ten thousand dollars for outside work. This sisterly church, progressive in its spirit and tolerant in its tone, now numbers nearly three hundred members, three hundred in its Sunday-school, and owns a church property valued at forty-five thousand dollars. Long may it live!

EMANUEI. M. E. CHURCH.

On the corner of Greenwood Boulevard and Oak Street, was organized, September 1890, with twenty- seven members. (Sunday-school, prayer and class meetings were first held, April 1890, the Sunday school having been organized May, 1889.) The pastor is Rev. Dr. S. F. Jones and the trustees are Harvey B. Hurd, William H. Jones, Frank P. Crandon, David B. Dewey, D. R. Dyche, John B. Kirk, H. H. Gage, J. J. Shutterly, Charles G. Haskin. The present membership (June, 1891,) 138; Sunday-school, 163; Epworth League, 40. The church edifice will be of Ashland stone and Gothic architecture; (Root and Burnham, architects). Estimated cost, $60,000.

OTHER CHURCHES.

The Roman Catholic parish was established in 1866, by Right Rev. James Duggan, Bishop of Chicago, with about eighteen members. Father Donohue, the first resident pastor, began his labors in 1872. The present membership of the parish is eight hundred. A new church building will soon be erected to accommodate the many parishioners, the corner-stone being already laid.

The Norwegian Methodist church was organized in 1870 by Rev. A. Haagenson, with about twelve members. The present pastor is Rev. E. M. Stangeland, and the present membership sixty, with a Sunday-school of seventy members. Their church property is valued at about three thousand dollars.

The Swedish Methodist church was organized about 1874. This pulpit was supplied by students for several years. The first resident pastor was Rev. Frederic Ogren, who came in 1877. Rev. N. O. Westergren is now the pastor, and the present membership is one hundred and seventy. The church property is valued at five thousand dollars.

The Free Methodist church was organized about 1881, and now has a membership of forty-five; Rev. J. D. Kelsey is the pastor, and the church property is valued at eight thousand dollars.

The African Methodist church was organized in 1882 by Rev. George H. Hann, with three members. This society owns a house of worship on Benson Avenue and has ninety members at the present time, with Rev. Mr. Dawson pastor.

ST. MARK'S EPISCOPAL CHURCH.

The Second Baptist church (colored) was organized in 1883 with twenty members. It has a present membership of sixty-three, but is without a resident pastor at this time. The church building was burned, but was rebuilt during 1890.

The Swedish Evangelical Lutheran church was organized in 1888, by Rev. S. A. Sandahl of Lake View, with thirty-four communicants. Rev. J. Edgren, the present incumbent, is the first resident pastor. The church has at this time one hundred and forty-five communicants, and church property valued at about four thousand two hundred dollars.

EVANSTON TOWNSHIP HIGH SCHOOL.

In the fall of 1881, a movement was started to establish in Evanston a Township High School in place of the village high school opened under Dr. Otis E. Haven in 1875. South Evanston had always sent a considerable number of tuition pupils to Evanston, and Rogers Park had been well represented among our pupils and graduates. The geography of the town, lying, as it does, along a single line of railroad, with numerous stations, makes a central high school easy of access. William Blanchard, N. W. Boomer and Professor William P. Jones were among the more active in promoting the movement, which was duly proposed to the people, and received a large majority of votes. It was organized under the state law, and was the fifth of its class to go into successful operation. The question of location excited considerable discussion, and the present site was chosen as a compromise among several conflicting views. Its principal defect is its proximity to the railroad, and the consequent interruptions to school work during the frequent passage of trains.

The building was erected during the summer of 1883, and was formally dedicated for school purposes August thirty-first. The township trustees, who by law constitute the board of education for a township high school, were William Blanchard, S. D. Childs and S. B. Goodenow. Henry L. Boltwood, a graduate of Amherst College, who organized, and for eleven years taught the first township high school in Illinois, at Princeton, in Bureau County, was called from the township high school in Ottawa, to take charge of ours. He had as assistants, Lyndon Evans, a graduate of Knox college, Miss Eva S. Edwards and Miss Ellen Lee White, who were in the Evanston village high school, and Miss Mary L. Banie, who came with him from Ottawa. The school opened with one hundred and seven pupils, and the total enrollment for the year was one hundred and thirty-nine.

Evanston Township High School

On the 20th of December 1883, the school building narrowly escaped destruction by fire, which caught from a defective flue. Half the interior of the building was destroyed by fire and by water. The pupils behaved admirably, and school was resumed after a two weeks' vacation, in the unconsumed half of the building.

In consequence of a change in the course of study extending it from three years to four, the first graduating class was small, numbering but five.

In the second year the enrollment was one hundred and fifty-five. Drawing was introduced into the course, and typewriting was introduced as a voluntary study. More than forty took this some part of the year. An industrial exhibit of the pupils' handiwork in drawing, wood carving, cooking and needlework was held near the close of the year with such success that it has been repeated annually, with increased attendance and interest. Twelve pupils graduated.

In 1885-86 the enrollment reached one hundred and seventy one, and an additional teacher was employed. Fourteen pupils graduated.

In 1886-87 the enrollment was one hundred and seventy-seven, and a sixth teacher was added. In this year wood-work was added to the school course as a voluntary branch. Over twenty lads took this branch and were regularly instructed by a skilled workman. The graduates numbered sixteen.

In 1887-88 the enrollment reached one hundred and eighty-five, and the graduates numbered nineteen. The introduction of drawing into the lower grades enabled us to enlarge and greatly improve upon our former work. The graduates numbered nineteen.

In 1888-89 the enrollment was one hundred and eighty-five, and the graduates numbered fifteen.

The school year of 1889-90 opened with an increase of nearly twenty-five per cent above the preceding year. Two hundred and sixteen have been enrolled up to date, and the graduating class will probably considerably exceed in numbers any of the preceding classes. The increased number obliged us to seat our large hall which now contains two hundred and five single desks. A new hard coal furnace was added, and the large lower room where the school formerly assembled is divided into two large recitation rooms. French, which had been dropped because of the small number desiring instruction, has been restored to the course.

The school has four times competed for honors in the competitive state examinations, and has twice taken almost everything competed for. One year, on twelve sets of papers presented, it took eight first prizes and two second prizes, with a general prize for the highest averages. The prize money, amounting to nearly one hundred and fifty dollars, was expended mostly upon pictures and books. The school is well equipped with library and apparatus.

Special stress has been laid upon literature and History, with good results. The sciences are taught practically and by laboratory methods. Our diploma admits to Amherst and Smith colleges, to our State University, the Northwestern University and to Ann Arbor.

Few communities have better material with which to build a school, and a public more generally in sympathy with good education. There would be a proof of great weakness somewhere if the school failed to have a good record.

Of the eighty-one graduates, thirteen have taken the Classical course, thirty the Latin Scientific, twenty-one the Modern language, and the other seventeen the three years' English course. The school is now represented by its graduates in Harvard, Yale, Amherst, Williams and Smith colleges; in the Boston Polytechnic School, and in our State University; besides nine who are now in the Northwestern University. Several have entered college without completing the high school course.

Of the eighty-one graduates, twenty-seven were boys. This proportion is far in excess of some high schools in our state. Of the present enrollment of two hundred and eleven, there are eighty-seven boys and one hundred and twenty-four girls.

OUR LITERARY PEOPLE.

"The ink of the scholar is more sacred than the blood of the martyr;" so Mohammed said, and he ought to know, for he had considerable experience with both fluids. Accordingly, Evanston ought to be at least a match with Mecca for sacredness, for the amount of scholarly ink which has been put to paper by Evanston pens will compare favorably with that of any other community of its size and age in the world.

A university is the magnet of thinkers, whether they are of large or less degree. "Atmosphere" counts for more than any other one feature of environment, whether it be an atmosphere actual, artistic or psychological. And from the first this has been the highest charm of Evanston. Something that said at first, and with gentle, quiet, but tireless insistence, has kept on saying ever since, that not achievement, and not wealth, but always character is the final factor that classifies humanity. Upon this truth concerning atmosphere all literature is builded; it is the force that swings Shakspeare in his sunlike orbit as well as lights the tallow dip in the peasant's window of mere talent or the pineywood match of "the casual contributor." So literary people, be they great or small, or lilliputian, hover by instinct around a center of books and thought and character. There are not less than thirty persons in our Evanstons—"proper" and otherwise—who have written books of their own,—such as they are. Some of us have perpetrated only one, but the worst offenders have gone well up to one dozen, and the end is not yet. Journalists here find congenial soil and flourish like the green bay tree. It is safe to predict that the coming thirty-five years will show ten times as much work of this kind as the past thirty-five can show. The history of the university up to the present has been the story of a constant struggle,— successful, it is true, but none the less absorbing and exhausting. When a professor has to instruct classes each day in four different languages, he is more likely, when his day's work is done, to look around for a feather-bed than for a quill. The past has been a period of pioneering, of hard work, of long hours, short purses and no leisure. This is true, not only of the university, but of the whole village, and in fact, of the whole west. But these things are gradually changing for the better; and yet we have no reason to complain or be ashamed, but rather have every reason to be proud; in testimony of which we submit the long list of Evanston authors and their books, which appears in the appendix of this volume.

EVANSTON SOCIETIES.

Ours is certainly a sociable community, if the number and variety of its societies is a criterion. Verily, we must be a community of "jiners," for there are in active operation among students and townspeople, over one hundred and twenty-five different societies, including the churches and their benevolent organizations. The rapid evolution which has brought about this result is but a type of the growth of the whole town. The glories of the Evanston Club, in its beautiful home on Chicago Avenue and Grove Street, are but the symbol of a score of great things that have grown from small beginnings in these thirty-five years.

IOTA OMEGA.

It is clearly my impression that the first literary society ever organized in Evanston, outside the colleges, was the "Iota Omega," (otherwise "Independent Order"), in February 1860. This was composed wholly of young women, their motto being. "No others need apply." We met at "Bannister House," as some of us used playfully to term that popular headquarters of intellectual enterprise. Thence we marched over in procession, with brooms on shoulders, dust-pan in hand and scrubbing brash alongside, and took possession of the upper front room of a house long ago transformed by Mrs. Chapin into a delightful home.

We took symbolic names copied verbatim from a yellow old "roll-call "in my possession.

We had fines,—set forth as follows in Mary Bannister's graceful chirography:

"For tardiness, one cent; for absence, five cents; for letting out secrets, one dollar; for voting both ways, one cent; for withdrawing membership from the society, two dollars."

We learned the manual alphabet and our gyrations were the despair of our student friends as we kept a dumb show of saying whatever we would "unbeknownst" to their high theological dignities. We had a constitution from which this is an extract:

> "Whereas, we, the undersigned, are greatly grieved in spirit and bowed down in dust by heaviness of mind, we do earnestly desire and crave communion with cur companions in the flesh, and in so doing expect to receive into our hearts joy and consolation, and at the same time to

excite the curiosity of the young men, who are all to be kept out, and whereas we would profit our souls by receiving instruction, ergo, etc."

I was president and Mary Bannister secretary of the society. From our "minutes" the following tidbits are selected:

"The council voted upon badges, that the president should wear a white rosette, the secretary a blue one, the treasurer a red one, and the rest straw-colored ones.

"Kate M. Kidder motioned that all members of the I. O. 'always conceal any hard feelings they have towards each other.' Carried unanimously.

"The president then agreed to pay fines enough in advance to purchase a book for treasurer's accounts.

"Mary E. Willard motioned the society go to prayer-meetings on Thursday evenings. Not carried.

"A committee was selected to propose a question for debate at the next meeting. The following was soon decided upon:

" 'Resolved, That the husband and wife are equal in power.' "

But the Iota Omega society erelong paled its ineffectual fires before the dawning glories of "The Reading Circle" (in 1861).

Here was richness indeed. Debate that sent the plummet line down to the origin of evil and up to the New Jerusalem; free will versus necessity; abolition, woman's rights, and every other great issue, past, present and to come, were dealt with, and in no gingerly fashion, either.

Enough has been said to give an idea of the fun and frolic of former Evanston, which, it may be truthfully remarked, was interspersed with such festivities as choir meeting, Sunday-school teachers' meeting, and an occasional boat ride, the best part of which was the singing of hymns to the rhythm of the summer waves and in the witching moonlight.

All these good times which we enjoyed every bit as well as our younger brothers and sisters do their Country Club, centered in the Bannister, Stewart, Kidder, Bragdon and Ludlam homes, and in our own "Swampscot" by the lake, but most of all at " Mary B's." In the midst of these festivities (?) came a note to each individual of "our set" from another "on the ridge,"—then the almost exclusive inheritance of the financially well-to-do. This communication set forth the fact, in courteous phrase, that we were invited to join what has since evolved into the Eclectic and afterwards the "Social" club, and taken permanent form in the elegantly housed Evanston club, on the cherished old site of the Ludlam homestead,—a landmark for whose loss old-timers can hardly be consoled, even by the intricate magnificence of the new edifice.

This old-time invitation caused a "state of mind" among our militant young Methodists, for by it we were informed that "at the *fourth* meeting of said club we had been invited to join." I very well remember saying to Miss Amelia Shackelford (now Mrs. Wm. K. Sullivan), one of the favorite friends of that halcyon period: "*Fourth* meeting indeed! Why didn't they ask us to the *first,* and let us have a hand in settling the whys and wherefores of the new society?" This was the general feeling, and in the foolish vanity and crudity of youth, we sent back word that " while we appreciated the kindness that prompted an invitation to the *fourth meeting* of their society, we did not see our way clear to join, etc.

Many a time, in wiser and less opinionated years, I have wondered if we might not have done each other good, the two sets of young people now not so young, and have always been sincerely glad that, going our several ways, we yet maintained the kindliest personal relations.

The little "Iota Omega" was followed by the large "Eclectic," of which our townsman, J. H. Kedzie, gives the following account:

"Evanston's four hundred first families' were the four hundred first arriving on the ground. The Eclectic club, though limited in membership by the limited seating capacity of our parlors, had no restrictions except territorial; membership, for convenience, being confined to residents of the West side.

"The objects of this club, like all clubs that have lived and died in Evanston, were twofold,—intellectual improvement and social enjoyment.

"The commencement in 1864 was spontaneous and quite informal.

"A few families were invited to meet at the house of Mr. C. Comstock for the purpose of listening to the reading of a few selections by Mr. Page. Rev. John Wilkinson, who was spending that winter in Evanston, with his wife, took an active interest in the readings thus commenced. An organization was formed, at first called simply the Reading club, with Mr. Page as president.

"The meetings were held regularly every Monday evening, at the houses of the different members in alphabetical order. The exercises consisted of two readings, one by a lady and one by a gentleman each evening, also in alphabetical order. Each reading was not to exceed half an hour, and the rest of the evening was devoted to music, conversation and refreshments. Sometimes a whole evening was devoted to music, sometimes to a Shakspearean play, sometimes to story-telling, sometimes to a scientific discussion, sometimes to tableaux, and once, at least, to the trial of a member for 'high crimes and misdemeanors.'

"These delightful meetings were continued with only a short summer vacation, for fifteen years. Why should they ever have ceased? Were not the exercises sufficiently attractive'? No one will say they were not, and still thisinstitution has gone to join the days before the flood. Other attractions camt with more of novelty, but less of quiet, inexpensive enjoyment and improvement. Some of the members died, some moved away, but their places might easily have been supplied by newcomers. Still, the club has passed away, but not without leaving an honorable record, full of pleasant memories that will live so long as a single member shall survive.

"Among the families connected with the club were those of C. Comstock, S. Goodenow, A. Shuman, H. B. Hurd, J. J. Parkhurst, George Watson, R. S. King, W. Blanchard, L. C. Pitner, G. W. Smith, George Lord, J. H. Kedzie, Thomas Lord, George Purington, Thomas Cosgrove, J. M. Lyons, C. J. Gilbert, C. L. Way, Charles E. Brown, J. B. Adams, H. W. Hinsdale, N. G. Iglehart, W. C. Comstock, C. S. Burch, and a number of others whose names I do not at this moment recall."

It is to Mr. L. H. Boutell that we are indebted for an account of the next society that brought together the Evanston clans:

"The Philosophical Society originated in a suggestion made by Dr. Bannister. At his request, several gentlemen met in the room of Professor Kistler, in the university building, 'to consider the subject of forming a society for mutual improvement in science and general knowledge.' On the evening of October 22, 1866, the Evanston Philosophical association was organized, a constitution and by-laws adopted, and the following officers chosen: President, Dr. Henry Bannister; vice president, H. B. Hurd; treasurer, Professor H. S. Noyes; secretary, L. H. Boutell.

"The original members of the association were Henry Bannister, Henry S. Noyes, Francis Bradley, W. J. Leonard, Daniel P. Kidder, Daniel Bonbright, Oliver Marcy, Louis Kistler, Leo P. Hamline, Lucius H. Bugbee, L. H. Boutell, R. S. Greene, J. H. Kedzie,,H. B. Hurd, F. D. Hemenway, James B. Duncan, P. B. Shumway, M. Raymond, Edward Eggleston.

"For the first year, the meetings were held in the mathematical room of Northwestern University. After that they were held at the residences of the members, until the fall of 1871; and from that time on they were held at the rooms of the public library. Special meetings, to which the public were invited, were occasionally held in other places.

"The regular meetings were held once a month, from October to June; but special meetings were frequently called, generally two weeks after the regular meeting. The work of the society consisted in the presentation of original papers on topics of philosophical, scientific, or literary interest. These papers and discussions took a wide range, and many of them were of a high order of merit.

"The association kept up for a time a course of free public lectures. Whenever the papers to be read were of sufficient general interest to warrant it, the public were invited to attend the meetings. The first village paper was started under the auspices of this society.

"The last meeting of the association was held February 13, 1882. Various causes, needless to enumerate here, led to the discontinuance of the meetings. During the sixteen years of its life it exerted a stimulating and elevating influence, not only upon those connected with it, but upon the entire community. Not the least of Dr. Bannister's many titles to honor and affectionate remembrance is the fact that he was the originator of the Evanston Philosophical association.

The presidents of the association were Henry Bannister, Oliver Marcy, Francis Bradley, L. H. Boutell, F. D. Hemenway, Andrew Shuman, D. H. Wheeler, N. S. Davis, M. Raymond, N. C. Gridley, J. G. Forest, H. S. Carhart, C. W. Pearson, H. F. Fisk. The secretaries were L. H. Boutell, F. D. Hemenway, E. N. Packard, C. W. Pearson, Robert Baird, L. E. Cooley, H. G. Lunt, John H. Hamline, David Cavan, James S. Murray, C. A. P. Garnsey."

Then came the "Pro and Con Club" organized by Mrs. E. B. Harbert in the interest of equal suffrage, and attended by Governor and Mrs. Beveridge, Judge and Mrs. Bradwell, Madam Willard and other progressive spirits. The education growing out of this society has illustration in the following paragraph, from Miss Anthony's "History of Woman's Suffrage:"[53]

"It was decided to celebrate the Centennial Fourth of July (1876) in some appropriate manner. Under the auspices of Mrs. Harbert this was done at Evanston. The occasion was heralded as 'The Woman's Fourth,' and programs were scattered through the village. The auditorium of the large Methodist church was tastefully decorated with exquisite flowers; flags were gracefully festooned about the pulpit, and all the appointments were pronounced artistic by the most critical. Of Mrs. Harbert's oration we give an extract:

"Because our lake-bordered, tree-fringed village was once her home, I lovingly trace first on Evanston's scroll of honor the name of Jane C. Hoge, while just underneath it I write that of our venerable philanthropist, who was the first woman in these United States to receive the badge of the Christian commission, Mrs. Arza Brown."⁶

In the University the first literary society was the Hinman, and in the Northwestern Female College, the Minerva. While Dr. Haven and I were at the helm in University and Women's College, the literary societies —Hinman and Adelphic in the college classes, the Philomathean and Euphronian in the preparatory— were open alike to gentlemen and ladies. This helped to keep out secret orders and greatly stimulated the interest of our young people in all the rhetorical exercises both within and outside of the literary societies. I have never known so keen and sustained devotion to composition, debate, speech-making and the study of parliamentary usage, as during this interval. But in 1874 a different policy was inaugurated, and the Ossoli society for young women gathered them again into a separate literary community, as the Eugensia did later in the Preparatory Department. The Greek letter fraternities which have absorbed so much of the life of the old literary societies, and whose only secret, so far as I have learned, is that they have no secret, began in 1864 with the Phi Kappa Psi for young men, and in 1881 with the Alpha Phi for young women. Now the college has chapters of the Sigma Chi, Phi Kappa Sigma, Beta Theta Pi, Delta Upsilon and Phi Delta Theta, while the Alpha Phi shares the field with Kappa Kappa Gamma, Delta Gamma, and Kappa Alpha Theta.

SECRET SOCIETIES.

Masonic.—Evans Lodge, No. 524, F. and A. M.; Evanston Chapter, No. 144, R. A. M.; Evanston Commandery, No. 58, K. T.; Mount Moriah Lodge, No. 28, A. F. and A. M.

I. O. O. F.— Evanston Lodge, No. 673, Canton Delta, No. 34, R. M.

I. O. C. F.—St. Charles Court, No. 44.

I. O. F.—Court Evans, No. 97.

United Order of Honor.—Crescent Lodge, No. 72.

Royal Arcanum.—Covenant Council, No. 558.

Royal League.—Northwestern Council, No. 149.

National Union.—Unity Council, No. 141.

G. A. R.—John A. Logan Post, No. 540.

Knights of Labor.—Ridgeville Assembly, No. 7328.

TEMPERANCE SOCIETIES.

Independent Order of Good Templars.—Willard Lodge.
Woman's Christian Temperance Union.
Willard W. C. T. U.
Young Men's Christian Association.

LITERARY SOCIETIES.

Village.—Chautauqua Circle, Legensia, Woman's Club, Browning Club.
College.—Adelphic, Hinman, Euphronian, Philomathean, Ossoli, Eugenia, Twentieth Century Club.

COLLEGE FRATERNITIES.

Alpha Phi, Beta Theta Pi, Delta Gamma, Delta Upsilon, Kappa Kappa Gamma, Kappa Alpha Theta, Phi Delta Theta, Phi Kappa Psi, Phi Kappa Sigma, Sigma Chi.

MISCELLANEOUS.

Evanston Club, Evanston Boat Club, Evanston Country Club, Evanston Cycling Club, Evanston Township Improvement Association, Benevolent Society of Evanston, Idlewild Club, Arlington Club.

Here is a partial list of Evanston societies—more than a hundred in all—and even this does not include the score or so of tennis, whist and fair weather social clubs of a more or less evanescent existence:

CHURCH SOCIETIES.

Baptist.—Emanuel Club, Seed Sowers, Woman's Foreign Missionary Society, Woman's Home Missionary Society, Young People's Society of Christian Endeavor.
Second Baptist.—Ladies' Aid Society.
Congregational.—Ladies' Home Missionary Society, the Light Bearers, Woman's Foreign Missionary Society, Young People's Missionary Club. Young People's Society of Christian Endeavor.
St. Mark's Episcopal. — Queen Bertha's Guild, St. Mark's Guild, St. Andrew's Brotherhood, St. Margaret's Guild, the Women's Guild, the Altar Committee, the Woman's Auxiliary.

German Evangelican Lutheran.—Young People's Society.
First Methodist.—Ladies' Aid Society, Mission Band, Woman's Foreign Missionary Society, Woman's Home Missionary Society, Young People's League, Young Ladies' Missionary Aid Society.
Norwegian Methodist.—Ladies' Sewing Society.
Presbyterian.— Ladies' Church Association, Woman's Foreign Missionary Society, Woman's Home Missionary Society, Young Ladies' Missionary Society, Young People's Society of Christian Endeavor.
Roman Catholic. — Catholic Order of Foresters, Ladies' Rosary, Sisters of Charity, St. Vincent de Paul, Young Men's Sodality, Young Women's Sodality, Boys' Sodality, Girls' Sodality.
Swedish Evangelical Lutheran.—Bible Tract Society, Young People's Literary Society, Woman's Benevolent Society.

EVANSTON'S WATERWORKS.[54]

Our waterworks system grew out of an annexation movement in 1873, by which the village of North Evanston was added to Evanston proper. By this means the value of the assessed property was raised to two million dollars, which permitted the united corporation to raise a loan of one hundred thousand dollars.

Bonds in the sum of eighty-six thousand dollars were issued and the money formed the original water fund, with which the plant was put into operation.

A Holly engine with a pumping capacity of two million gallons of water daily, together with the necessary boilers and other apparatus, took up twenty-five million dollars of the fund.

A handsome building was put up on land donated by the Northwestern University, and the rest of the fund was put into a modest system of mains, which was considered sufficient for the time. The new engine was started in the month of November, 1874, if my memory serves me rightly, and secured a sufficiently ample supply of water from an iron crib located on the pier. Two years later it became evident that the supply of water for the pumps was not sufficient, and an iron inlet pipe, sixteen inches in diameter, was run out into the lake one thousand six hundred feet. Through this the Holly engine pumped into a well twenty-six feet deep and of a diameter of fifteen feet. A few years ago a succession of hot spells demonstrated the fact that Evanston had again grown beyond the supply of water, and a new engine was contracted for with the Holly company having a capacity of five million gallons every twenty-four hours. This engine was completed last winter, but not used regularly until last summer, the old pumps being adequate for all ordinary emergencies. The new pump is of the compound order, is of the Gaskill make, and cost eighteen thousand dollars as it stands. It has a capacity beyond what the village can now use, and also beyond what the inlet pipe can supply. The two pumps running together will have a nominal capacity of seven million gallons of water daily, whereas not more than three million per diem can pass through the inlet pipe. It will be readily seen, therefore, that a new inlet pipe is one of the necessities which must be provided for in the near future, though it now furnishes all the village can use, unless in case of some big fire. The figures show that the consumption of water has risen from six hundred and eleven thousand four hundred and thirty-nine gallons August 1, 1875, to one million nine hundred and sixty-one thousand one hundred and seventy-nine gallons July 25, 1889. That this vast amount of water is supplied economically is shown by the report made to the board of trustees, by which it appears that during the month of July fifty-eight million one hundred and seventeen thousand five hundred and ninety-seven gallons of water were pumped, or an average of one million five hundred and fifty-two thousand one hundred and eighty daily. The coal burned averaged three thousand two hundred and ninety-three pounds daily, costing one hundred and ninety-one dollars and thirty-three cents for the month. The average total cost of pumping each million gallons of water was only ten dollars and fourteen cents, of which three dollars and ninety-six cents was for coal. These figures, I think, speak for themselves, and show conclusively how carefully and economically the water system of Evanston is managed by the trustees elected by the people.

The waterworks system of Evanston, according to the inventory submitted to the trustees by Mr. C. J. Gilbert, one of the best friends of the waterworks, on his retirement from the board, shows that the whole cost to that date had been one hundred and sixty-eight thousand three hundred and thirty-nine dollars, or, adding the assessments for the extensions to be made in the spring and summer, one hundred and ninety-two thousand and forty dollars.

The property belonging to the water system includes sixteen hundred feet of inlet pipe, with crib, piers, well, well house, engine house, boilers, Holly engine with two million gallons daily capacity, Gaskill. engine with a daily capacity of five million gallons, engineer's residence, one hundred and twenty-two hydrants and ninety-seven thousand four hundred and ninety-five feet, or more than eighteen and one-half miles of water mains, besides the usual valves and connections.

The first superintendent of the works was George Story, who was in charge for six months, and was succeeded by Ira A. Holly, who remained at the head for two years. John Ebert was the chief engineer for three years, and Jones Patrick for five years. My assistants are Robert F. Grahame, second engineer; Charles E. Bendixson, third engineer.

Evanston has every reason to be proud of its system of supplying an abundance of pure water, and has, through its various boards of trustees, demonstrated its claims as a comfortable and progressive place of residence, fully abreast of the times, and a worthy suburb of the great city with which it is so intimately connected.

EVANSTON AND TEMPERANCE.

There is a celestial Evanston, there is a terrestrial Evanston, and there is a diabolical Evanston. They intersphere at every point and every moment of the day. But we all think the celestial Evanston is in the ascendency, and one of my reasons for the belief that is in me is Evanston's noble stand against the evil of strong drink. The happiest thought of those good men who founded our classic village was to incorporate in the university charter a provision that no intoxicating liquors should ever be sold within four miles of the college campus. The very announcement of this fact was the magnet to draw hither a class of people who were total abstainers and who desired for their children the surroundings of sobriety.[55] Owning most of the land on which original Evanston was located, the university trustees placed a clause in every deed of transfer, declaring a lapse of title in case intoxicants were ever vended. Moreover, so soon as the village was incorporated a local ordinance was passed in harmony with the university charter, and now that Evanston has become a municipality of twelve thousand souls, the provisions of this ordinance have been steadily strengthened until it is iron-clad. Hence it has come about as the result of honest hard work according to a plan, that Evanston is the ideal temperance town of the great Northwest, for it never had a legalized saloon or bar-room; its costly club house explicitly declares in its by-laws against the use of intoxicants within its walls, and the sentiment of the town is so strong in favor of prohibition that the subject of granting licenses has never yet come up in the local elections.

Judge Hurd gives me this interesting incident:

> "One of the notable epochs in the history of Evanston was our contest over the exclusion of the sale of liquor within the four-mile limit. For a time there was a determined effort to break down the limitation, and, as we understood, this was supported by the liquor league in Chicago. Many suits were brought, fines inflicted, and some paid, until the disputants agreed to take a case to the Supreme Court, and settle the validity of the law, which was done; and the case, 'O'Leary vs. Cook County,' is the leading case in the Illinois reports on that subject. One of the lawyers engaged in that litigation on the part of the liquor men was the afterward famous Gen. Mulligan; and on the part of the university, Governor John L. Beveridge. I took some part in these suits after these men had left for the war, and argued the case in the Supreme Court. There was a funny

J. H. KEDZIE.

WILLIAM DEERING.

HON. H. B. HURD.

H. H. C. MILLER.

incident connected with this argument, namely, that the attorney on the other side was so drunk that I had to submit his side of the case to the court as well as my own! Inasmuch as the question was whether such a law was germane to the establishment and maintaining of the university, I was greatly tempted to put my antagonist in the case as a part of my argument. The court may have done that for me in his personal summing up of the case."

Mrs. Julia Atkins Miller, an early valedictorian of Northwestern Female College, writes of the following occurrence, about the year 1858:
"When a midnight raid was made on the liquor saloon, on the ridge near the railroad crossing, I was suspected of knowing who were the maskers, but I did not. It was the only effort of which I ever heard, to establish a liquor saloon within the limits of the corporation."

Away back in 1860, Dr. Charles Jewett, of New England, lived here, and gave us admirable scientific temperance lectures; and Parker Earle, a leading officer among the Sons of Temperance, sometimes spoke before his fellow-citizens, always to excellent acceptance.

About this time, L. L. Greenleaf and family became residents of Evanston. Mr. Greenleaf was the western representative of Fairbanks & Co., St. Johnsbury, Vt., and knew the blessedness of living outside the sickening atmosphere of the saloon. He knew also that moral suasion must go hand in hand with prohibition. Through his influence a "Temperance Alliance" was formed, which met in his own and other chief homes of the village, for several years. But not until the great crusade of 1873-74, did temperance sentiment crystallize into an organic force that was steadily and strongly felt. On March 17, 1874, under the divine influence of that wonderful uprising, a few earnest Christian women met in Union Hall, and formed what was called the "Women's Temperance Alliance." Among their objects were the prosecution of violators of the university charter law, the circulation of the pledge, and the visiting of all places within the four-mile limit where liquors were secretly sold or gaming was carried on. The first president was Mrs. A. J. Brown, and the following are the names of some of the ladies present at these initiative meetings, who perfected the organization, and determined the policy of the society and its methods of work: Mrs. Rev. Dr. Noyes, Mrs. Edward Russell, Mrs. Dr. O. Marcy, Mrs. A. P. Wightman, Mrs. Francis Bradley, Mrs. Arza Brown, Mrs. Charles E. Brown, Mrs. Emily Huntington Miller, Mrs. John E. Kedzie, Mrs. T. C. Hoag, Mrs. Helen E. Hesler, Mrs. J. F. Willard, Mrs. Mary B. Willard, Mrs. Rev. F. L. Chappell, Mrs. Dr. Fisk, Mrs. Caroline F. Corbin, Mrs. M.

C. Van Benschoten. While this organization was being completed here, thousands of like societies were rapidly forming all over the country.

May 1, 1875, the society changed its name to "Woman's Christian Temperance Union," and fell into line with the ever lengthening ranks of the national organization that now numbers ten thousand local auxiliaries, and the World's W. C. T. U. now represented in forty different governments. Circulation of the pledge, house-to-house visitation, public meetings,—indeed all the usual methods were faithfully employed. But the person who deserves special mention for enthusiasm and untiring devotion to the work, is Mrs. Arza Brown. Although then eighty years of age, she went fearlessly to the most forbidding places; she searched diligently the statutes concerning the liquor traffic, and, by the concise manner in which she presented the results of her investigations before the association, aided largely in the elucidation of judicial questions. To all of this she added the impulse of fervent prayer. The Christian men of the town lent their ready aid and encouragement. Dr. Briggs, pastor of the M. E. Church at that time, was an ardent temperance man. Dr. N. S. Davis, then a resident here, was always ready with his help at the public quarterly meetings, held in the different churches. Rev. Mr. Packard, of the Congregational church, lent active aid and hearty sympathy in the movement, Rev. Mr. Chappell, the Baptist minister, spoke for us at our public meetings. Many pleasant thoughts return to the pioneers in this good cause, as the past comes up again,—thoughts of kind words and helpful deeds and memories of unrecorded names of those who at the time could not have realized the help they gave to the trembling hands at the helm of the new ship W. C. T. U.

February 23, 1875, Mrs. S. M. I. Henry organized the Star Band of Hope, whose first president was Eben P. Clapp, now one of Evanston's physicians. Mrs. Andrew J. Brown was secretary and the presiding genius always. A simple form of military drill was introduced, conducted by Captain Julian R. Fitch. Evanston ladies met in large numbers to make caps and belts for the young "soldiers fighting for good habits." There was a "Girls' Brigade" connected with this Cold Water Army, of which Mrs. Ed. Russell,[56] always an ardent temperance woman, was chief.

This Band of Hope lasted five years, and tided scores of bright boys over the danger-shoals that all must pass in getting their life-craft launched far out upon the deeper waters of confirmed good character.

In September 1879, a Sunday afternoon temperance meeting was started by the W. C. T. U. under the inspiration of Mrs. M. M. Conwell, who was then acting president. Its meetings were held for some time in the waiting-room of the old Northwestern depot, later in a rented store, corner of Davis and Maple streets, and now they have been regularly maintained for years in Union Hall. Here hundreds of men have signed the pledge and sought the Lord; and here all phases of the reform have been ably discussed from the standpoint of Christian discipleship and Christian patriotism. At this meeting, started by Mrs. M. M. Conwell, Frank P. Crandon, Esq., made the first address, standing on a dry goods box in the railroad station, and I made the second, by way of celebrating my fortieth birthday. People who never went to church flocked like doves to their windows, and accomplished musicians among our young folks furnished the music.

It should be mentioned that Mrs. Leander Clifford, one of our most revered pioneers, was associated with the earliest movement to establish these Sunday afternoon meetings, which continue to the present time with unabated interest.

Meanwhile a Young Woman's Temperance Union was formed by Anna Gordon and Edward Murphy, during the meetings held here in 1885, by Francis Murphy, the blue-ribbon evangelist. This had as its chief spirit Miss Mary McDowell, now a national worker, who for several years did excellent service in emphasizing the social features of the temperance movement. It also maintained a kitchen garden for girls. Miss Anna Gordon's Loyal Temperance Legion has since been organized and has become a prime favorite among the children of Evanston. Probably no two persons in the town receive so many warmhearted greetings on the street, as when red-cheeked girls nod and bright-eyed boys lift their caps to Anna Gordon who has gathered so many of them into her Bands of Hope, and to Mrs. Walker, teacher of the Free Kindergarten.

In the winter of 1885 Mrs. Mary Bannister Willard, with the true missionary spirit, trudged through cold and snow and succeeded in raising funds enough (in the form of fifteen-dollar scholarships) to establish what the W. C. T. U. has since christened the " Mary B. Willard Free Kindergarten." Its motto is "Give us the children until they are six years old, and we will risk the rest of their lives." Mrs. Hester E. Walker has had the school in charge since its beginning, and by her unselfish devotion has endeared herself to all the children's hearts and won over many a desolate and careless parent to a better life.

The "Good Time Club" of girls, organized to illustrate the truth that the best of good times consists in doing good to somebody else, was organized by Mrs. Addison DeCoudres and helped to confirm in the pleasant ways of philanthropy many young girls of Evanston.

It has been the latest work of the W. C. T. U. to organize the colored women of Evanston into a local auxiliary. They were invited to belong to the original society, but preferred to form one by themselves, and they have been kind enough to name it the Willard W. C. T. U.

The list of our W. C. T. U. presidents from 1874 to 1890 is as follows: Mrs. E. E. Marcy, Mrs. Mary Thompson Willard, Mrs. W. E. Clifford, Mrs. Francis Bradley, Mrs. A. J. Brown, Mrs. Mary B. Willard, Mrs. Mary H. Hull, Mrs. William Bradley, Mrs. Gertrude M. Singleton, Mrs. Lucy Prescott Vane. Along with these should be named Mrs. T. C. Riley, treasurer, and Mrs. Jane Eggleston Zimmerman, superintendent, of the Sunday meeting, as among the pioneer "stand-bys" of the society.

In 1886, a lodge of Good Templars was organized by Mr. and Mrs. John B. Finch; it is doing excellent work and has fitted up headquarters on Davis Street. Its chiefs have been Mrs. Franc E. Finch, Mrs. C A. Warner, Mrs. E. A. Warner, Rev. Frank A. Scarvie. It is named the Willard Lodge.

The pastors of all our churches, including the Catholic, have been, so far as I know, "ensamples to the flock" in their total abstinence principles, and almost without exception champions of prohibition; certainly all have believed in it for Evanston. There is hardly a distinguished temperance speaker in America who has not addressed audiences here, and at one time the heads of the World's Good Templar Lodge, of the W. C. T. U., and of the National Prohibition party, had their homes here, while Chicago has become the headquarters of the National W. C. T. U., with the largest temperance publishing house in the world; and Rest Cottage, Evanston, is a branch of the National W. C. T. U. office in the city.

The late President Cummings of our university, was one of the most solid temperance men in Christendom, along political as well as legal and moral suasion lines, and the chief citizens of Evanston have stood staunchly for the enforcement of our prohibition ordinances. The Law and Order society was formed at the suggestion of Rev. Dr. Bannister in 1883. Dr. D. R. Dyche has always been the president and moving spirit. To this good man and his coadjutors Evanston owes more than can be told. The municipal officers are in hearty sympathy with the law, and although Chicago is but eleven miles away, and enforcement can not be made perfect, it is nevertheless true, that, in the main, prohibition properly prohibits in "Evanston proper," and no single feature of our town is more appreciated by our people.

EVANSTON IN THE WAR.

No town in America met the shock of the Civil War more bravely than our own. I well remember the Sunday morning just after the defeat at Bull Run when Julius H. White (afterward General), one of our leading business men stood up on the cushion of his pew at the front of the old church, after the benediction was pronounced, and in a voice of intense earnestness called for a "war meeting" the next evening in that same church. Nothing could have been more incongruous with the soft air of that spring day or the sweet peace of our idyllic village. A *war* meeting in Evanston! The congregation walked homeward in the solemn hush of a great sorrow; there were so many young men in Evanston, dear by ties of kindred or of heart to almost every home, and if there must be war then *they* must go! Perhaps the most fervent prayers that ever went up to God for courage and for resignation pierced the sky that Sabbath day, when the sunshine was so golden and the great lake so blue and calm. Monday night came, and it seemed as though the entire village had congregated at the church. The grave faces of Dr. John Evans, of Rev. Dr. Dempster and of acting President Noyes were at the front with those of other professors from the eldest to the most youthful; three gallant figures who were afterwards generals, White, Beveridge and Gamble, that night placed their names upon the muster roll; students vied with each other in signing the patriot's pledge while the most stirring airs were sung by the Ludlam family, Robert Bently, Frances Harvey, Jenny Wheeler, and others, Miss Kellogg presiding at the organ. Besides the three who became generals, Beveridge, White and Gamble, (Major) Edward Russell, Harry Pearsons, Alfred and William Bailey and many others signed that night. General Beveridge raised a company and joined the 8th Illinois Cavalry. General White opened a recruiting office in the city, resigned the office of collector of customs and took the field at the head of the 37th Illinois Infantry, a regiment of one thousand men, among the officers of which were Gen. John C. Black and his brother William P. Black, both now well known. Henry M. Kidder enlisted and became colonel. To secure a complete record I have made many efforts, but find our veterans unwilling to discourse upon the theme.

The following extract from the journal of my sister Mary, gives a graphic picture of the situation as realized in a typical Evanston home:

"April 14, 1861. — News came yesterday of the evacuation—we don't like to say the surrender—of Fort Sumter by Major Anderson.

When I think of all the blood that must be shed, of all the treasure that must be expended to retrieve the honor of my native land, it almost takes away my breath. Think of the thousands of men, living at home and in peace to-day, who must fall in the strife! How it hurts me to remember that every man of them is somebody's husband or father, somebody's brother or son; and that while they yield up their lives on the battlefield, the dear ones at home are many of them going to meet death by a longer path, and one just as painful to tread, — the path where mourners walk clad in their sable robes.

"April 20.—Oliver has succeeded in getting up a great war enthusiasm in the minds of his two sisters this morning, by reading exciting passages from the daily papers and 'interlarding' them with frenzied speeches of his own. At last Frank and I broke forth with one accord into singing the 'Star Spangled Banner,' which, by the aid of his melodious (?) voice, was rendered in a style that seemed peculiarly exciting to his imagination; so much so that, when we came to the chorus of the last verse, he rushed into the closet for a broom, which he waved frantically to and fro to symbolize to himself the fact, as I suppose, that the glorious banner *did* yet wave 'o'er the land of the free and the home of the brave.' While this amusing scene transpired, I thought, with a sad heart, 'Will my brother, my only brother, go to the war?' But who are we, that our hearts should not be broken as well as other women's hearts?

"April 23.—This evening we went to a war meeting at the church. When the 'Star Spangled Banner' was sung, as I joined in the chorus, I was half wild with enthusiasm, though I stood there so quietly. Above the pulpit hung the national flag, arranged in graceful folds around a portrait of Washington, who looked serenely down upon us, as if confident that we would not desert a cause in which he thought no sacrifice too dear. Several speeches were made, and there was a call for those who were willing to volunteer to come forward and sign the muster-roll. I shall never forget the scene that followed. Rapidly they went; young men whom we all know and esteem; students in college and in theology; men who had wives and daughters looking after them, with smiles of pride on their lips though there were tears of sorrow in their eyes; and beardless boys, with their slight forms and flushed young faces. Cheer after cheer went up from the excited audience as each one took the pen and wrote his name as a volunteer in the army that goes to save the Union. One young man told us that he did not join here, because, although he came last week from a distant town to enter college, 'he would throw books aside and return home to-morrow to go with his father and his brothers to the field.' Dr. McFarland was loudly applauded. He said that 'he was a Virginian, and he should start for his native State to-morrow to join with his relatives, who are all loyal, in fighting for the Union. He said his mother was buried there, and he meant that no traitor should set his foot upon her grave.' I am afraid that we didn't realize how solemn was the scene; how eternal destinies were being fixed that evening by a mere penstroke. God pity the man who is not prepared to die before he joins the army. Oh! if we could have known the agony that will result from what was done then in the church we love so much, and where we have worshiped so peacefully together, I know we should have filled the house with sobs, and tears would have fallen like the rain that beat against the windows as though nature herself were grieving. A large fund was immediately subscribed for the support of the families of poor men who will go into the army. The liberal subscriptions showed plainly enough the patriotism which glowed in each heart. It seemed very generous to hear Dr. Evans give his name for hundreds of dollars, and hardly less *so* when seamstresses, and young ladies who support themselves by teaching, pledged themselves for the payment of smaller sums.

"War! What a new meaning has the term for me since the fall of Port Sumter only a few days ago! Truly

> " *We are living, we are dwelling*
> *In a grand and awful time;*
> *In an age on ages telling;*
> *To be living is sublime.*' "

From Rev. Liston H. Pearce, graduated in 1866, we have these anecdotes:

"It was war times and we were a patriotic set, at least most of us. But there was White from Baltimore. He could neither conceal his Southern sympathies nor control his temper. One evening as we came up from supper where the discussion had been heated, he became exasperated, and cried, 'Then down with the stars and stripes, and up with the palmetto!' There was instantly a rush made for him with shouts of ' To the lake with him!' But he held his pursuers at bay on the stairs. In the tumult, he cried, 'I'm for the country when she is right,' to which Fowler, now the reverend bishop, shouted back, 'We're for our country, right or wrong; if she's wrong, we'll right her.' W. went at last to his room a wiser if not a better man.

"It was about the commencement of the last year of the war, though we did not know it. Things looked dark. Students were dropping out of the university and entering the army. At last a number of the boys resolved that they would form a university company if Professor Linn would go as captain. I chanced to be Linn's room-mate at Auntie Bragdon's, and was commissioned to make the proposition to him. I shall never forget how serious and thoughtful he was when he said it must be the voice of God and his country, and he would go. 'Old timers' at Evanston will remember how we marched off to the war and how we came back, some in coffins, and among them the brave, noble, generous Linn. In the company of which he was captain, went Henry Meacham, I. W. McCaskey, Charles Bragdon and many others."

Mrs. Julia Atkins Miller, valedictorian of the class of 1860, writes:

"You must well remember the spirit of patriotism that prevailed in Evanston when Bishop Simpson preached the sermon after the fall of Fort Sumter. Bunting could not be procured at any price in anything like sufficient quantity to meet the demand. It must be manufactured for the entire country. Dr. Charles Jones happened to think of an old flag, then stored in Chicago, belonging to his brother Wesley. He brought it to Evanston, torn and mouse-eaten, as it was. I worked all day making over that old flag. Perhaps you recall the enthusiasm exhibited by the university students that evening when they saw it floating on the college building during their sunset walk! I need not tell you how elated Professor and Mrs. Jones were when our flag was the first to wave."

From Mrs. Dr. Kidder's Journal:

"It was an Evanston woman who suggested a movement that would have rolled into Abraham Lincoln's office a petition with more names of women than were ever before attached to any paper, if his official pen had not anticipated its advent and issued the Emancipation Proclamation. Mrs. Hyde, her heart too deeply burdened with sorrow to bear it longer alone, came to see me and ask if we women, who had not such cares as engrossed all of her time, would not put into circulation a petition and let it come before the president as the voice of the women of the land. A few other women were consulted and a petition was prepared. Copies of it were sent to religious newspapers of different churches requesting its publication, accompanied by a note, asking women who should read the petition to cut it from the paper, attach it to a blank, obtain signatures, and when filled, forward it to a place specified; all to work as speedily as possible. A considerable number of papers commended the movement, women gladly circulated the petitions, and many had been returned to the offices named. The *Northwestern Christian Advocate* in Chicago reported that a mammoth roll, almost beyond the capacity of a man to carry, was being daily added to the petition. Senator Harlan had been engaged to see that the petition was presented to the President, when lo! the Emancipation Proclamation sounded through the length and breadth of the land."

Major Edward Russell says that all who went from here were in the Army of the Potomac during the war. He adds the following:

"The fight at Gettysburg commenced by the Eighth Cavalry, the Evanston regiment, under the command of Major Beveridge. After the battle commenced and got fairly along, our brigade was placed at the enemy's right, our left in a commanding position, where we could see everything. It was a splendid sight to see one side charge across the valley in front of Seminary Ridge, and then the other charge in turn.
"In our regiment were Gov. John L Beveridge, who was commander; Capt. Joseph Clapp; Lieut. Harry Pearsons, Alfred Bailey, W. R. Bailey, Edwin Bailey, George W. Huntoon, George Hide, George Kirby, K. S. Lewis, James Milner, Charles McDaniel, Charles Pratt, George H. Reed, Peter Schütz, James A. Snyder, Charles Smith, A. P. Searle, C. P. Westfield, Harry and Will Page, Charles Wigglesworth, O. C. Foster, E. R. Lewis, Philo Judson, J. D. Ludlam, also Dr. W. A. Spencer, who is now one of the secretaries of the Church Extension Society of the Methodist church."

Evanston's war record has as its sequel the efficient activities of the John A. Logan Grand Army Post. By means of frequent lectures and entertainments they keep alive the sense of old time comradeship. Probably their most notable exploit was a magnificent reception given to Mrs. General Logan, in the First M. E. church, October 24, 1889.

We can not better close this chapter than with the following summary of the history of the post, and a soldier-preacher's unique comment on it:

"Gen. John A. Logan, Post No. 540, Department of Illinois G. A. R., was organized October at, 1885, under the name of Gamble Post. The name was changed on the death of Logan. Its commanders who now rank as Post Commanders are EH R. Lewis, William H, Langton and E.

S. Weeden. Present commander, J. W. Thompson. Number of members, one hundred and eight. It has on its roster many distinguished citizens, amongst whom might be named Gen. John L. Beveridge, Judge David T. Corbin, Chaplain W. A. Spencer, Professor William H. Cutler, Frank P. Crandon, D. B. Dewey, P. N. Fox, Holmes Hoge, W. S. Harbert, Dr. I. Poole, H. A. Pierson and Gen. Julius White. Many others might be added did space permit. Evanston was well represented in the War of the Rebellion, but the Eighth Illinois Cavalry probably stands highest amongst the organizations prominently represented from our village.

J. W. Thompson."

"The above is Brother Thompson's own; 'tis the best he could do from his resources. It is worth while to say of him,— Thompson,—that he is one of the bravest and purest men I have ever known.

H. A. Delano."

I have this testimony from one of these brave soldiers:

"The ladies of Evanston, during the entire period of the war, were active in aid of the soldiers in the field in various ways, holding frequent meetings, sending hospital supplies, such as bandages, lint, hospital garments, mittens and bed clothing, and in assisting the Sanitary Commission in Chicago; one of the citizens of Evanston, Mrs. A. H. Hoge, having been distinguished for her great and invaluable services as a member of the Sanitary Commission.
"The great fair held in Chicago in aid of the Sanitary Commission was largely conducted under the auspices of these ladies, and it was to this fair that Mr. Lincoln gave the original draft of the Emancipation Proclamation. It was sold at the fair to Hon. Thomas B. Bryan, who paid three thousand dollars for it, and gave it back subsequently to the Soldiers' Home in Chicago, which institution grew out of the Sanitary Fair, having been established partly by funds which the Sanitary Fair had produced, and partly by the aid of the State. The Emancipation Proclamation, being the property of the Soldiers' Home, thus acquired, was in its possession at the time of the great fire in 1871, and was destroyed in the rooms of the Historical Society, where it had been deposited for safe keeping."

EVANSTON IN POLITICS.

At my request Hon. Edward S. Taylor has, with his usual kindness of heart and felicity of pen, treated this subject.

Mr. Taylor, as everybody knows, has represented us in the legislature, and has been for years secretary of the Lincoln Park Association; he has had a hand, too, in that successful undertaking, the Sheridan road. He says:

> "Evanston has not been forgotten in the past in the distribution of public offices. Again and again have her citizens been called to positions of honor and trust.
>
> "Julius White more than thirty years ago became a resident of our town, and the hospitality of his house is a pleasant memory of those early days. A social event of that date, well remembered by many, was the visit of Abraham Lincoln to Evanston as the guest of his old friend, Julius White. In 1861 Mr. White was appointed by Mr. Lincoln collector of the port of Chicago, perhaps the most honorable of the presidential appointments in the northwest.
>
> "Soon after the breaking out of the war, Mr. White resigned his office and organized the Thirty-seventh regiment of Illinois. At the close of the war, he bore the commission of a major-general of volunteers.
>
> "General White was elected a member of the board of county commissioners organized under the constitution of 1870, and became its first president.
>
> "In 1872 General White was appointed by President Grant, minister to the Argentine Republic. He resigned this mission in 1875, and thereafter until his death resided in South Evanston, and was one of the most enterprising and efficient promoters of that suburb.
>
> "In 1863 Dr. John Evans, an esteemed friend and neighbor, after whom our village was named, removed from our midst to Denver, having been appointed by President Lincoln governor of the territory of Colorado; although Evanston lost him as a citizen he remained bound to our people by his official ties, the trustees of the Northwestern university having retained him as the president of the board. His munificent contributions to the university will ever endear him to our citizens. He still resides in Denver, and is identified with many of the railroad and mining enterprises of the Centennial State.
>
> "Again did President Lincoln call upon Evanston to furnish the right man for the right place; in 1862 he selected as consul to China, one of our earliest acquaintances here, Prof. W. P. Jones, the founder and for many

years president of the Northwestern Female College, the bud which blossomed into the present Woman's College, an annex to Northwestern University. It was during his residence in the celestial kingdom that the old Chinese wall, which prohibited intercourse with other nations, was broken down, the portals of the ancient empire opened, and the wealth of its early civilization blended with the progress and thought of modern times. While in China Mr. Jones was sent on a special mission to Pekin [sic][57], which resulted in a settlement of the difficulties growing out of the opium war and the destruction of American property at Canton. Rev. Dr. Talmage once said of Mr. Jones' work as consul at Canton: 'No account of his life in China, and effort to do good to these people would be complete without a record of his efforts to have the surplus of the indemnity paid by China to the United States repaid to China in a way that would render to her the greatest and most permanent advantage.'

"Returning to this country, Professor Jones connected himself with the Chicago press but longing for his chosen vocation, that of a teacher, he assumed the presidency of the Fremont Normal School, Fremont, Nebraska, where, in the midst of his years of usefulness, he received the final summons, leaving the precious memory of a life devoted to the elevation and betterment of mankind.

"For twenty-two years consecutively (with the exception of the thirty-third general assembly from 1883 to 1885) Evanston has had a representative in the state administration—either in the executive or legislative department. In 1866 Edward S. Taylor, who had for three years represented Evanston in the board of supervisors, which at that time was charged with the administration of the county affairs, was elected a representative in the twenty-fifth general assembly, and re-elected to the twenty-sixth general assembly in 1868.

"During his term in the legislature the park system of Chicago was inaugurated, with which he has since been identified. Mr. Taylor is at present a member of the state board of equalization from this, the Fourth congressional district.

"John L. Beveridge, Esq , our honored neighbor, was one of the earliest settlers here. In 1861 he enlisted a company in Evanston, for the Eighth Illinois Cavalry, and subsequently organized the Seventeenth Illinois Cavalry; he emerged from the service in 1865, having worthily worn successively the emblem of a captain, major, colonel and brigadier-general. In 1868 he was elected sheriff of Cook county, but having no warrant to hang any one during his term, he was not subsequently elected chief executive of the republic.

"In 1870 Gen. Beveridge was elected to the state senate and after serving

a portion of his term resigned, having been elected in 1871 member of Congress from the State at large. In 1872 General Beveridge was elected lieutenant-governor, and by virtue of his office became president of the senate; by the election of Governor Oglesby to the United States Senate, General Beveridge became governor and served in that position the unexpired term of three years. In 1882 he was appointed by President Arthur sub-treasurer, which office he held until the accession of Mr. Cleveland. Since his retirement from the position of sub-treasurer Governor Beveridge has held no official position but has been engaged in banking,—and was at one time "president of the Lincoln National Bank.
"In order that Evanston might again be identified with state affairs, the late Andrew Shuman, Esq., well known as editor of the Chicago *Journal* for many years, was elected lieutenant-governor in 1876, and presided over the state senate during the terms of the thirtieth and thirty-first general assembly. It is well remembered that in his administration as president of the senate his uniform courtesy and dignity gave a charm to its sessions. Mr. Shuman served a term as commissioner of the penitentiary by appointment of Governor Oglesby. Governor Shuman, as we Evanstonians were pleased to call him, retired from the editorial chair seeking rest to revive the energies exhausted by thirty-three years of continuous journalistic service. But alas! this precaution came too late.
"In 1880 John H. Kedzie, Esq., was selected as a representative in the thirty-second general assembly; after his retirement in 1882, the people of the district which comprised the towns of North Chicago, Lake View and Evanston, gave Evanston a rest for two years. In 1884 Harry S. Boutell was elected to the thirty-fourth general assembly. Harry had grown up in our midst, was a graduate of the Northwestern University and was equipped both by nature and acquirement for the position to which he was called. He was the peer of any in that general assembly in debate and excelled all as a brilliant speaker. In 1886 C. G. Neeley was elected to the thirty-fifth general assembly. He was heard upon most of the important questions which were discussed by that body, and he rarely spoke without saying something. Mr. Neeley is now one of the assistants to State's Attorney Longenecker, and has charge of all trials in one branch of the circuit court.
"George S. Baker, for several years at the head of our public schools in Evanston and subsequently a member of the bar, was elected in 1888 to the thirty-sixth general assembly. During the session Mr. Baker acquitted himself creditably; the people of Evanston are in a large measure indebted to him for the law which makes the Sheridan road a possibility. It would subserve the public interest if he were returned to

the next general assembly.[58]

"Harvey B. Hurd, Esq., who came here before Evanston was, is not unknown in public life. In 1871 he was one of a commission of three to revise the laws after the adoption of the present state constitution. On account of his fitness his associates on the commission burdened him with the work. The result of his labors is embodied in a volume known throughout the state as 'Hurd's Revision.' He has been for many years a professor in the law department of the Northwestern University. He served by appointment for a short term as a member of the board of county commissioners.

"Mr. Hurd is a devoted believer in drainage, and his self sacrificing spirit in endeavoring to provide adequate drainage for our village for the next hundred years, marks him as one of our most enterprising and public-spirited citizens.

"W. N. Brainard, a long time resident here, is perhaps one of the most widely known of our citizens. He was at one time a canal commissioner, and subsequently a most efficient member of the board of railroad and warehouse commissioners; he has recently contributed to the Chicago press several very readable articles on early life in California, replete with personal reminiscences.

"James H. Raymond, Esq., well known to us all, a graduate of Northwestern University, was for a time secretary of the railroad and warehouse commission, and he largely aided in framing the rules of that board. He is now engaged in the practice of patent law, and as we are informed is doing a large business.

"For many years Mr. Daniel Shepard (familiarly known as Dan) was identified with our village. He has been for time without mind secretary of the Republican state committee, and what he does not know about politics is not worth knowing. He is probably as well posted as any man in this country on its politics and public men. Dan is said to be tougue-tied; he was talkative early in life, but when he became a man he put away childish things and adopted the idea that 'silence is golden.' Though afflicted as stated, his eyesight and hearing are unimpaired; he can gather more and impart less than any one we know. It is this faculty coupled with a wonderfully retentive memory that makes him the general he is. To Mr. Shepard more than any other was the lamented Logan indebted for his election to the senate in 1885, such election being assured by the election of a Republican representative in an overwhelmingly Democratic district, through tactics admirably planned and successfully executed under Mr. Shepard's personal direction.

"Judge Walter B. Scates, who resided in our village for several years preceding his death (which occurred three years ago), was at one time chief justice of the supreme court of Illinois. He, with another, compiled the statutes of Illinois after the adoption of the constitution of 1848, known as the 'Scates and Blackwell revision.' In 1866 President Johnson appointed him collector of the port of Chicago.

"Hon. Burton C. Cook, now residing in a lovely home overlooking the lake, was, before he became a resident of Evanston, a longtime in public life. He was a member of the state senate from 1852 to 1860. He was a member of the peace conference in 1861, by appointment of his old friend President Lincoln, and was representative in the thirty-ninth, fortieth and forty-first congresses, from 1864 to 1870.

"So far as I recollect the above embraces all who have borne the burden of official life."

A STUDENT'S POINT OF VIEW.

Among the students of that elder day none were more esteemed than the two Strobridge brothers. They were strong in body and mind, self-supporting, genial, and devotedly in earnest. The elder brother is Rev. Dr. George E. Strobridge, now pastor of a Methodist Episcopal church in New York City. The younger, Rev. Thomas R. Strobridge, is pastor of the church in Princeton, Illinois. Mrs. M. M. Conwell, known as the founder of our Union Hall Gospel Meeting, at the time of starting which she was president of Evanston Woman's Christian Temperance Union, is the mother of these two gifted and useful ministers; and their sister, Mrs. B. F. Foster, is with us active in every good work.

I wrote Rev. T. R. Strobridge for his experience, which is typical and will greatly encourage our young people who are "working their way."

He says:

"My going to Evanston in 1861 I have always considered as a turn in the course of my life for which I could claim a providential guidance. Those were days of simplicity, compared with the present state of that renowned educational center; days in which the fair present and more prosperous future were in anticipation.

"I was a clerk in a store in Cincinnati when Mr. Lincoln, in 1861, passed through that city on his way to Washington. I can see myself yet as I walked across the city beside his carriage, looking up into his good but homely face, while he stood bowing to the crowd, with his hand on a board that had been torn from a fence and laid across the carriage for his support. On that day I went back to my employer, Mr. Shillito, the Marshall Field of Cincinnati,[59] and told him that I was going to study for the ministry. He asked me if we had any creditable institutions in the Methodist Episcopal church for giving the necessary training to young men. I told him I knew of one, located at Evanston, Illinois, called the Garrett Biblical Institute, to which I was going. He was a strong Presbyterian and kindly offered to send me to an institution in that denomination, where he would pay the bills if I would enter that ministry. My poverty made this a tempting offer, but my father, up to his death, had been an official in Wesley Chapel, Cincinnati, and I had read what my Scotch grandfather called 'Flatcher's Chacks.' So the financial temptation was overcome, and with ten dollars, which my employer gave me, as he said, 'For Christ's sake,' I paid my fare to Chicago, reaching Evanston early in May 1861. My brother George had been there since the previous March. I had fifty dollars in my pocket which Rev. J. J. Mitchell had raised for me in the official board of Wesley Chapel without my knowledge, and on the recommendation of that board (required of us as intending students of the Institute) I at once became a boarder with the other 'bibs' in Brother A. C. Langworthy's ecclesiastical hotel, at one dollar and seventy-five cents a week, for which amount I always felt assured Brother Langworthy rendered me a full equivalent:

"Evanston was then a village with a few plain stores, comfortable dwellings, a postoffice and one church,—an oblong, wooden structure, with papered walls and plain furniture. It stood on Church Street in a grove, near the corner of Orrington Avenue. Those were happy days, when we knew every one in the town, and all the Christians in the place filled up the "meeting house" during the pastorates of Brothers Tiffany, Bibbins, Dandy and Raymond, the latter of whom took Dr. Dempster's chair in the Institute, and gave us for three years strong and eloquent sermons, in which the students of Watson could see whence came the line of thought and the helping inspiration. A variety of pulpit ministration was furnished us by the distinguished visitors who tarried over the Sabbath.

"At the time I became a citizen of Evanston there were, besides the church, but four public buildings,—the public schoolhouse, the female college, presided over by Professor Jones, the frame building which stood opposite T. C. Hoag's home and bore the proud name of 'Northwestern University,' and a building of similar proportions and dignity, located about half a mile farther north on the lake shore in the grove, which was the only Institute building, and within whose accommodating walls were the chapel, library, recitation rooms and the "biblical hotel " aforesaid.

Here with about seventy students I was soon at home, trying to carry five studies. When I first took my seat in the chapel and swept my gaze about me I was amused at the coats of many colors which the students wore. But I grew sober as I observed the central figure upon the platform,—an aged man, not large of stature, with a genial, thoughtful face, wearing the same kind of a garment, made of dark red, figured calico. This was Dr. Dempster, whom I frequently saw afterwards working at his wood pile. There sat also Dr. Bannister, whose sturdy form, strong face and noble character were in perfect harmony; Dr. Kidder, whose erect carriage denoted the courteous gentleman and methodical student; and Professor Hemenway, accurate, clear, industrious, and upright in form as in soul. He was my instructor and class leader. We met at his home. My brother George, Miss Katie Kidder, Miss Frances E. Willard and her sister Mary, who was so soon to end her "nineteen beautiful years," together with other earnest-hearted young people, often gathered at his home to profit by the professor's spiritual counsels and elucidations of the Word.

"The fall of 1861 found me with an empty purse and a full conviction that I needed a better basis of college training as a foundation for a biblical finish. As the Northwestern University offers its advantages to students for the ministry free of charge, I turned my ambitions in that direction. I was fortunate enough to take the place of J. O. Foster as chore boy in Dr. Kidder's family, my work being considered an equivalent for my shelter and board. Here I remained for nearly two years, making myself useful in the garden, barn and at the wood pile. I was then under the superintendence of Professor Noyes, acting president of Northwestern University. He was above the medium stature, and slightly lame by reason of a stiffened knee. I can see that fine face now. His eyes were large and blue, his forehead high and correspondingly broad, and never did clay yield better to the moulding touches of thought and generous impulses from within, than it did in his benignant countenance. His coadjutors were Professor Bonbright, whose knowledge of the labyrinthine relations of the Latin subjunctive was truly marvelous in my eyes. Although he is rarely gifted as an instructor, his success in certain cases when he would impart a knowledge of that mood was, if my memory serves me now better than then, a little doubtful in some cases! Professor Marcy, in the prime of his power, was soon placed over the scientific department. I used to think in those days that we were especially favored as pupils in having such willing and able instructors, and our classes being small, we received more individual attention than would have been possible in large and crowded institutions.

"When I left Dr. Kidder's I went to housekeeping with several other bachelors in the top story of the University building, now used as a preparatory department, having been moved up to the classic grove. My domestic companions were my brother George, Robert Bently, L. H. Pearce and James Swormstedt. My brother and I were janitors of the building, for which we received two dollars per week. Upon this we lived. Our supply of meat was rather limited and our supply of meal mush was rather large. Miss Rebecca Hoag made us welcome visits with pastry, which her generous mother had prepared and sent. For two years we thus and there subsisted. When we heard Mr. Lincoln's last call for troops, the summer vacation being near, we made up a company among the students, and taking Alphonso C. Linn, one of our tutors, as captain, we went into the army and remained in the service until the war closed in 1865, which gave us six months' military experience. Our noble captain, however, never returned, having died of typhoid fever. Upon coming back in the fall, George became a tutor in the university, and I, having broken a colt of Dr. Kidder's, began on the Sabbaths my first pastoral labors, riding over to Bowmanville. This enabled me to occupy a room in Heck Hall, which was opened in 1866, and to take my meals at the hotel. I graduated at the university in the spring of 1867. I then went to New York City, where I labored in the city mission work and attended the Union Theological Seminary, but the more I heard of Calvinism the less I liked it I was very grateful, however, to those who permitted me to attend the lectures of Dr. William T. Shedd, Dr. Edward Hitchcock and Dr. Smith, in that worthy institution. I returned to Evanston and graduated at Garrett Biblical Institute in 1868. The manner in which the way opened before me causes me to conclude that any young person in this country who desires an education may expect providential assistance in that honorable endeavor.

"It was my pleasure during those years to witness the building of Heck Hall, and be among the first to enjoy one of those new and comfortable apartments, which were furnished by the ladies of the different churches of the northwest. Also during those seven years the stately central stone building of the university arose in the beautiful grove. Pleasant memories do I cherish of those students; of those wise, cultured, Christian gentlemen, who were our instructors; of those kindly citizens, who sought to know and help the students who were temporarily among them; of those officials in the church, who, with their families, fostered and furthered our interests; Messrs. Haskin, Hoag, Vane, Beveridge, Pearsons, DeCoudres, Reynolds, Clifford, Judson and others ; the latter three of whom have passed onward, while some of their loved ones still remain. With the good people of Evanston during those seven years, I was permitted to mingle as a student, a believer, and a citizen. That was also the period of the great war. With them my soul was moved by the gathering and marching of armies, the shock of awful battles, the assassination of our great Lincoln, the fear for our sacred institutions, and the final glorious hour of victory."

SARAH ROLAND CHILDS,
First Lady Graduate of N. W. U.

JANE M. BANCROFT ROBINSON,
Former Dean of Woman's College.

MARY McCRILLIS, M. D.

SARAH BRAYTON, M. D.

LETTERS FROM DEAN BANCROFT AND DEAN SANFORD.

After much importunity, as her life is one of great pre-occupation, Dean Jane M. Bancroft, Ph. D.,[60] furnishes her reminiscences. Her years of study in Europe and the devoted work she is now doing for women in the Methodist Episcopal church, and as author of a most helpful book on "Deaconesses in Europe and Their Lessons for America," have evidently not at all interfered with this gifted woman's clear memory of her active and helpful work in Evanston.

My Dear Miss Willard:

It is not neglect that has so long delayed the answer to your request to write you a few impressions of the eight years that I was dean of the Woman's college at Evanston. Neither are the impressions slight ones. So long a period of one's active life maintains its well-defined place in memory. Before going I had corresponded with you and had formed one of the three at the first interview of prophetic forecast at Sing Sing when three successive deans of the Woman's college met for the first time, yourself, Nellie Soulé and myself. How curiously girlhood names sound in later life, but Mrs. Carhart evidently remembers the interview in that way as she has set the fashion of using the name.

I reached Evanston just at a transition period. The Woman's college had been occupied four years and a term. For a year and a term you had reigned in the building that had claimed so much of your love and loyalty from its origin to its completion. For two years Miss Soulé had given the best of her time, talent and ripe experience to like duties. Then came Mrs. Sanford who occupied the position for a year before I entered upon the office at the opening of the college year of 1877. The largest number of girls who had been inmates of the college building up to that date in any one session was thirty-two or thirty-four.

The university was weighted by a heavy debt and its very existence threatened by a lawsuit which was dragging its slow length along. Dr. Marcy was the president, a man to whom the university owes an amount of grateful thanks that can not well be computed in the ordinary returns of commercial life. Whenever an emergency arose he stood ready to sacrifice his personal tastes and preferences, and to fit into any place that would best serve the institution with which the work of his life was associated. As to what a college for women ought to be there was a wide diversity of view, a diversity that was reflected in the opinions of the people of the town, in the mothers who brought their daughters to the college, and in the young women themselves; such a diversity as invariably marks the transition stages of a new enterprise.

In the decade of years and longer that has elapsed since then public opinion has crystallized into a more definite consciousness. The successful experiences of Vassar, Smith and Wellesley have shown that a college of high grade can be combined with a more immediate care and personal interest in young woman students than is wont to be exercised at colleges for men only. At the period of which I write, however, it was not unusual for a mother to ask me if teachers accompanied the young ladies in their walks, if the bureau drawers of the students were inspected at regular intervals, and if the Saturday mending was under some one's supervision. The next visitor might be an independent young woman who would introduce herself by announcing with plain decisiveness that she had come for college work only and desired no limitations that were not equally imposed upon young men. The dean had sympathy with the general principles thus stated, but found they had slight practical application in the social life of a building a very small minority of whose inmates were students in regular college standing.

I well remember the faculty meetings of the College of Liberal Arts. With what hesitant step I at first entered the president's room, the only woman present in that faculty of able and experienced professors, the majority of whom had been associated with the institution for years! Very pleasant memories are stowed away among my mental treasures, of the words and deeds belonging to those meetings. Then I count it an unusual privilege to have had such close familiarity during so many years with college usages and requirements. I learned, too, that self-sacrifice and denial enter into the lives of all connected with large interests affecting the welfare of others, for whenever an emergency arose the professors had an opportunity to relieve the straitened circumstances of the instigation by relinquishing a portion of their salaries. Meanwhile, as time passed on the outlook became more promising. The supreme court decided the lawsuit in favor of the university.[61] The students quickly responded to the good news; they expended their enthusiasm in rockets and bonfires, and still having a surplus, formed a procession and marched to the president's house. They were greatly elated by obtaining a speech from Dr. Marcy, who, as report goes, shares the disinclination that General Grant had for "words, mere words." Coming down to the Woman's college they asked the dean to voice some sentiments that should express the general joy. The short speech that followed cost the one who made it far greater effort than more elaborate ones that have followed since then, but the good will of the hearer compensated for the defects of the endeavor.

Four years passed away and Dr. Cummings came to us. Immediately new life and vigor were breathed into all portions of the university system. The great debt that was standing as an obstacle to any progressive effort must be lifted. The era of beneficence had arisen. A united effort upon the part of those who gave with princely generosity through all gradations of contributions to those to whom the smallest sums were as the "widow's mite," wiped away the indebtedness that had so long paralyzed growth. One improvement after another followed. Special departments were strengthened. The teaching force increased, and the university began to assume an appearance of progressive activity in distinction from the condition of merely holding its own. Students were attracted in larger numbers. This would have been the case in some degree from the added population and wealth that during these years were rapidly adding to the resources of the patronizing territory, but the added attractions and resources of the university had their share in the increase. Four years more passed on. The number of girls in the Woman's college had increased to an average of between fifty and sixty, as the figures show in the records kept by the dean.

The college cottage, that valuable and indispensable adjunct of the college life, had enlarged its accommodations until from fifteen or sixteen, over thirty girls were accommodated. A band of noble women were those with whom I used to meet at the monthly gatherings. Convinced that there must be some way provided by which girls in limited circumstances could have a home with suitable environments, the women connected with the board labored unobtrusively but indefatigably to this end. No one, not within the small circle of administration, can realize the patient, unwearied efforts of years, that have been needed to produce the results of the present time. I have in mind some of the students that have been there; now useful, busy women, filling places of trust and importance. Such women, both of the college and cottage, I am constantly meeting, and when they recall a word or act of mine that has combined with the numberless other lines of influence that have made them what they are, I feel that I am obtaining the real reward for much labor and endeavor that went into my life at Evanston. It gives a sense of permanence, as of something surviving out of the fleeting years; a strong enthusiasm to work in the present with a prophetic hopefulness that the "good that is desired shall one day become real."

Such, my dear Miss Willard, are some of the reflections that come to me as, at your request, I review the eight years and more that I occupied the office of dean in a university for which I wish all noble prosperity in its high mission of uplifting the civilization of our times.

Yours very truly, JANE M. BANCROFT.

Mrs. A. E. Sanford was dean of the Woman's college, and at my request sends her recollections:

BLOOMINGTON, Illinois, Oct. 19.

My Dear Miss Willard:

I gladly give you a few lines concerning the eventful year 1875-6, when, as dean of the Woman's college of Northwestern University, it was my privilege to follow you in the educational work. It was not my good fortune to meet you there, since you were absent most of that year with Mr. Moody in the east. This has always been a regret to me, but as I turn the pages of the past, memory lingers very lovingly over the pleasant days spent in that charming village of classic fame, Evanston, beautiful for situation on the shore of fair Lake Michigan. My eyes wandered frequently from my class room to the blue waters which sparkled and danced not far away, and no walk was so restful as that within the campus, beside the lake.

Many who were very near and dear appear at memory's roll-call, but I can mention only a few of the faithful friends or the many attractions which made Evanston for me, as it has been for many, a charmed spot. I shall mention first Mrs. Bishop Hamline, whose saintly face was enshrined with its circling halo of silver hair. From her lovely home the door to heaven seemed always ajar, and beautiful glimpses of "the better country" did we, who were accustomed to gather there on Sabbath and Thursday afternoons, gain as we talked of the way to the "prepared mansion." Mrs. Hamline's words were an inspiration and a benediction, and many a young soul has been equipped for its warfare from her strong words of helpfulness. There Christians learned to tread more surely the restful paths of peace, and many from her lips learned the way to the " celestial city," whither she has since gone. Here I frequently met Mrs. Mary B. Willard, Mrs. Elizabeth Wheeler Andrew, and Dr. Kate Bushnell. At Nashville, with the latter two, I reviewed the Evanston days of 1876 and 1877 and recalled many of their scenes.

Here I frequently met dear Mrs. Arza Brown, who realized Cicero's beautiful ideal of old age, not permitted to become wearisome or inactive. Her constant contact with the great minds of every age made her a delightful and instructive companion. Delighting herself with untangling the misty thoughts of classic lore, she freely shared with others the treasures she gained by diligent effort. A student to her death, with mind clear and vigorous, with heart sunny and warm, she was one of the strong attractions to Mrs. I. R. Hitt's home, where I always found the latchstring out. This was one of my resting places when weary in spirit, and here I never failed to find the helpfulness of loving sympathy. My thought turns ever fondly to this pleasant home and its genial, cultured mistress.

Mrs. Emily Huntington Miller contributed much to the cheeriness of my college home, by transferring to it some of the fragrance and beauty of her own home, in choice plants, which were a continual delight. A box of ferns, in which, unexpected, one plant after another appeared, a constant surprise and joy, reminded me of her own beautiful character, in which new beauties and graces every day appeared to surprise and charm. This ideal woman, in her ideal home, was a comfort and a joy, and I count it one of my life's greatest blessings to have known her, and enjoyed her friendship. What Monday's dinners, which her own deft hands had prepared, have I relished with her! Always neat and attractive at home, busy with her literary work a large part of each day, but devoting herself to her husband and boys in the evening, her artistic taste and touch making her home a bower of beauty, where rest awaited the weary ones. Alas! that the family circle is broken, and the strong, true heart that beat in accord with hers, is still.

Dr. Kate Bushnell was one of my helpers there, a missionary in spirit as much as when she carried her message of Christ's love to China's benighted women. Constantly seeking to uplift and help those whose acquaintance with Christ was more limited than hers, she was often found among the college girls, drawing them to a higher, purer life of real happiness and usefulness. On Sabbath evenings, she, with Mrs. Andrew, often led the girls' prayer-meetings in my room.

I have pleasant memories also of your brother Oliver, who placed his valuable library of American history at my disposal to aid me in my Junior class work. Our plan was to study by topics without text books, and we ransacked the university library for information in this work, which was full of fascination for us all. Your brother's library, in this department, was a treasure-house of rich stores. This was the winter also when he came to Christ, and I was impressed by his earnestness as he sought to atone for "lost opportunities." Surely God permitted him to lead many to Himself before He called him home! I recall your dear old mother also, as I heard her speak frequently in the church prayer-meetings; Bishop Harris, as he stood before "my girls" one Friday afternoon to tell them of the women of heathen lands and the debt of American women to them; Professor Hemenway, as he skillfully unraveled the meaning of God's word to his attentive Bible class of Sunday afternoons; Professor and Mrs. Marcy and their genial home surroundings; Professor Cumnock, whom it has been my good fortune to meet and enjoy in other places, as I did then in my visits to his class room. Here I met and enjoyed one of my girlhood's friends, Mrs. Cornelia Lord, who, like myself, had exchanged her New England home for one in the Prairie State.

I recall the missionary meetings in the Methodist church, and the eager enthusiasm of the women. I recall many young men and women whom I have followed with loving interest as they have gone out into life's active work, some to foreign fields, some to positions of honor and dignity here, and I count no year of my life more favored than the one spent in Evanston, Chicago's classic suburb, blessed with that city's privileges, but free from her vices and perils. Thinking of the grand women who have gone out from Evanston to push forward the world's grand enterprises, I am constrained to believe that the atmosphere of this village by the lake is favorable to the development of heroic qualities. Scanning the achievements of Evanston's clear-brained, brave-hearted sons and daughters, I pray earnestly, "Long live and prosper this home of refinement and culture and devotion." May she be in the future, as in the past, the refuge and resting-place of heroic souls, who shall go out to do valiant service for God and humanity. I remain as ever, sincerely yours,

A. E. SANFORD.

WM. F. POOLE,
Librarian of Newberry Library, Chicago.

WM. S. LORD.

VOLNEY W. FOSTER.

M. M. KIRKMAN.

OUR LIBRARIES.[62]

NORTHWESTERN UNIVERSITY LIBRARY.

The history of the library dates from the beginning of the university. The first circular of the university, issued in 1856, speaks of a certain appropriation to "be expended during the current year in books for a library." An early catalogue states that " it is accessible to all students." From the first the policy has been, a university library used but not abused. Through the years the number of volumes has been increased until the library contains (May 31, 1891,) twenty-four thousand one hundred and sixteen bound volumes and many thousand pamphlets. In 1869, Luther L. Greenleaf, of Evanston, purchased the library of Hon. Johann Schulze, Ph. D., Member of the Prussian Ministry of Public Instruction, from his heirs, and presented it to the university. About half of this library of eleven thousand volumes and nearly as many pamphlets pertains to classical philology, it contains a notable collection of the Greek and Latin classics, early and late, and in many editions. In 1878, William Deering and L. J. Gage purchased and equipped with the books needed as auxiliaries in the study of the Book of books.

FREE PUBLIC LIBRARY.

The Evanston Library Association, organized in 1870, was the forerunner of the Free Public Library. Under its auspices a library containing about nine hundred volumes was opened February 9, 1871. The use of the library for reference was free, and any resident of Evanston could draw out books on the payment of an annual fee of five dollars. The largest gift to the new enterprise, five hundred and seventy-five dollars, was made by Luther L. Greenleaf.

In 1872 the Legislature passed an act enabling the municipal corporation of Illinois to establish free public libraries, and in April 1873, at the first election after the passage of the act, the citizens of Evanston voted the two-mill tax for the public library. The first Board of Directors consisted of J. H. Kedzie, L. L. Greenleaf, Thomas Freeman, L. H. Boutell, J. S. Jewell, Samuel Greene, E. S. Taylor, O. A. Willard, Andrew Shuman. To them the Evanston Library Association transferred its books and other property, on condition that the library be maintained

T. C. HOAG.

GEN. JOHN L. BEVERIDGE.

S. A. KEAN.

REV. E. D. WHEADON.

as a free public library for the citizens of the village of Evanston. The library was opened under the new regime, July 3, 1873.

The present Board of Directors are N. C. Gridley, president, L. H. Boutell, C. A. Rogers, J. S. Currey, J. H. Thompson, W. A. Lord. The library occupies rooms on Sherman Avenue near Davis Street; it is open afternoons and evenings three days in the week, and it contained (May 1, 1891) 9,609 volumes. In 1890 the income from taxation was $2,950. New books are added each month to the several departments of the library. Miss Mary Morse is librarian.

THE DESPLAINES CAMP GROUND.

Old time Evanstonians were devoted to "Desplaines." We used to go over to that blessed gospel camp ground in big wagons, packed with household goods and good householders, singing hymns on the way, and setting at work to fix up a tent or cottage when we got there, with all the zest of youth and good fellowship. We used to promenade around the circle, when on big platforms of turf the evening fires were lighted, and think as they gleamed upon the under edge of the great forest trees, decked in their livery of green, that Paradise need hardly be more beautiful. Holiness seemed easy as we watched the holy stars so high above the sheltering trees, and the world seemed to our young hearts like a sweet and tranquil place, as we heard, in the deep twilight of the quiet woods, the liquid notes of whip-poor-wills. Kind faces smiled upon us, earnest voices spoke of God, and like a heavenly orchestra the great congregation poured forth its grateful heart in that endeared old hymn:

> *"Come, thou fount of every blessing,*
> *Tune my heart to sing thy praise."*

Every house in the great circle was a home to us; every face in the perched up "preachers' stand" was a friend's face; the kindly figures at the front, beside whom we loved to kneel in prayer and sympathetic counsel, though ourselves young in the sweet Christian life, were often familiar figures of Sunday-school scholars, public school pupils, or comrades of those pleasant years.

So much a part of Evanston has Desplaines camp meeting ever been that some record of its origin is here in place. To many of us ho figure stands out quite so clearly as that of Elder Boring, then in the zenith of his powers, genial, active and devoted, as he took his place of leadership in that odd old "preachers' stand," and blew the horn for services to begin, its explosive notes calling us from grove and riverside to our hard seats in the primitive but delightful auditorium.

From an interesting sketch of the Desplaines, dictated to a stenographer, I quote what Elder Boring says concerning its origin:

> "In 1857 I was transferred to the Rock River conference. When I came to the district the first thing I met with was that there was a great desire to have a camp-meeting. That was in 1860. Some initial steps had been taken by the people for a Chicago district camp-meeting. A committee had been appointed to select a place. The first thing I did was to act with that committee in selecting a place for the Chicago district camp-meeting. I continued to reside in Waukegan until the fall of 1860, and I naturally wanted to locate the camp-meeting on the lake shore. Among other places, I looked at the present site of Lake Bluff with that committee. I liked Winnetka; and I wanted the camp-meeting located there,—on the lake shore at Winnetka; that was my personal preference. When the people of the district met to fix on the place for the camp-meeting, they were called to assemble at Desplaines. This had been arranged before I came on to the district, and it was voted to have the camp-meeting located at Desplaines, and ground was secured of Squire Rand (I do not remember his first name), on his farm. It was there we held the first camp-meeting, in August, 1860.
>
> "We continued on those old grounds five consecutive years. It was then determined to purchase the present site, as now occupied by the Desplaines camp-ground; and then T. C. Hoag, Esq., of Evanston, came in as one of the trustees. He was living in Chicago at the time, and I think was one of the committee that made the original purchase. George F. Foster may have lived here in Evanston then. He was a very active man, a trustee, one of the committee on the old ground, and one of the trustees that bought the new ground where the camp-meeting is now held. He was the father of Frank Foster, who lives here now. T. C. Hoag became very prominent as one of the trustees, and has remained

continually in trusteeship, I think, from that time to this; and Evanston has continued to give the full weight of its influence in behalf of the old Desplaines camp-meetings."[63]

PERSONALIA.

ORRINGTON LUNT, DISCOVERER OF EVANSTON.

Of Mr. Orrington Lunt it should be said that from the first he has been a member of the Executive Committee, and from 1875 first vice-president of the board of trustees of Northwestern University. He has been one of the trustees of Garrett Biblical Institute and its secretary and treasurer from the beginning. He has superintended the erection of its buildings, and given himself to the institutions at Evanston as if they were his own children. After the fire, when he was burnt out in home and business, his first thought seemed to be to save the books of the Institute and University, and he went at once to the Rock River conference which was in session a day or two after the fire, and made such statements about the needs of the schools at Evanston, as to give an impetus to Northwestern Methodism on that subject, and to secure substantial help in the hour of darkness. He was, at this time, placed on the executive committee of the Chicago Relief, and devoted himself to public interests with the enthusiasm that most men bring to private interests alone. He is a typical Methodist of the old regime, a man of unblemished record in every particular, of benignant aspect and great modesty of character. Had he been like most men of his merit in respect of the qualities that seek or compel public attention, he would to-day have been a man of wide reputation outside his own church, as he certainly is within its pleasant borders. He began in Chicago as one of the earliest pioneers in the grain trade, and has helped to develop the city along the line of its highest and best purposes. Orrington Lunt was born in Bowdoinham, Maine, 24th December 1815. His father, William Lunt, was a merchant, one of the leading citizens of the place, and a member of the state legislature. Orrington is descended in a direct line from the family of Henry Lunt, Newburyport, Mass., who emigrated to the United States from England, in 1635. He was at one time president and treasurer of the board of water commissioners, Chicago. In 1865 he went abroad with his family, and spent two years in foreign travel. He was one of the early members of the trustee board of Clark Street M. E. church, and has given liberally to all the different enterprises of Methodism in Chicago. Mr. Lunt discovered Evanston, as is recited in the opening chapter of this book, and no one man's name is more indissolubly connected with the history of the university during its first thirty years. He was a leading member of the Committee of Safety

DR. JOHN EVANS.
Chief among the Early Founders.

and War Finance organized in Chicago after the fail of Fort Sumter, was prominent in starting the first regiment from the city, and was present at Fort Sumter when, four years later, the old flag was flung to the breeze in its rightful place once more. For some years, Mr. Lunt was vice president of the Galena and Chicago Union Railroad, now merged in the famous "Northwestern." By a large gift of land in North Evanston (one hundred and fifty-seven acres, fifty-four of which still remain unsold and will constitute an endowment) he has founded the Orrington Lunt Library Fund of the university, besides making numerous other gifts. He has been twice a lay delegate from Rock River to the General Conference, and a member of the Methodist Ecumenical Council held in London in 1881.

His domestic record is brief, as happy ones are apt to be. On the 16th of January 1842, he married Cornelia A., daughter of Hon. Samuel Gray, a leading attorney in his native town of Bowdoinham, who served as Republican senator, and member of the Governor's Council of the State, and was prominently identified with commercial pursuits during the whole of his adult life. Mr. Lunt has two sons, Horace, a graduate of Harvard University, an attorney of rising prominence, and George, a sturdy business man. His only daughter, the accomplished Miss Cornelia G. Lunt, seems to have inherited her father's philanthropic nature, and is foremost in good words and works relating to philanthropic, intellectual and artistic progress in Chicago and Evanston. Mr. Lunt lives in peace and honor at his beautiful lake shore home in Evanston,[64] still active in the enterprises of the church and town. We may truthfully claim for him not the dazzling brightness of literary or Christian genius, but the steady mild light of persistent effort, sterling integrity, and unweariness in well-doing, while around all his acts has shone the radiant glow of true Christian charity toward men.

DR. JOHN EVANS,

CHIEF AMONG THE EARLY FOUNDERS.

Ex-Governor John Evans, whose name is inseparably associated with our town, is of Quaker ancestry, and Ohio nativity. He was born in Waynesville, Ohio, in 1814; studied medicine, and graduated from the medical department of Cincinnati College in 1838. He lived in Attica, Indiana, acquiring a large practice in his profession. But it was in the town of Delphi, Ohio, that Bishop Simpson found him, and Mrs.

Simpson has told me the story in this way:

"There was a bright doctor in that village,—a widower with a lovely little daughter, Josephine. He had come from Ohio and was a Hicksite Friend by education. He was not, however, a Christian, but of a speculative mind, as men of his stamp are apt to be. He went out to hear Rev. Dr. Simpson —as my husband was then called—give his lecture on education, and he took a remarkable liking to the lecturer, so much so that he went to hear him preach next day. The tender, earnest words of the sermon wrought upon the physician still more, and he proposed to go on with 'the Old Doc' (as Matthew Simpson was playfully called by his friends), which he did, traveling with him three days, and thus began a devoted friendship between these two ardent natures, one that deepened with the years. Dr. Evans—for it was he—came to our next commencement, at Greencastle, Ind., and after hearing my husband's baccalaureate sermon, he said to me, 'That man's words make my ears ring with the name of God.' He became a Christian and joined the Methodist church. My husband felt that a man of intellect like him should have a larger field, and urged him to come to Chicago, which he did in 1848, investing in real estate and soon ceasing to practice medicine. Then followed the great enterprise at Evanston—which, by the way, Dr. Evans asked my husband's permission to name for him, but Mr. Simpson felt that the new village should be named for Dr. Evans."

He occupied a chair in Rush Medical College for eleven years, and was in 1852-53 chairman of Chicago's Committee on Public Schools, laying the foundations of that magnificent system of education. In council with Bishop Simpson he led the contest for lay representation in the General Conference of the M. E. Church, calling the convention in Chicago for the promotion of that cause. He has been a member of every General Conference since laymen were admitted.

In 1862, through the active influence of Bishop Simpson and his friendship with President Lincoln, Dr. Evans was made Governor of Colorado. Here he at once began organizing troops for the war, young and sparsely settled as the country was. Bishop Ames organized the Colorado Conference in 1863. Oliver A. Willard had been appointed pastor at Denver city, having been invited by Bishops Simpson and Ames and Governor Evans to enter that difficult field. Governor Evans has been the father of Methodism in Colorado and has contributed besides his munificent gifts to churches there, one hundred thousand dollars each to Northwestern and Denver universities.

He is now seventy-seven years of age, but active as ever, and since he went to Colorado,[65] he has constantly grown along the line of his greatest genius, which was as a man of affairs. He has a sixth sense for large capitalistic movements. He built the South Park railroad, the Texas and Gulf railroad, two cable roads in the city of Denver, and is now building an electric. He early set the keynote for the metropolitan and magnificent city which Denver has grown to be. He is the founder of its great university, and president of its board of trustees, as well as since the founding of the university at Evanston, president of the board of trustees here. His munificence to both institutions is well known. He has built a church in Denver as a memorial of his beloved daughter Josephine, Mrs. Governor Elbert, and given largely to other churches of his own denomination. The newspapers in Denver call him the "Grand Old Man," and on his return from some great business exploits when he had "put through" some financial measure of vast importance to the city, the horses were taken from his carriage, and it was drawn through the streets by the applauding populace.

I am informed by Mr. O. Lunt (who told me with the characteristic twinkle in his eye) that Mrs. Margaret Evans (Mrs. Lunt's sister) is the person who gave final form to the name of Chicago's classic suburb. "I know you will rejoice that a woman named the Woman's Paradise," said that good man, and so I do.

ONE OF OUR PIONEERS—
MAJOR EDWARD H. MULFORD.

Evanston has been remarkable from the beginning for pronounced individualities among its men and women. My good friend, Mr. Hesler,[66] will say that it is "contrary to experience" when I affirm that negatives have been few and photographs many, but of negatives in *character* Evanston has been less prolific than any town of its size with which I have been conversant. Perhaps this is because of the clear-cut outline and emphatic color set before Evanstonians in the types of early days. Among these, none "stood out" more strongly than Major E. H. Mulford, of Oakton, better known to moderns as the neighborhood of the Kirk homestead, which was once the Major's home.

Chicago was nothing but a cluster of trading houses in the midst of the swamps when he first appeared upon the scene and predicted that this lowland settlement would become the "Queen City of the West." Men laughed at him then, but "he laughs best who laughs last," and the grand old pioneer who heard the cow-bells tinkle in the pasture on what is now our Court House square, lived to see his every prophecy not only fulfilled, but vastly outrun by the solid facts of the magic city's greatness. Born in New Jersey, in 1792, he had a quiet life until, on becoming of age, he went to Fredonia, Pa., and soon afterwards to Philadelphia. Still later he moved to Chautauqua County, N. Y., and as an enthusiast in the militia service and a master spirit in those "training days" of which the present generation knows so little, he acquired the honorable title of Major. In this capacity he was appointed escort to General LaFayette, and he retained a delightful memory of that great man, concerning whom I have heard my mother say that, as a girl, she used to sing with her enthusiastic mates:

*"We bow not the neck and we bend not the knee,
But our hearts, LaFayette, we surrender to thee."*

In 1835, when forty-three years old, Major Mulford came to Chicago with his family and built a log house on what is now called Kinzie Street. He and his sons started the first jewelry store in the West during the five years he remained in the city. But the Major had pre-empted, at one dollar and twenty-five cents per acre, two sections of government land southwest of Evanston, on which, about 1840, he built a log house, and called the place Ridgeville, by which name it was known for many years. This appellation was later changed for Oakton—a name that it is a pity to lose from our local gazetteer. Indeed, if our South Evanston neighbors *will* change theirs—which may they determine not to do—they would outrank us in chronological distinction by naming their beautiful village Oakton. Inasmuch as it is so largely located on land once owned by him, there would be special appropriateness in this designation. When the Major moved to Oakton, the country was full of Indians, and directly through his land ran the long trail from Milwaukee to Chicago. His log house, 30x40 feet, was the scene of the first court held in Cook county, for he was the first justice here appointed; and the earliest agricultural labors performed within a mile of the present town of Evanston were his, for he was a Cincinnatus in cast of mind and mode of life. The two sections of land that he first "took up," as the phrase is, were afterward increased to three, and one was sold in later years for three thousand dollars per acre. Mr. Thomas Hoyne, who was long associated with Major Mulford in business and social relations, used to relate an incident of the manner in which the first justice's court was held at Oakton House, which was hotel as well as home. There being no room for the jury in the house, the trial was held in the open air, Major Mulford being the presiding magistrate and Mr. Hoyne defending the prisoner at the bar. Before this honest judge have pleaded many of Chicago's foremost lawyers, when they were mere striplings in years and sprigs of jurisprudence. He was an enthusiast in politics, and in the early days his name was the war-cry that called the Democratic hosts to caucus, convention and ballot box. Had his health held out, he would doubtless have become distinguished in public life, but after 1850 it did not permit him to hazard the rigors of political warfare.

As everybody knows among "old timers," Major Mulford was a man of pure life and chivalric nature, a philanthropist in temperament and a Christian in faith, one of the founders of the Baptist church and a deacon therein from the date of its founding until, in 1878, he died at the age of eighty-six. His two sons went South and died there; his only daughter Anna (Mrs. Gibbs) was one of the brightest and most genial ladies ever known to Evanston. Major Mulford's estimable wife, who shared with him all the hardships of their pioneer life, died in 1873, and his remains now rest beside hers in Rosehill cemetery. Probably no one in Evanston was more generally beloved than this well-poised, upright and most genial gentleman, whose life and character were a link with the century that saw the birth of this republic. His house was the center of hospitalities on New Year's day, but not a drop of wine sullied its honest joys.

The only misdemeanor that disturbed the tranquility of Evanston's earlier years was the entrance one summer night of masked robbers into the peaceful home of the beloved Major, who gagged him and rifled the house at a time when his health was in a very critical condition. The unusual exemption of our citizens from such dastardly assaults probably results from the fact that some of us are known to have nothing worth carrying off, and the rest are well provided with pistols and burglar alarms. The freedom of our town from saloons also does much to render it unattractive to thieves and thugs.

One of the best results that came to us from Major Mulford's pioneering disposition was the visit to the West of Dr. Jacob W. Ludlam (father of the celebrated Dr. Reuben Ludlani, and the well-known Dr. Edward M. P. Ludlam, of Chicago's homeopathic annals) who came from New Jersey to visit the Major in 1845^ and was by him persuaded to make this his home. The elder Dr. Ludlam and Major Mulford were of similar character and presence: tall, portly and dignified in form and bearing, with dark eyes, handsome and expressive countenances, strong intellects, sturdy common sense and great geniality of tone and manner.

These two friends and comrades were among the best specimens of what we are wont to call "gentlemen of the old school" that I have ever seen, and were in character and conduct, models worthy of study by those who aspire to the fine distinction of becoming gentlemen of the new.

L. I. GREENLEAF,
THE MAECENAS OF EARLY EVANSTON.

A man of senatorial face, figure and bearing; one to be noted anywhere, even as was Saul among the prophets; a model of ethical exactitude, warm with brotherly kindness and open-handed in deeds of charity—such was L. L. Greenleaf, long the leader among "men of means" in Evanston.

Upon the request of Mrs. Dr. Kidder, that pioneer in all good works, he founded the Temperance Alliance; he gave prizes to the Grove school, and a choice library (once the property of Germany's superintendent of public instruction) to our university. He was foremost in all our enterprises, looked with manly zeal and pride upon the growth of Evanston, and was, no doubt, our favorite citizen. Few acts of my life have gone against the grain more thoroughly than this: As a young Christian, in the dawn of a heavenly revival season at the old church, I went timidly to that man of unmatched dignity, in deportment as in character, and asked him to kneel at the altar of prayer. He looked down upon me benignantly and sadly, and said, "I thank you for your kindly interest Miss Frank, but I can't go."

The years passed on; our college for women was projected, to which, as to every other village enterprise, he liberally contributed. His gentle wife was one of the charter members of our board of trustees, and when our institution became a department of the university she was president of our board and signed the papers of agreement; their two daughters were my pupils, and no girls in Evanston were better students or more unassuming in heart and life.

Mr. Greenleaf lost his little son, and at the funeral looked into the casket where his dead hope lay, with a father's agony on the face that we had always seen so calm. The Chicago fire came, and in a night the fortune of the gracious Greenleafs was swept away. With it seemed to go health and hope in that good man, whom we all loved. His wife gathered up the scorched threads of his great and intricate business as best she could; her daily visits to the grimy city are remembered by all who knew the olden time.

KATHRYN KIDDER.

KATHERINE WILLARD.

After a while the family removed to Beloit, Wis., and kept boarders. I was their guest when, in 1878, at the commencement exercises I addressed the Archean society, of which my brother had been a member in his college days. Going over with the Greenleafs to the church, my host said simply, but not sorrowfully, "If we were in the olden days in Evanston I should preside at your meeting, but to-night I am one of the crowd." Something in my throat choked me a little, and this sensation grew painful as he gently continued, "My chief occupation now is to take care of Professor Emerson's horse, and I try to do it well."

I thought of him presiding when a United States senator made the speech at our great Fourth of July celebration on the university campus, eight years before; I saw his majestic figure heading the procession, as it formed on the campus on college commencement day; I remembered him as he introduced the dignitaries on state occasions at the church, but to my mind he was never so truly great as in those words of a masterly humility, without impatience and above complaint. He grew more and more spiritual through glorious discipline and sacred sorrow, and with a Christian faith as sweet as any little child's he passed to heaven in 1886,—November 23d.

The Evanston *Index,* in noticing his death, contained the following:

"As a benefactor he was a liberal contributor to churches, to Heck Hall (the theological college of Evanston), and charities in general, and will be especially remembered for his donation to the university of the valuable Greenleaf library of 20,000 volumes.

"The fire of October 9, 1871, proved a severe shock to Mr. Greenleaf, both physically and financially, never to be regained. Only the day preceding the conflagration he estimated his wealth at $200,000. Alas! sometimes "riches suddenly make to themselves wings." Jan. 1, 1872, he retired from the firm, as previously arranged agreeably to his request. During the winter his health broke down, and to complete the catastrophe, an unfortunate co-partnership was formed."

"One woe doth tread upon another's heel,
So fast they follow."[67]

Of that other Evanston transplanted to Rosehill, the lifeless form of our beloved friend became a resident, but his citizenship is in the New Jerusalem.

MISS LUELLA CLARK.

Of the Northwestern Female College, was a genius, and the world would have known it had the motor matched the intellectual forces of her being. She was a poet born, but poets must be made as well as born. If ever anybody loved Evanston with something akin to worship, that woman did. Each tree had for her an individuality, and each shady nook cherished her footsteps. There was a sheltering juniper by the lake shore named by her "L'Asile,"[68] where we used to spread down shawls, and with our favorite books hide ourselves in the silence and sweetness of a place always sacred in memory to us and our near friends. The Boat club building now stands in the neighborhood of that vanished retreat. Miss Clark was a cousin of Professor Noyes and had the entree of all that was literary and scholastic in the village. Books from the professor's ample library were always on her table at the Northwestern Female College; Bayne, Bunsen, Arnold, Ruskin and Carlyle were among the most familiar names. She was "composition teacher," and gave strong and noble impulse to our proclivities for writing; she taught us mental philosophy and was a spiritual uplift not less than a mental stimulus to her pupils. She was a most sensitive and refined nature, upon whom the world's rough winds might not play without imparting pain. In our sorrows she was at one with us, but the bright smile and telling repartee ofttimes added flavor to our joy. From Evanston Miss Clark went to Cincinnati Female College, where she taught her favorite subjects for several years, and then returned to her native New Hampshire to be the caretaker and solace of her invalid mother for many years more. Her mother having passed to heaven, Luella Clark lives on in loneliness in the old family home at Lisbon, New Hampshire, where all old-timers of us who live in Evanston and shared it with her once, send her our love and tender condolence.

DR. JOHN DEMPSTER.

When I hear the brakemen call out "Dempster Street" I am reminded of Longfellow's saying that "every place is haunted, but none so much as the place where we lived in our youth." To me there is a sacredness about that name which even the rough handling of custom can not wear away. John Dempster, founder of Garrett Biblical Institute, was one of God's great heroes. Without advantages, a tin peddler in his youth, but lifted to the peerage of character and culture by a camp meeting conversion that struck *in,* not out, he became so polarized toward Christ that his whole life afterward seemed saying

> *"Happy, if with my latest breath*
> *I may but speak his name;*
> *Preach him to all and cry in death,*
> *'Behold, behold the Lamb!'* "[169]

His soul was at white heat with zeal for an educated ministry in the church that had transformed his being. Poor and unhelped, he hammered out for himself such mental acquisitions as made him perfectly at home among the ablest theologians, and lifted him from the deepest obscurity to such prominence that he headed an embassy to President Lincoln during the war and was regarded as a leader among Arminian theologians on this continent. Clearly as if he stood before me now, I can see that first president of Garrett Biblical Institute; tall, attenuated in figure and physically past his prime, not more by reason of age than of relentless mental grip and unmitigated toil; stately in bearing as a prince, and gallant as a courtier in manner; with square jaw, corrugated brow, beaked nose that nothing sublunary ever balked; mouth firm but kind, and eyes blue and dominant as an eagle's, glowing with primeval fire. This was the man who, having already founded one theological school, persuaded Eliza Garrett to give her money to the Institute at Evanston, and fully purposed to found a third on the Pacific coast before he passed to heaven. Who of us that heard him in the old church forgets that incisive utterance, each syllable clear-cut, each like a stone in its place, and the whole a Roman mosaic of brilliant workmanship? Some persons we remember by a sentence that flashed into our spirits with supernal power. Dr. Dempster often cleft my dreamy thoughts like that. One sentence, enforced with that penetrating gesture and pointed glance so peculiar to himself, was this: "Never forget that the sensorium of the universe is on its throne!" He lived "up by the Institute" in the house that was my brother's for several years and was afterward burned. Calling on his kind old wife one day she showed me where she wanted her husband and herself to rest at last, under the spreading branches of a tree near where Rev. C. H. Zimmerman now lives. "The doctor says, 'Bury me if you can catch me,'" smiled the old lady, unconsciously quoting Socrates as well as her liege lord. November 25, 1863, Dr. Dempster suffered a dangerous surgical operation; rallied wonderfully; we all took heart of hope; then, suddenly, he passed away.

Oliver Wendell Holmes tells us the time will come when one flashing glance between two disembodied spirits will reveal more than all philosophies and histories have told. This is true, I fervently hope; and a hint of it comes to me when the brakeman's call of "Dempster Street" lights up in my private picture gallery a tablet whereon all I have written here of Dr. Dempster, and vastly more, is traced forever and for aye.

REV. DR. AND MRS. KIDDER.

The first house that the stranger-student was invited to enter in Evanston, between the years 1856 and 1871, was likely to be that of Rev. Dr. and Mrs. Kidder. That roomy mansion among the trees near the corner of Chicago Avenue and Church Street, and now known as the Hitt homestead, was officially the social center of old-time Evanston. Its sway was undisputed; its associations were delightful. True Christian hospitality has rarely had a more adequate exponent, for here were comfort, cordiality and culture, without luxury, fashion or display. The timid girl working her passage through the college elbowed the distinguished head of the university, and the youth who sawed wood or milked cows to earn his board, met the rich Chicago business man without feeling any gulf between them.

Elizabeth Stuart Phelps in her recent marvelous article in *The Forum* on "The Christianity of Christ," has a paragraph that reminds me of that chief family in early Evanston. She says:

"In a luxurious home whose invitations are not declined, whose hospitality is familiar to many distinguished men and women of our land, there may be found, any day, mingled with the most gifted guests, plain, poor, obscure people, quite unknown in 'society.' I once saw at a breakfast at this house, the foremost poet in the country seated next a massage rubber, a poor girl training herself for the practice of medicine, and in need of two things,—a good breakfast and a glimpse into the cultivated world. She had both in the Lord's name, in that Christian home. Yet the spirit of that ideal hospitality is so rare that we tell of it as we do of heroic deeds. The Christianity of Christ would make it so common that we should notice it only as we do the sunrise."

As has been said in a sketch prepared by Rev. George E. Strobridge: "Scarcely ever did the family sit down without some guests at table. A feature of Doctor Kidder's cordial treatment of the students was his regular practice of inviting them to take tea at his house and spend the evening. For this purpose he would select them in groups or companies until the whole number in attendance at the institute had been thus

MADAME WILLARD,
Rest Cottage.

MRS. BISHOP HAMLINE.

MRS. DR. KIDDER.

MRS. LUCY K. BANNISTER.

pleasantly entertained."

It was of incalculable benefit to us, whose opinions were then forming, that the Kidder home, with its large library lined with well-filled bookcases, its roomy parlors and its broad piazza on which we delighted to promenade when summer nights were fair and sweet, brought to our young hearts the conception of Christ and Christians as a social force. From some of our hearts, at least, the heavenly vision has never faded, and no "society" after the stratified regulation pattern has ever had one charm for us since then.

Early pictures of that Evanston home show a young man, —afterward Col. Henry M. Kidder, one of the university's first graduates, a genial, stalwart youth, fond of outdoor life, agricultural editor of the *Northwestern Christian Advocate,* and brother in general to all the young ladies. I think my first book reviews were procured for me by him in his editorial capacity. One was Sidney Dobell's poems, another, somebody's entomology, and I got the books in exchange for the review, which was remarkably good pay. The young farmer-editor marched away to the wars, emerged at the close thereof as a colonel, married gifted Miss Sallie Ravenhill, and lives, as everybody knows, at North Evanston, whence womanly Kathryn Kidder has gone out to a wide career on both sides of the sea.

Rowena was the doctor's eldest daughter and the sister of Henry (both being the children of the doctor's previous marriage and both natives of Brazil, where their missionary mother died). We were all fond of this generous-hearted girl, whose death was the first in our circle of young people, and made a deep impression on us all. Miss Kate Kidder used to be called the "belle of Evanston," and was a most interesting commingling of the traits herein attributed to her parents. She married noble George Strobridge, and the beneficent work of their united lives is well known to the Methodist Episcopal church, especially in New York city.

Handsome Dan Kidder and lovely Eva completed the family, the latter having, like her sister, married a student of Garrett Biblical Institute (Rev. Mr. Wilson) and passing early to the better country, when her little ones seemed most to need their mother's care.

No home is really such unless a woman is its central figure, and while the kindliness and urbanity of Rev. Dr. Kidder are among Evanston's clearly defined memories, the remarkable intelligence and earnest good will of Mrs. Henriette S. Kidder, his wife, merit especial recognition in any story of those times.

In the opinion of the present veracious and "impartial historian," the union of two lives like those of Harriet Smith and Daniel P. Kidder is an incalculable augmentation to them both, and by this means a woman of high native endowment made sure of companionship that was intellectually worthy of her, which is no small matter. There are persons who strengthen, develop and build up in a day as others could not in a lifetime. Somebody said of Walter Savage Landor that "to catch one flash of his eye was a liberal education." Garfield said of Doctor Mark Hopkins, "Set him on one end of a log as teacher and me on the other as pupil, and you have a university." By how much more ought two persons, both endowed, educated and earnest, who spend a whole lifetime together, to build each other up in the most holy faith of humanity and God! Rev. Dr. Kidder has always seemed to me "an Israelite indeed." Like many another little Methodist girl, I used to wonder as I read my *Sunday School Advocate* and Sunday-school books, all of them "revised by D. P. Kidder," how one man's head "could carry all he knew." When we came to Evanston, and here he was, I had great curiosity to see him, and when his handsome daughter Kate came to my room at Professor Jones' college and invited my sister Mary and me to take tea at the finest house in the village, I said with inward joy and quakings about equally mixed, "and I shall then see Daniel P. Kidder!" Behold, when I gazed upon him, I saw "a man who bore without abuse the grand old name of gentleman." He was of medium height, elastic step, had a voice of great sweetness, a rarely intellectual brow, and a face of equally rare refinement and gentleness. He did not make us at home in the off-hand, genial way so natural to some men and women, but rather with that perfection of politeness in which he excelled most other men, and even women—do I live to admit it! He was so noted for this choice trait that the "biblicals" had it for a saying that once when he entered his barn in abstracted mood, studying out a sermon, he even went so far as to remark to a flustered sitting hen, "Do not allow me to disturb you, madam." The doctor impressed us all as a man of immaculate character and conduct; his habits had great exactitude; his industry was marvelous. John Wesley was hardly more careful of his minutes. Indeed, method was a prime characteristic of this model Methodist. When not in his library at work at that high desk by the pleasant window looking out on the Beveridge lawn, he was in his class at the Theological seminary, or on horseback on his small sorrel horse, going to his farm on the ridge or attending to errands for the institution or the home. His fair, handsome, accurate, handwriting, so pleasant to read and worthy to form copybooks, has always been to me the completest emblem of his character. What wonder that he revised eight hundred Sunday-school books in the twelve years that he was corresponding secretary of the Methodist Sunday-school Union, or editor of its publications! In the fifteen years of his life in Evanston, he wrote his "Homiletics" and "Christian Pastorate." Besides these and his well-known " Sketches of a Residence and Travels in Brazil," he has published four other volumes, edited twenty, written thirty articles for reviews, encyclopedias, etc., many of them requiring great research, and some full enough to make a book apiece.

THE BANNISTERS.

"The Bannisters!" Here is a subject on which it is impossible for the present historian to be impartial! But so signally endeared to "old timers" is that memorable household—that the danger of writing out one's heart is greatly mitigated. The lifelong relationships that lend zest to the writing of this chapter are thus playfully hinted at in extract from my sister Mary's journal as given in "Nineteen Beautiful Years":

"July 24, 1861.—About twenty years ago, in the state of New York, 'might have been seen' a young mother playing with her only son, who had arrived at the interesting age of six years. She made with her own hands his little clothes; she curled his soft brown hair; and/gazing into the blue eyes of the boy, she no doubt thought him uncommonly innocent and charming. Well, this small boy lived on, year after year; he grew, he cried and laughed, he rocked the cradle of his youngest sister, and, I make no doubt, he dropped her on the floor when he got tired of her, so that she might cry and be taken care of by his mother. He went to school, he made mud-pies, and studied his lessons with unusual diligence. 'When quite a youth, he lived upon a farm; he milked cows and tended sheep; he made a swing, he swung his sisters, he hunted, fished, and learned to swim. Later in life he went to college, assumed superior airs at vacation time, wore paper collars, carried a slim little cane, and quoted Byron. Subsequently, he graduated, in a creditable manner, from Beloit college, lived at home for a few months, grew serious, commenced to study for the ministry, —*fell in love.*

"Nineteen years ago, in the State of New York, a dark-eyed little girl made her appearance among the ways of men. She grew, she throve, she went to school, and had her little affections for fellow infants. She came with her parents to reside in a beautiful western village. She developed into a refined young lady, religious, educated, and accomplished. She studied four languages besides her own, exhibited great musical talent, possessed all the domestic virtues, such as patience, mechanical skill, tact, and so on.

"The boy and girl whom I have thus glowingly described became acquainted a few months ago. Recently they have exchanged hearts, and seem to be at present in a happy state of mind.

"After all that I have said, but one more remark shall be offered, viz.: My brave and noble brother can no longer be depended upon as an escort 'o' nights,' by his feminine relatives; and of late spends such a number of evenings abroad as can be accounted for on only one hypothesis."

In brief, my brother Oliver and Mary Bannister, after a year's engagement, merged their destinies, July 3, 1862. Therefore it stands to reason that I can not write with impartiality about the house of Bannister, but surely it is safe to say that there was not a home in early Evanston where "we young folks" better loved to go. If each of the "old set" that formed our "reading circle" and the girlish club mysteriously called "Iota Omega" should write out such personal incidents as we can now recall, they would make a medley unique and readable. Mary Bannister was a central figure in all our young proceedings. She had extraordinary fineness and alertness of mind, remarkable scholarship, and was the soul of geniality; she treated young men and women almost precisely alike—in a fashion full of sisterly directness and good will, which, combined with her piquant vivacity and many accomplishments, made her, in my judgment, the most generally attractive girl in early Evanston, and I believe this would be the general verdict of those who have "grown old along with me." When we went to visit her we always had good talk—of books, art, life. She seemed incapable of commonplace, and her own bright ways, with the cordial welcome of her parents, gave to that home-its chief attractiveness. Music here had its rendezvous, the Ludlam family, all of them singers, being among Mary's most devoted friends, and the chief singers at the Northwestern Female College (her *alma mater* in 1860), joining in the festivals so frequent at dear old "Bannister House."

In the earliest days, when Bishop Foster lived next door (corner Chicago Avenue and Church Street) the two families were almost like one, and to my mind the Evanston paradise centered at a point equidistant between those two most favored homes. Florence Annie Foster was a feminine edition of her father, and he was, to our young imaginations, the Christian Apollo of our Parnassus, and his daughter chief of the Muses. What that keen-minded girl of twenty did not know of all a

Christian maiden could discern in the great worlds of thought and life, it had never dawned on us to dream. Books she had at her tongue's end, and gifts of speech and pen beyond us all. But the "wonderful Fosters" went back to New York city in 1860, leaving the greatest void our village has yet known from any family's departure. That corner house[70] where they once lived, Dr. Tiffany's family succeeding them, and many years after, our beloved physician, Dr. James S. Jewell, has passed into history as one of Evanston's rarest and best centers of high thinking. Doubtless the good men and women, who, for purposes restorative, still frequent its sometime classic shades, will rejoice to know to what high dignities they have succeeded.

REV. DR. HENRY BANNISTER, THE SCHOLAR.

Rev. Dr. Henry Bannister was a strong, sturdy, steadfast, square-shouldered man, of dark complexion, eyes and hair, the latter of a quality remarkable in fineness—even more so than that of women. He was of medium height and stocky build—in figure not unlike a German. He was a born scholar— devoted to his Hebrew studies, writing a commentary on Isaiah, and was sitting at his work in that cozy library, with ever-glowing grate, tall book-cases and engravings of apostles and church fathers, whenever he was not in the recitation room, or on calls about town in his neighborly, yet blunt, staccato fashion. A man of intense earnestness, absolute honesty and most refreshing simplicity of character, but sensitive to a fault; desirous of every one's good will, and worthy of it, but too proud to confess the dependence his sympathetic nature felt on those about him; a man with one of the noblest foreheads ever uplifted for the handwriting of destiny, and a face and smile full of hearty good will, but carrying weight always, on account of a somewhat phlegmatic physique unequally yoked to a spirit full of "the hate of hate, the scorn of scorn, the love of love"; a mind devoted to books and art, to adventurous thought, wide observation, and most of all to friendship's hallowed face. A brave man he was, of sturdy old New England stock, who had fought his way to classical scholarship, high position as an educator, and a comfortable financial outlook, through the most difficult conditions. To me he was a sort of Methodistic Dr. Samuel Johnson. His clean-cut, concise, well-ordered conversation, always seasoned with grace, had not the characteristics that Boswell makes immortal in his story of the great Samuel, but his learned presence, his love of letters, the sweet nut of his kindness beneath the husk of his sometime brusquerie; his reverence for woman and his worship of religion, all called to mind the mighty Englishman. Dr. Bannister was at heart a radical. Many a time have I heard my mother say, "Your father and Dr. Bannister were arguing, and the Hebrew scholar said, with a thump of that ever-present cane, 'Brother Willard, you may as well give in first as last; the woman question is upon us—and it has come to stay.' " Once when I was talking with him about that lovely young preacher, Miss Mary Phillips, whose graduation with so much honor from our theological school was such a hope and whose early death such a sorrow, he said, as I urged that she be admitted, "I tell you once for all, while I am here any reputable woman that wants to study shall study, and any one that wants to graduate shall graduate." Thump went his cane, punctuating these declarations, braver seventeen years ago than they would be to-day.

In 1862 I went to him in his capacity of chairman of the public school board, and asked to be chosen teacher in what was afterwards called "the Benson Avenue school," then the only one in Evanston. He was walking along near his own pleasant home on Chicago Avenue when I overtook him and tremulously preferred my request. He stopped, abruptly asked, "Do you think you could make it go, Frank?" I answered, "Yes, I do." He smiled, said nothing further, but marched on, and the next evening sent me word that I had been unanimously chosen. What a rare, good friend he was and how full his life of kindness! Above all things he hated shams. One could not well be other than true and simple-hearted in his presence. I remember it was his custom to bow to everybody. Like me he was troubled with blurred and defective vision. When I lamented to him my inability to recall faces well and inaptitude at the recognitions that are so pleasant in church or on the street, he said, "Well, never mind it. Just bow to everybody. That's a safe rule in a village like ours, and then all will be well." He hated aristocracy. Humanity was so royal in his eyes that, more nearly than almost any man of my acquaintance, he treated all alike. When he first came to Evanston, and in common with other professors built a pretty home, one of our good old-fashioned brethren came into the barnyard where Dr. Bannister, who was always ready to "put a shoulder to the wheel," was working, and said, "Evanston is getting very much set up with aristocracy since you college men are building these handsome houses." The doctor nourished his scepter, a three-tined hay fork, and from the throne whereon he stood, roared out, "Yes, Brother Blank, here's a case in point for you—of aristocracy on a dung-hill!"

He was a very modest man—morbidly so. He always said he didn't know enough to write a book, and had to be strongly persuaded before he undertook his commentary. As a preacher he was keenly discriminating in expression, and, though he used manuscript always, was intensely earnest and convincing—at least he was to me, so much so that it is written in my religious records that while a sermon by Charles H. Spurgeon, read on the old farm, first set me thinking, one by Dr. Bannister and another by Bishop Foster first stirred my heart. The experiences that came to many of us under the preaching of Dr. and Mrs. Palmer, in the winter of 1866, were strongly shared by Dr. Bannister. Always undemonstrative and almost diffident in his expressions of Christian experience, he became clear and pronounced, attending regularly the meeting for the promotion of holiness, so long maintained at the home of Mrs. Bishop Hamline, and speaking out with no uncertain sound in the church prayer-meeting. His staunch profession of this high grace drew down upon him something of criticism, as must always be the case, and most of all when a pronounced character of somewhat hasty speech strikes out for Beulah Land. But the honesty and manliness of Dr. Bannister were so thoroughly known that his advocacy of a doctrine so often and so ignorantly spoken against, gave it great strength among our people. He was a most public-spirited citizen; he was a liberal orthodox in theology, a devout inquirer, a man of profound spiritual nature. Not a Methodist by birth, and a Presbyterian in theological training, he was in intellectual sympathy a cosmopolitan, while devotedly loyal to his mother church, her creed and institutions. He thought, however, that her polity might be profitably improved by increasing its simplicity, and had little use for ecclesiastical hierarchies or denominational red tape.

Common schools, the free library, philosophical society, and temperance alliance, all had in him a steadfast advocate and helpful friend. He was generous to a fault with money, and never turned away a needy one whom he had power to help. Nothing could be more unostentatious than his manners, and his whole conduct of life was such as becometh godliness. He had almost all his days been under the conscious influence of the Holy Spirit. "As a child he read the life of Benjamin Abbot, by which his deep heart was deeply stirred. When twelve years old he was 'convicted,' as Methodists say, by a sermon preached in a country schoolhouse by Rev. B. G. Paddock, and about two years later, under the teaching and guidance of a pious schoolmaster, he was clearly and soundly converted. When about nineteen years old he walked a hundred and fifty miles to reach Cazenovia, where, with only his own resolution and his trust in God, he completed in two years his preparatory studies." Later on he was *principal* of this institution for thirteen years, and was greatly beloved. At Wesleyan University, from which six years after graduation came his well-earned degree, he had the advantage of companionship with men since famous in our church. That intellectual giant (who declined the bishopric!), Wilbur Fisk, was president, and D. D. Whedon was one of the professors; Dr. Kidder and Bishop Clark were classmates.

Among his thousands of pupils at Cazenovia were Charles Dudley Warner,[71] Gen. Joseph R. Hawley,[72] Senator Stanford,[73] of California, Bishop John P. Newman and Eliphalet Remington.[74] He was a thorough disciplinarian, almost stern, but so true and tender of heart and so unimpeachable of purpose that his name is precious in the historic old seminary of Cazenovia as in beautiful Evanston, where he lived and taught twenty-seven years, coming in 1856.

In 1869 Dr. Bannister went abroad in a party "personally conducted" by that most musical-natured of men, Dr. James Jewell, once a beloved physician in Evanston, whose untimely loss we all lament. The regular continental tour was made by these two in company, after which Dr. Bannister and his favorite friend and comrade, Dr. Bonbright, were together for some months in Berlin, and about Christmas Dr. Bannister came to Rome, where Kate Jackson and I had been for some months studying antiquities and Italian. Under his fatherly escort we went to Egypt, and while he and Rev. Drs. Daniel March, E. P. Goodwin, H. R. Hayden and several other less celebrated clergymen made the difficult trip through the desert to Mt. Sinai and Jerusalem, Miss Jackson and I went up the Nile as far as the first cataract, then returning, crossed to Joppa, and in the holy city found our faithful Evanston friend, who was not a little distressed for fear his ministerial brethren might not be minded to accept the incumbrance of two ladies; indeed we were now three, Mrs. John S. Paine, of Cambridge, Mass., with her husband, having come with us, or rather, we with them.

But such a showing did Dr. Bannister make for us; such vehement representations of our physical endurance and powers as travelers, that on his "goodwill" we were allowed to join. I remember how thoroughly "on our mettle" we felt ourselves to be; with what diligence we "kept up;" with what Spartan firmness we repressed every exclamation of distress over atrocious roads, a villainous dragoman and treacherous steeds; and how good Dr. Bannister was wont to ride up alongside at least once a day and whisper, "You know you must bear me out in all I said, girls."

At the end of three weeks' camping out—during which Bishop Kingsley's fractious horse had kicked Rev. Mr. Hayden, and after hairbreadth 'scapes not a few—we straggled into sight of Beyrout [75] and civilization, when Dr. Bannister came with that peculiar half-pensive, half-apologetic smile, and said, "You've won the day. These ministers admit that not one of them has borne the trip better or hindered the party less or grumbled as little." That was a red-letter day indeed, and we have always been grateful to the good men who risked detention for our sakes, in a trip to which for a lifetime they had been looking forward. It was at Beyrout that Dr. Bannister met with one of his life's most sorrowful experiences, in the sudden death of dear Bishop Kingsley, whose only companion he was at the time, the rest of us having gone off to Damascus. A great grief indeed was that to Dr. Bannister,—one of the greatest in a life notably fortunate and almost without personal bereavement, for his wife and children all survived him and his own transit was a quick and painless one. As Bishop Ninde beautifully said of this quiet, unobtrusive, but remarkably gifted man:

"The unseen world was to him an everyday reality; its mysteries were in his most familiar thoughts. And so in his company, as one of his students well expressed it, 'there was the strange sense of other worldliness.' His very presence was a benediction and his daily life a prayer unspoken."

Two most impressive extracts from the Doctor's private journal I am permitted to give through the kindness of Mrs. Ella Bannister Merwin, who in response to my earnest request copies them from a book found under lock and key after her father passed away.

EXTRACTS.

March 1, 1867. Commenced this day another year of sacred instruction. Prospered hitherto for ten years in this blessed work, too unworthily performed, I give praise to God. And I, now, with a more perfect submissiveness than ever heretofore, consecrate myself anew to my duties to the young men resorting to this school of the prophets. I desire no reserve of my powers. All belong to this work for the sake of Christ and his cause. O God, help me with steadfast purpose to be unreservedly devoted every day and every moment to thy service in this work to which I am appointed. Give me all spiritual preparation for it. Destroy within me all remains of selfishness and sin. Make me like Christ—subdued, calm, of the purest aims and motives in all things, with unflagging purpose to do my whole duty when I see it clearly, full of love and faith, *full of Thee.*

Give me true intellectual fitness. Help me to see truth in its brightness—in the pure light native to it—and to present it, when thus seen, with a result to be known, in its full extent, only in the future ages.

November 1, 1867.—Closed the term yesterday, with twelve noble young men, handsomely furnished, as we think, for their glorious work. They are all well educated, first in the colleges whence they came to us, next by most assiduous devotion to their studies in the institute. They are also holy young men— full of zeal for their Master and his cause, consecrated to do just what God shall indicate as their duty.

One is already on the ocean bound for China to commence his life work. All of them appear to possess true missionary qualities.

No year has passed with such evidences of self-sacrificing devotion among students. Brotherly love has uninterruptedly subsisted in the school. Christian character has, to all appearance, marvelously matured. To me, the lecture room has been like heaven. Never has my work been more delightful. Nothing is of such interest to me as to see, in prospect, the young men under our care, utterly forgetful of the rewards of earth, utterly ignoring all honor seeking, all money getting, all self-preferring in any form, passing the days of their pilgrimage, the time of their holy calling, like lines of light and fire among the masses of souls darkened and besotted by sin. I love to think of our men as feeling impelled to seek out the poor and unprivileged classes as well as those elevated in social life. And only a true-hearted consecration, every moment sustained by heavenly help, can secure this. To such a consecration have they this year, especially, been urgently exhorted.

It was the year of his own greater consecration.

He returned to Evanston and went on the even tenor of his way, varied by serving as a delegate in three successive General Conferences, and on the book committee; also, by President Grant's appointment, he went as a visitor to the Military Academy at West Point. In the spring of 1883, after a week's illness, during most of which he heard recitations in his own library, he passed away as the church bells were ringing on Sunday morning, April 14. His faithful eldest son, Henry M. Bannister, M. D., was in attendance; a slight stroke of paralysis smote the revered father toward the close; his lips moved and he uttered the characteristic words, *"We are in the hands of God."* He asked to see his wife, who by her own illness and helplessness had been kept from his sick chamber. As she was brought to him he tried to put his arm around her, murmuring, " My dear, dear wife, how much we have been to each other, for more than fifty years!" His children and grandchildren were summoned, and my mother, with his and our dear sister Bragdon, were there when, with perfect consciousness and complete composure, he sank into his rest.

The *Index* said of him that week, "Evanston has sustained many losses by death, but it is safe to say no other death has so stirred our community to its very foundations." More than thirty ministers attended the funeral, and in the "Evanston plat" at Rosehill was made the honored grave of one who, as Dr. Whedon said, "lived well, died well, and, dying in life's early afternoon, enriched the world by his good name."

REV. DR. FRANCIS D. HEMENWAY.[76]

The words "conscientious fidelity" give this man's life keynote. Converted in a Methodist revival when but twelve years of age, he thus wrote out, when but sixteen, the solemn dedication that seems to have penetrated every fiber of his being:

> "Eternal and unchangeable God, this day do I, with the utmost solemnity and sincerity, surrender myself to Thee, desiring nothing so much as to be wholly Thine. I renounce all former lords that have had dominion over me and I consecrate to Thee all I am and all that I have—the faculties of my mind, the members of my body, my worldly possessions, my time, my influence with others—to be all used entirely for Thy glory, and resolutely employed in obedience to Thy commands as long as Thou shalt continue my life; ever holding myself in an attentive posture to observe the first intimations of Thy will, and ready with alacrity and zeal to execute it, whether it relates to Thee, myself or my fellow creatures.
>
> "And when I shall have done and borne Thy will upon earth, call me from hence at what time and in what manner Thou pleasest; only grant that in my dying moments and in the near prospect of eternity, I may remember Thee, my engagements to Thee, and may employ my latest breath in Thy service. And do Thou, Lord, when Thou seest the agonies of dissolving nature upon me, remember this covenant, too, even though I should be incapable to recollect it; look down, O my Heavenly Father, with a pitying eye upon Thy languishing, Thy dying child; place Thine everlasting arms under me for my support; put strength and confidence into my departing spirit and receive it into the embraces of Thy everlasting love, welcome it to the abodes of them that sleep in Jesus, to wait with them that glorious day when the last of Thy promises to Thy covenant peoples shall be fulfilled in their resurrection, and to that abundant entrance which shall be ministered them into that everlasting kingdom which Thou hast assured them by Thy covenant, and in the hope of which I now lay hold on it, designing

to live and die with my hand upon it. Amen."

Upon no student among the hundreds that loved him has Dr. Hemenway's mantle seemed to fall so manifestly as upon Rev. Dr. Charles F. Bradley, his biographer and devoted friend. Dr. Bradley writes of him thus:

"First among the powerful impressions which Dr. Hemenway made upon us, his pupils, I place the emphasis which he ever laid by precept and example upon the sacred and precious character of truth. 'Buy the truth and sell it not;' 'buy it at all cost, and sell it not at any price,' were his injunctions. Because God's word is truth, because Christ is 'the truth,' they deserve absolute allegiance from us. Sham, pretension and deception he abhorred. As in doctrine, so in character, he demanded, as chief and fundamental, genuineness, sincerity and truth. To many of us, I am sure, he made the truth more sacred and supreme. From this characteristic and unswerving devotion to truth sprang, I believe, other important traits of character, such as fidelity to duty, loyalty to his convictions, his skill and justice as a critic, his clear and accurate judgment and his marvelous power of analysis.

"His home, the institute and the church are the three points through which the perfect circle of his life was drawn. But how minutely faithful he was to all his duties in these! No man could love his home and his family more devotedly. In the public and social services of the church he was ever active and ever welcome; but for more than twenty-five years the class-room in the institute was the center of his life. The professor's chair was his throne of power.

"I may not pass over the keenness of his criticism or his use of it as a teacher. He wielded a Damascus blade which many of us learned to fear. But to students whose very talents and virtues had won for them a perilous degree of attention and praise, whose prominence in the home church or popularity in an early pastoral charge had fostered self-esteem and self-confidence, this discipline was of unspeakable value.

"I think that no one part of Dr. Hemenway's great nature was less widely understood than the depth of his sympathy and the warmth of his heart. He was not demonstrative, and he did not ask demonstration in return. He had a warmer appreciation of his students than they generally knew. He seldom praised them to their faces; but in this he was consistent. No doubt he valued appreciation, but it would have been impossible to deceive him with flattery, and it was most difficult to praise him. He would turn aside the sincerest words of admiration. He was naturally reserved, but let the slightest appeal of real need touch what seemed a wall of reserve, and there came forth refreshing streams of wise counsel and heartfelt sympathy. Where shall we turn for one to fill his place when we desire again such sympathy and advice? He himself taught us that what a man is means more than what he does, or rather, that what a man really does depends on what he really is. Herein lay his greatest service to us—he was a man of God. His inner spiritual life was«pure and deep and strong. Well do I remember his saying, 'The religion of Christ meets every want of my nature and condition;' and his whole life bore out the testimony.'

So much for the testimony of Dr. Hemenway's distinguished pupil. My own first vivid recollection of this remarkable man goes back to the time when he became my class leader, the first one I ever had, in the year 1861, shortly after I joined the Methodist Church in Evanston. I had known him up to that time as the youngest professor in Garrett Biblical Institute, his specialty being Biblical literature and exegesis; also as probably the most interesting speaker in our prayer-meeting, and certainly the most spiritual and attractive leader of that spontaneous singing which is a feature so delightful in the Methodist love feast, general class, and regular church prayer meeting. He was of medium height, slight figure erectly borne, with an air of quiet alertness, self-poise and dignity, a notable forehead, thoughtful eyes, lips of unusual expressiveness in respect to refinement and good will, with perhaps a certain reticence. In manner he was always most courteous, but possibly somewhat absorbed. His home was on the lake shore, where the Country club now holds sway, a pleasant cottage house that had a sense of home-likeness palpably present, even to us young people who gathered in, Tuesday evenings, to class meeting. We were nearly all students. The young men were incipient theologians; the young ladies, daughters of professors in the university, with a few of their schoolmates. My sister Mary and I were regular attendants, going usually with our friend Mary Bannister, or else with Kate Kidder or one of the Bragdon girls. I remember that George Strobridge and his brother Thomas were perhaps the most edifying among those who spoke. They always had something to say, and a clear-cut way of saying it, while their spirit was most devout and earnest for growth in the deep things of God. Our leader had a tuneful voice in speech as well as in song. There was a ring in it, a peculiar vibration or *timbre*, as the French say, different from any other voice that I have ever heard. I am sure I should have known it from all others, if in the Desert of Sahara he had said "good morning" to me on a sudden, and still more if he had started his favorite hymn, "Lead, kindly Light, amid the encircling gloom." It was his custom to stand during the meeting in thoughtful attitude, listening most intently to what we fledglings had to say, and making some commentary most brotherly and considerate, and especially suited to our respective characters and difficulties. There was nothing off-hand about him; we always felt ourselves to be upon our good behavior, and the gentle reticence of Professor Hemenway impressed me strongly. I felt that he was a man devoted to Christ and His cause, that his whole life lay in that of his Master, that there was no cant in his religion, but it was really cheery and thoughtful, and that he had an ever-outstretched hand of helpfulness. After a while he went away. Possibly, it was on account of financial stress, which was very much felt by all our institutions in those days. I think he spent some time at Andover in devoted study, for he was born a scholar, and books were his world. While he had enjoyed classical advantages in Vermont, I think his education was not collegiate, but it became practically such by private study.

He came to us with powers even more deeply schooled, and seemed beyond most men whom I have met, to have his abilities well in hand, to have made the most of every faculty, to have applied an unremitting industry to capabilities of an unusual order, so that beyond others he might say to the Lord, "Thou deliveredst unto me five talents, behold I have gained beside them five talents more." For years his quiet, studious life went on. He was a man universally respected and beloved. Vastly considerate of others, they repaid his consideration in kind. A most polished preacher, each sentence carefully wrought out, he was in much demand, not only in our own, but in other denominations, and became perhaps the most popular pulpit supply that Evanston could furnish. In addition to his professorial duties, he had charge for years of the church at Winnetka, and later on at South Evanston, where stands a beautiful monument to him in the form of the Hemenway M. E. church[77] of that thriving suburb. But undoubtedly his best monument is the hymnal of our church, for, while other gifted and accomplished men were associated with him, it is perhaps not too much to say that they brought less love to their high duties than this lover of the hymn book, who himself sang with the spirit no less than with the understanding. Although we were neighbors on Chicago Avenue for many years I had no sense of personal acquaintance beyond the good will of those belonging to the same church and social circle. Perhaps this resulted from the great preoccupation of us both, and the somewhat recluse life which it was natural to Professor Hemenway to lead. I think his fragile health, of which, however, he never spoke, caused him to husband his resources to the utmost, for he had heavy and varied duties, as has been shown.

In 1870 he was made a doctor of divinity by our own university, an honor that does not always fall where it is merited, but I doubt if any one who knew him could fail to feel that in his case it was bestowed most worthily, by which I mean that it had been fairly earned. Dr. Hemenway was not a prolific, but a most acceptable, contributor to the periodicals of his denomination, and wrote commentaries on the books of Jeremiah and Lamentations, of which scholars have spoken in high terms. He loved his church, I think, as truly as any man I ever knew, and yet was no more a bigot in religion than he was a pedant in scholarship. When I emerged from my work as a teacher, and set out to try to speak in public, I said to my mother one day, "I am going to ask Professor Hemenway to let me give in his hearing the address I have prepared, and to criticise me in every particular, for I do not believe any one to whom I can go is more kindly disposed, or better qualified to give me just the help I need." My generous friend, Professor Cumnock, had for weeks taught me gratuitously, and I sincerely appreciated this rare opportunity, but I thought Dr. Hemenway, coming freshly to the consideration of the problem, and seeing me under a new angle of vision as an intending speaker, would bring a new element of light to my difficult pathway. So I went around to his quiet home, being warmly welcomed by my ever kind friend, Mrs. Hemenway, and asked if he would take the time to hear me speak my piece. "I am entirely at your service," was his kind reply. So he took his hat and we repaired to the university and to Professor Cumnock's room, which had been placed at my disposal. It seems strange that I could proceed to set forth to this grave and reverend man, soberly seated in a far corner of the room, paper and pencil in hand, my views of the great curse of intemperance and what could be done by women in this land to mitigate the same. However, this had to be, and was, the ordeal to be survived by the professor and the novitiate. When I had finished, speaking first with a brother's interest and kindness concerning what I had tried to say, he called my attention to certain errors in pronunciation, figures of speech, etc. Although this was some years before he died, I never had another meeting with him, but I thought this characteristic, and have related the incident not because it was personal to myself, but for the reason that such little traits and features of character often bring out in better relief that which we wish to convey concerning an impressive and unique personality.

Of Mrs. Dr. Hemenway, the playmate of his boyhood and the

companion of his life, known and loved by me for over thirty years, I had desired to write, but her letter in response to my request for the facts of her life, closed with a paragraph that holds my pen. She says:

"As regards my own life in Evanston or elsewhere, it has been too quiet and uneventful to be mentioned except as the privileged home-maker of one of the purest, truest and best of men, who fully appreciated the meaning of that sacred word, 'home.'"

REV. DR. MINER RAYMOND.

This senior member of our Evanston faculties is rightly named "Miner," for in his eighty affluent years he has delved many a nugget of gold out of his rarely original mind, for the enrichment of his thousands of pupils and tens of thousands of auditors.

Going to his sheltered home the other day, I asked if I might "interview" him, and, as he spoke in that deep voice known to us all so well, while his fatherly face, snowy hair, scholarly brow and keen eyes were memorably outlined before me, as we sat in his pleasant library, I wrote down almost verbatim the following frank words:

"From my earliest recollection the old style Methodist circuit preachers were the greatest men I knew;—my father's family the only Methodist family in Rensselaerville, N. Y., for twenty years or so. The good Methodist people came in from four miles around and we were the one village family. The avocation in life of those preachers was the greatest thing I had to think about, but I don't think so big a thing as ever to be like them entered my mind as possible. It was too great for me. The next thing in my recollection is this fact: When I was twelve years old the superintendent of public schools told father it was no use for me to go there any more, and kindly said: 'Send him to Greenwich academy.' Father answered, 'Glad to send him if I could, but there's no money. He must not be idle though,' and he set me on a shoe bench, drawing the cords of affliction on the stool of repentance for six years and I wanting to go to school all the time. I did the best I could, but wanted to go to school—didn't know why. M. E. preachers interested themselves in me and wrote to Dr. Wilbur Fisk and got me off to Wilbraham in 1830, when I was nearly nineteen years old.

"From that point till to-day things have gone right along straight. I had been there but a few weeks when I was licensed to exhort, and went with older students that asked me and held meetings. Pretty soon I went as a regular supply. I had a change of heart when I was twelve years old, but didn't join the church because our folks didn't know of any one so young that belonged;—people didn't think of children joining in those days.

"If I had had the modern Sunday-school training I should have joined at twelve. It was a revival that waked me up at twelve, and I had a distinct experience—but from fourteen to seventeen years of age I was on the lookout. I began to say, 'I'll have to be a Methodist as things are, but if I was Deacon A's son, why wouldn't I be a Presbyterian? and if I was Squire B's, I'd be an Episcopalian, and if I was a Hottentot's son, then I'd be a Hottentot.' So I said to myself, 'I'll not be in a hurry to settle this thing—it is perhaps a matter of education.' So then I began to read Tom Paine, Voltaire, etc., and thought that maybe I could lay the Bible away. But that experience at twelve years old kept coming back and I made up my mind it was no use for me to try to be an infidel.

"The summer I was seventeen, when general training day was being held in our village, I worked right along in the shop all day. At three P. M. my father came in and said, 'I've tried to find somebody that owed me money, but I can't, and yet we've got to have some to pay that last leather bill. Go out, my son, and see if you can get any of our bills that these fellows owe.'

"They were coming in from the training and I took off my apron and stood on the doorstep of the old shop looking them over. Near by was a man I knew very well;—he was forty years old and dead drunk. I said to myself, 'Did he think at seventeen that he'd be where he is at forty? No. What security have I that I sha'n't go the self-same road, and when I'm as old be as big a failure as he is?' I saw a group of men fighting, and said to myself, 'What security have I that I sha'n't be there when I'm as old as they?' And a voice in my soul answered, 'You have just one sure refuge;—the religion of the Lord Jesus Christ.' Before I went to bed that night I had resolved upon a life of prayer, and that resolution I have kept until to-day. It led me right along;—all was plain sailing. The next spring I was baptized and joined the church. By God's grace I have never once profaned his name by an oath. Everything worked well with me.

"In 1833 I began to teach in Wilbraham, Mass., and taught seven years. I then became pastor in Worcester two years, in Boston four, in Westfield two. I then returned to Wilbraham as principal—stayed sixteen years—came here in 1864 as professor of systematic theology, and was pastor for the first three years. I have lived here twenty-six years. Have been a member of six general conferences. I have always taught and had my own living to earn, hence had no time for closet writing. Have made my sermons by solitary thinking as I had opportunity. When I was called to preach a special sermon, I was accustomed to select the text or topic, read all I could get upon it, that is all I had time to read, which wasn't much. I then formed an outline of the plan and began to preach the sermon to myself. If there was a piece of woods anywhere about, I would walk and talk that sermon there. If the first formula didn't suit me I would go back and start again, and so on till it was satisfactory. If I went through the sermon fifty times I could always give the same words that I had thought out in the woods. When I was principal of the academy I had to prepare the sermon on Sunday morning, that I gave that day. My line of thought has always been the philosophy of theology, and I have read more in ten years on that topic than in all my life before, and have had wonderful satisfaction in finding that the views I had thought out I still retain.'

"At this point I said, 'You are orthodox, doctor, but liberal orthodox.'
"He answered 'That is true; and I'll give you the basis: The general outline of what is called orthodox Christianity commends itself to my reason. Of course I know that no man is wholly right. I may be wrong, so I feel obliged to exercise a liberal charity toward those who think differently. That is all there is of that. They give me credit for being very liberal, but I'm sure God is still more so. There are more good people in the world than it gets credit for.'

" 'Now, doctor, as to your marriage?'

" 'Well, Elizabeth Henderson, of Worcester county, Mass., was the mother of my children. We were married, August 20, 1837. Her niece, Isabella Hill (widow of Rev. Amos Binney), is my present wife. Elizabeth's father was a thorough Methodist and a native of Ireland. He used to tell us that he "might have heard John Wesley," his family having once gone to a meeting for that purpose, while he, a boy, remained at home. His name was on the class book fifty years and never had au "S " (for "sick") nor an "A" (for "absent") after it; but after his children married there was a "D" (for "distant") once a year when he went to visit them.

" 'My children couldn't well be any kinder to me than they are; I still keep about my work, though I was seventy-eight on the 29th of August. [1889.] By the way, here's a letter that came from the only one that doesn't live in Evanston; ' and the great-hearted man showed me a note, in a bold, business hand, reading as follows:

" *My Dear Father:* I congratulate you and everybody else that you have lived seventy-eight years. May you live many years more, for your years are full of dignity, honor and peace.

Your affectionate son, SAM B. RAYMOND. August 28, 1889.'"

Some of Dr. Raymond's distinguished pupils have written of him in connection with his great work on systematic theology, and here are their estimates. Bishop Gilbert Haven, that Saul among the prophets, wrote as follows:

> "Those who have heard Dr. Raymond preach have never failed to be delighted with his strong, clear, bold statements of gospel truth. He preaches as from a lecture-chair in his precision of statement; he lectures as from the pulpit, in his force and fire. Many of his admirers urged him for years to put his words on paper. But ink and paper have been as far from his desire as they were from that of Father Taylor. He never wrote a composition, we venture to assert, in his school days, but with great reluctance. And when chosen to preach the Massachusetts election sermon, his greatest task was to put the sermon on paper. For such an anti-scriblerus to write out two bulky octavos,—over a thousand pages,—shows what changes time and fate may determine. These lectures are the sermons of his youth, set off with the critical growth of years. It is fruit in old age. Fat and flourishing must be the tree that bears it. His old pupils, who number thousands, will gladly secure this reminder of the days when they hung entranced upon his lips, and when they said one to another, 'Did not our hearts burn within us when he opened unto us the Scriptures?' Without any show of learning, with even the few Greek words put into English spelling, with no references to other authors, any more than Calvin's Institutes have, the great work rolls on and out, Serene and resolute and calm, And strong and self-possessed.
> It is a refreshment—every page; as easy to read as the author is to hear. It is fresh with the times; he handles Hodge as he would the composition of a boy; handles modern scientists, when they poach on the theological manor, as a huntsman does a rabbit; never breaks the thread of argument; never falls into drowsiness, and hardly ever into dilemmas and difficulties. It is a good lesson in writing. Dean Stanley is not clearer, nor half as orthodox."

One word of ill-will toward any living thing I never heard from Dr. Raymond's lips; his ways were ways of pleasantness and all his paths were paths of peace. As to his catholicity of opinion, take the incident at a dinner-table where some budding theologian was laying it off about the impropriety of woman's rights, when the good doctor, grown tired of the inane discussion, ended it by thumping the table, with the words: *"If she can do it well,* I am willing to see a colored woman president of the United States." That was literally "a climax and a half."

BISHOP SIMPSON.[78]

Probably no single spirit has ever breathed itself on Evanston with such a strong yet gentle sway, as that of Bishop Simpson, though he dwelt among us less than four years. But he was here during the most eventful period included in the annals of any population, great or small, that of the civil war. In the plenitude of his manhood; the central figure of the church he loved; the trusted counselor of Abraham Lincoln; the foremost patriotic orator of that unequaled crisis into which he threw himself with all the ardor of his enkindled soul, it was an education to have known him. As of all the truly great, it could be said of him that

> *"He hath borne his faculties so meek*
> *And was so clear in his great office"*[79]

that with him a little child might feel itself at home "and the birds of air might safely light upon his laurel wreath." There was in him a mildness that betokened mighty powers in perfect equipoise; majestic sweetness was enthroned upon his brow. I like to remember that a form so noble walked our streets and a face so loving looked into our own. Like the Corliss engine, he was best studied in action. One hour see him writing in a school-girl's album words forever memorable to her from that time forth:

> *"Without haste, without rest;*
> *Bind the motto on thy breast,*
> *Bear it with thee as a spell,*
> *Storm or sunshine, guard it well."*[80]

The next he passes from his home on Hinman Avenue along Church Street to the white meetinghouse among the trees, leading his little son Vernon by the hand; enters the pulpit, kneels in prayer, and a few minutes later is leading the whole congregation to such an assault upon heaven for the overthrow of human bondage and the triumph of our Union arms, as no soul among us ever thought to hear from human lips. The very air seems surcharged with the thunder and lightning of God's wrath against secession and slavery.

Always trained to the utmost decorum within the house of God, I do not ever remember lifting my head save once, to watch the face of one who prayed, except that of Bishop Simpson, when he stood in our old pulpit during the war of the rebellion. And that face was terrible to see—sublime with righteous wrath as ever was Isaiah's, and expressive of communion with the Most High as one in apocalyptic vision. It is said that his speeches at Cincinnati and other great centers so aroused the people that they rose *en masse* with shouts and waving of canes and handkerchiefs. I did not hear him make a war speech; such were not needed in Evanston, where our best manhood, young and middle-age, rallied grandly at once, under the inspiration of Generals White, Beveridge and Gamble, Major Russell, Alphonso Linn, and other never-to-be-forgotten heroes. But at Desplaines camp meeting, what an epoch to many Evanstonians was his mighty sermon on "Faith"! I have heard great preachers; Beecher, Talmage, Spurgeon in England, Pére Hyacynthe[81] [sic] in France, but, to my thought, no flight was ever so steady, so sustained, so lofty, as that of Bishop Simpson on that memorable day amid the leafy groves of dear old Desplaines camp ground.

For beyond all these he was an emotional orator; his whole soul was on fire in every utterance, and flew on tireless wings as eagles' toward the throne of God, carrying with it us, who could but follow with him, "gazing steadfastly up into heaven." Like a cathedral organ, with many stops and pipes and banks of keys, the bishop could give forth music sublime, tender or sweet, as he desired. We asked him to speak in Sunday-school on Christmas, and he began by saying, "Children, I can prove to you that but for Him whose day we are here to celebrate, you'd have no buttons on your coats." From this he pictured that ever unfolding and greatest of gospel miracles, a Christian civilization, in words so apt and by illustrations so telling that at nearly thirty years' distance I can clearly recall their vivid impression on my Sunday school class and me. Before a conference of ministers in Indiana, whom he was to ordain, he made such an address as I feel sure no other ever did, and it was urging them to stand by the cause of woman's ballot, —that it was sacred, sure to win, and Methodist ministers with memories of Susannah Wesley, Hester Ann Rogers, and other elect ladies not a few, should champion the coming of the home forces into government with might and main, because this meant Christ's triumph. He was the devoted and progressive friend of the temperance cause, and I have no more treasured memory than of being entertained in his Philadelphia home, almost at the outset of my work, accompanied by him to Spring Garden M. E. church, and introduced to a small meeting in the vestry by my princely friend, who eulogized the crusade and warmly indorsed the W. C. T. U.

Knowing the fearless character of his mind, how often have I said, in common with other radicals of our communion, "Oh for an hour of Bishop Simpson to point us forward on the path of progress!"

A gentleman who was his secretary and companion for months, on a difficult journey, taxing all his powers of endurance, once told one who reported his words to me, that in all the press of people and cumbering cares, he did not hear an impatient or unkind, and in all their intimate companionship not an imprudent word from Bishop Simpson, nor was there an utterance or deed that would have been unworthy the most refined of women. Beyond this, praise of a man's life and character can hardly go. It is the last analysis and microscopic test of a great character; not dress parade, but fatigue uniform and private hours. It is for this reason that (almost) "no man is a hero to his valet." But then we must remember that the valet is not a hero, and men are never justly judged save by their peers.

While he lived in Evanston—1860 to 1863—the bishop's official duties called him to California, and half the town formed in procession, going with him to the train,—an honor never before or since accorded to mortal, that I know of, by our staid and thoroughly equipoised Evanstonians, When he returned (coming all the awful distance overland by stage and in peril of the Indians a large part of the way, no doubt shortening his precious life by what must seem to us now a wholly unwarrantable strain upon his health, which was never robust), we all turned out again, and carrying the Bragdon melodeon[82] and led by the Ludlam voices, we young folks serenaded our revered chief with

"Home again, home again,
From a foreign shore."[83]

He spoke thirty times for us in Evanston, during the few years he lived among us. When he came home, utterly worn out, we did not realize the situation; were wont to urge him to "give us a treat now —it was our turn." When I was in California in 1883, the statement was repeatedly and sorrowfully made to me by Methodists, "We killed your Bishop E. O. Haven out here, literally killed him with kindness. He was so approachable and we were so appreciative, and we had never had a bishop to come and make his home with us before, so that with pulpit work, lectures, receptions, and the like, his delicate physique broke in a few months, and he vanished almost before we realized that he was ill."

Something like this was true of Bishop Simpson, than whom no human being was ever more "gentle and easy to be entreated." Mrs. Senator Blair told me that the last time he was in Washington, when utterly spent, engagement was added to engagement, until his Sabbath was crowded, and a reception on Saturday night capped the climax of unreason. Mrs. Blair saw him for the last time on that occasion, bemoaned his tired face and worn-out voice, and a few weeks later learned of his transition to the realm where work and worry never meet and weariness is known no more.

On my recent trip east (May 17 to June 4, 1889), I spent a morning with Mrs. Bishop Simpson and her accomplished daughters, Misses Sibbie and Ida, at their stately home on Arch Street, Philadelphia, and we talked of olden times. Evanstonians will be especially interested in some facts about the honored founder of our village.

As is well known, Bishop Simpson was a native of Cadiz, Ohio, was largely self-educated under the care of that remarkable man, his uncle, Judge Simpson, whom "old timers" remember as having been, with the bishop's mother, in his extreme old age, an inmate the family home at Evanston. When a young man the bishop became a professor in Allegheny College, and from there in 1839 he was called to the presidency of Indiana Asbury University (now DePauw). In a recent conversation Mrs. Simpson said to me, in substance:

"I went to Greencastle a bride but seventeen years old. We lived there nine years and built a brick house, which has lately been made the art department of the institution, and named Simpson Hall. My husband, though a young man,—then about twenty-eight years old,—was affectionately dubbed the 'Old Doc' by some of the students, afterwards better known as Secretary Harlan, Governor Porter, the new minister to Italy, General Luce and others. He was dressed in the gray homespun of those early days, and wisely went forth among the people with the purpose of bringing our new college to their knowledge and endearing it to them through their confidence and interest in him. Railroads were few and he traveled itinerant fashion, with his own conveyance. In the progress of this journey he lectured in the little town of Delphi. The people liked him, and urged him to stay over Sunday and preach, which he did.

"It was there that he formed the acquaintance of Dr. Evans, who, after the founding of Evanston, came to see us in Pittsburgh, and insisted that we must go there to live, which we did, and would have remained there but for two reasons; the lake air was trying to my husband's lungs, and the trains were infrequent in those days, so that to wait several hours or drive out from Chicago was the wearisome alternative often presented to him on returning from an exhausting trip. We love the Evanston people, and spent delightful years among them. Our home was that handsome house of Mr. Haskin's, just in the rear of the still finer one he afterward built, now, I think, the home of Mrs. Philip Shumway."[84] Many other most interesting things were told me by this remarkable woman, who to-day shares with Mrs. President Hayes the honor of being a central figure in the church she has loved and served so faithfully.

I am sorry the house in which Bishop Simpson and his family lived was burned, some years ago. "Old timers" remember a saying relative to Dr. Evans (as we called him until President Lincoln made him governor of Colorado), to the effect that "when any other of our eloquent preachers is to occupy the pulpit, one pocket handkerchief is enough for our warm-hearted founder, but when Bishop Simpson is to preach he invariably fortifies himself with two."

HENRY BASCOM RIDGAWAY, D. D.[85]

On a pleasant summer day about fifty years ago, a bright-faced lad was playing in the streets of Baltimore. He was a gentleman in every fiber, with good lineage, good training, and an appetency for the good, the true, the beautiful. His elder brother pointed to a man of striking form and features, but shabbily dressed and under the influence of liquor, and pointing, said, "Henry, that is Edgar Allan Poe." Hardly could there have been a greater contrast in the destinies of two representative men than in that of the pure-faced schoolboy and the ill-starred genius, whose life circles thus intersphered for a moment upon a Baltimore Street. Doubtless the sight, which must have pained his kindly heart, of a great soul in chains, helped to make him more than ever God's own free man, as he has been always, with no thralldom of evil habit, however small, throwing its fetters over body or soul. Henry Bascom Ridgaway's Methodistic antecedents are revealed in his beautiful name—that of Henry Bascom being the synonym for pulpit eloquence, borne as it was by one of the Methodist bishops of the South who was contemporary with Henry Clay and every whit the peer of that great orator. Dickinson College is the most historic seat of learning that the Methodist church in America can show. Founded in 1783 as a Presbyterian institution, its classic shades shelter traditions of the best English culture, and its graduates seem to have acquired a polish and precision that mark them through life as men of choice refinement. Rev. Dr. McClintock's mighty spirit broods in the air of Dickinson—the man who was such a blending of scholar and Christian,

REV. MINER RAYMOND, D. D.

REV. MILTON TERRY, D. D.

REV. H. B. RIDGAWAY, D. D.

REV. CHAS. W. BENNETT, D. D.

litterateur and saint, theologian and man of the world, as our church has not produced before or since his time. Young Ridgaway was just the student to be moulded by this preceptor. The Cincinnati *Gazette* said of him when making his memorable speech before the General Conference of the M. E. church South in 1882: "As all who know him are aware, the doctor is gentility personified. His action in public address is as smooth and graceful as his flowing rhetoric." The editor of Boston's *Christian Register,* having heard him on a yacht excursion to Martha's Vineyard, wrote: "His subject was 'The Attractive Power of the Cross,' and though some things were said that we could not accept, we found ourselves deeply impressed. His face is one of great spiritual beauty, and his whole manner most engaging." A New York paper says of one of his dedicatory sermons:

"At first the preacher proceeded with calmness and deliberation soon we were charmed with the sweetness of his voice; then his countenance lights up more and more; he delights you with a lovely picture, sketched with the utmost delicacy and precision; then comes a flight of thrilling and impassioned eloquence."

Preaching has always been the Doctor's chosen work, and he has had the chief churches of our Zion; twice he has served St. Paul's, New York, (where he preached the funeral sermon of his chief parishioner, James Harper, founder of the famous publishing house and at one time mayor of the city); Washington Square, New York, St. James', N. Y., St. Paul's, Cincinnati, besides Chestnut Street church, Portland, Me., Sing Sing, N. Y., and several leading churches in Baltimore.

He has written several books, one, "The Lord's Land," being a record of his trip to Palestine in 1870, and one of our best books on that oft-treated theme; "The Life of Bishop Janes," who was his personal friend, and of Alfred Cookman, to whom he has been likened in character and manners. In 1882 Dr. Ridgaway accepted the chair of historical theology in Garrett Biblical Institute, Evanston, (theological department of the Northwestern and several other institutions,) and upon the election of Dr. Ninde as bishop, in 1884, Dr. Ridgaway became president. In connection with these duties he acted as pastor of the M. E. church in 1885 and filled that difficult position to universal acceptance. Dr. Ridgaway was married in February, 1855, to Rosamond, only daughter of Professor Merritt Caldwell, that man so loved by all that knew him that though he died so long since, his name is more frequently spoken at Dickinson and elsewhere by those who knew him than are the names of some who are in active life. Professor Caldwell's wife was the sister of early Evanston's good Samaritan, Mrs. Bragdon, and one of our physicians seems to have inherited with his "Uncle Merritt's" name his happy cast of character.

Mrs. Ridgaway more than fills out the role of wife to a distinguished man and hostess to his constituency, superadding to these ceaseless cares, the most intelligent and sedulous work as a foreign missionary leader.

Dr. Ridgaway is a man of refreshingly progressive spirit. He believes in temperance reform, speaking of it thus in that greatest epoch in his life, before the General Conference of the M. E. church South:

"What shall I say—what *can* I say—that will be adequate to the subject, when I attempt to speak of the uprising of our women on the great temperance reformation? Their prayers, their petitions, their heroic struggles and eloquent pleadings, have fired the great heart of the North and yours. Nor is it all fire. I mean it does not end in blaze and smoke. It is a generating, intelligent power—power that is seizing on the ballot-box and legislatures * * * and will yet seize upon the national Congress, and from the great capitol itself shall issue temperance laws. The Christian wives, mothers, sisters and daughters have taken their stand as Luther did of old: 'I can do no otherwise, so help me God.' "

Dr. Ridgaway believes in the ballot for woman, and the remarkable chivalry of his nature has nowhere been more manifest than in his treatment of the two young evangelists, Miss Eliza Frye and Miss Anna Gleason, who have been enrolled as theological students since his presidency. Their own brother could not have been more hearty in the effort to make them feel at home. When all the theological seminaries that center in Chicago united in a banquet, the Doctor invited Miss Frye to go with himself and Mrs. Ridgaway; and recently on the day of prayer for colleges, after wise D.D.'s had been appropriately and duly heard, and tall young theologues had "improved the time," the president came forward, saying to whoever was presiding at that hour, "Will you give me a few minutes?" and when the request was granted and all rejoiced to think that he would speak again, Dr. Ridgaway turned to Miss Gleason, that quiet, scholarly young woman, saying with one of his captivating smiles, "I only asked that time that it might become yours." Was ever act more delicate, more like that "knight of the new chivalry" that Dr. Ridgaway is? May he be a bishop yet, and help to let the women into their full heritage in the wide realm of modern Methodism!

REV. CHARLES F. BRADLEY, D.D.,
PROFESSOR OF NEW TESTAMENT EXEGESIS.

Rev. Charles F. Bradley, A.M., D.D., was born in Chicago in 1852. He graduated from the high school of Chicago in 1869, and from Dartmouth College in 1873. He spent a year in Garrett Biblical Institute, and two years as instructor in Greek in Dartmouth College. Subsequently he attended Andover Theological School one year, and Garrett Biblical Institute one year; graduating therefrom, he joined the Minnesota conference, and was pastor at Duluth one year. He married Miss Susan Chase, of Lowell, Mass., and was stationed at Fargo, North Dakota, two years as pastor, going thence to Hamline University, St. Paul, as instructor in languages. While there he was appointed assistant to Dr. Henry Bannister, Garrett Biblical Institute, with one year's leave of absence. While he was abroad Dr. Bannister died, and Professor Bradley was given full professorship. He is at present traveling abroad and studying, being an indefatigable student, and for his age, unexcelled as a scholar in the denomination of which he is, alike by character and achievement, an ornament. His mind and heart are hospitable in nature; he is everybody's friend; a soldier of Christ, devoted and devout, but in touch with new ideas and abreast of the great army of progress that still goes marching on.

REV. MILTON S. TERRY, D.D.,
PROFESSOR OF OLD TESTAMENT EXEGESIS.

Rev. Dr. Milton S. Terry was born near Albany, N. Y., Feb. 22, 1840; prepared for college at Charlotteville Seminary, Charlotteville, N.Y.; attended Troy University; afterward Yale Theological Seminary; was pastor in New York conference twenty-two years, occupying pulpits at Hamden, Delphi, Peekskill on the Hudson, Poughkeepsie, Kingston and New York city. He was presiding elder New York District four years. He received in 1879 the degree of D.D. from Wesleyan University, at Middletown, Conn. For seven years he has been Professor of Old Testament Exegesis in Garrett Biblical Institute. Dr. Terry is author ot eighteen or twenty publications, of which the most important are his Commentaries on Genesis, Exodus, Judges, Samuel, Kings, Chronicles, Ezra, Nehemiah and Esther, also a large volume on Biblical Hermeneutics, and a translation from the Greek of the Sibylline Oracles, besides a large number of articles in the *Methodist Quarterly Review*, the *Old Testament Student*, the *Sunday School Times*, and various other periodicals. He was married in May 1864, to Miss Frances Orline Atchinson. They have two children, a daughter, now about to graduate in the classical course from Northwestern University, Evanston, and one son, a lad thirteen years of age. Dr. Terry traveled abroad in 1887 pursuing special studies in German universities, mostly in Berlin. He again went abroad in 1889, visited the principal cities of Europe, Bulgaria, Turkey, Greece, and Sicily. He is now at work on one or two new volumes. A man of great learning and most brotherly spirit, Dr. Terry has made for himself a warm place in the hearts of all Evanstonians. He and his noble wife are foremost friends of the temperance and every other good cause, and ready always to lend hand as well as heart, wherever the wrong needs resistance or good can be done.

REV. DR. CHARLES W. BENNETT.

When I went to Lima, N. Y., in 1866, as preceptress of Genesee Wesleyan Seminary, it was by invitation of Rev. Dr. Bennett, principal. But he had left for his sojourn in Berlin before my duties began, and so I missed seeing him. Naturally enough I inquired of his former associates as to his gifts and graces, receiving replies full of gracious revelation. The one that lingered longest in my mind was this from a wide awake student: "He's the sort of man that can play ball with us fellows on the playground, and then go in and maintain perfect order in the recitation room."

Methodism has had few educators in this era whose manner and spirit were so nearly allied to genius. A vigorous personality, a rugged honesty, a great, sympathetic nature balanced between brain and heart,— these are features of a make-up that stands for power among men of all classes and conditions. By my request, a friend long loved by me writes out this sketch of our Christian scholar and honored brother:

"*My Dear Miss Willard:*

Complying with your request to write a sketch of the life of Charles W. Bennett, involves simply a labor of love, with regret that I can not make the story longer and tell it better.

"Dr. Bennett, after five years in Evanston, seemed as thoroughly acclimated as if his first breath had been of breezes from the prairie instead of from the fragrant clover fields of the famous Genesee country of New York. If ever he be weary waiting for your late sunrises out of Lake Michigan, or homesick for the hills of his native state, no one is the wiser, so thoroughly does he identify himself with this place and this people. For here, in the chair of historical theology in Garrett Biblical Institute, he finds scope for his most congenial work.

"His earlier life was spent chiefly in the class-room, though pastoral duties claimed several years. In the summer of 1866 a way was opened for him to realize the long-cherished desire to study abroad. Accordingly, he resigned the principalship of the Genesee Wesleyan Seminary, at Lima, N. Y., and went to Berlin. There he availed himself of the lectures of Professors Semisch on church history, Dorner on New Testament exegesis, Trendelenburg and Michelet on history of philosophy, Friederic and Courtius on classical art and archaeology, and of the veteran Piper on archaeology. He studied also in the libraries and museums in which that city is so rich. Leaving his family in Berlin, he traveled extensively in Italy and afterwards in Palestine, Egypt and Greece, gathering materials for future use. In 1871 he was elected to the chair of history in Syracuse University, where he spent thirteen years. It was after no light self-conflict that he was induced to leave an institution endeared to him by so many years of sacrifice, while bravely sharing its fight for life. But the call was to work to which special preparation had been directed, and so, in December 1884, he came to Evanston.

"One outgrowth of his study is a volume issued last year, entitled 'Christian Archaeology,' being volume IV of the 'Library of Biblical and Theological Literature.' Of this book, Dr. Piper says in his introduction, 'It is the first work on Christian archaeology which has appeared on American soil. With hearty good wishes I welcome it to a position of prominence, even before it has come into my hands. The acquaintance I have with the method of the author's studies, his protracted connection with our university, his travels in the old world and their purpose, give assurance of its solid worth.' Another result incidental to his first, and to later visits in Germany, was the suggesting and securing, for Syracuse University, the Von Ranke library, the possession of which makes that young institution the envy of several older ones.

"There is a phase of this life, which, to those who know him best, is more precious than any public achievement. This is the depth and sincerity of his sympathy. This element has entered largely into the basis of his influence, especially over the young. Ever encouraging the despondent and checking the forward, he gave his most wayward pupils the remonstrance of an elder brother, or at most the admonition of a father, and not the cold rebuke of a master.

"It was nothing that with the income of a preacher or teacher his gifts for church and charity should exceed the measure of the tilting scale; it was nothing that he should keep open house for those whose home-hearth was desolate; nothing, compared with the generous sympathy which prompted it all, and which made him the confidant of hundreds, young and old. Yet it would be an interesting calculation to find the sum of small loans frequently made to straitened students; only *he* would not tell if he could. They tell it sometimes, and one young woman, graduated in one of his classes, a brilliant student, but unfitted by lack of early training in personal habits for the place of teacher, said to me; 'He talked to me like a mother—it nearly killed me, but I shall *never* cease to thank him for it.' Faithful indeed, the wounds of a friend; wounds which hurt most the hand that opens them."

CHARLES HORSWELL, PH. D.,
ADJUNCT PROFESSOR OF BIBLICAL LANGUAGES AND EXEGESIS.

This favorite and promising young professor was born in Kingston, Canada, Nov. 27, 1857. He entered our preparatory school in 1877, and was graduated from the university in 1884, and from the theological department in 1887, having just completed a course of study at New Haven for the degree of Ph. D. He was appointed instructor in Greek and Hebrew the year of his graduation from Garrett Biblical Institute. He was elected in 1891 Associate Professor of Biblical Languages and Exegesis.

Professor Horswell was married, Sept. 3, 1887, to Miss Helen M. Redfield, a graduate of the university, and a woman of studious purposes and tastes.

NELS E. SIMONSEN, A. M., B. D.,
PRINCIPAL OF NORWEGIAN AND DANISH THEOLOGICAL SEMINARY.

Our University wisely prefers to put her own graduates in positions of trust. What they are in talents, scholarship and conduct, she has learned, and in those trained within her own great halls, her heart doth safely trust. Professor Simonsen, a Norwegian, born (1855) in Alderly, Dodge Co., Wis., came to Evanston in 1873; and seven years later was graduated from the university with the degree of B.A. (in 1880), from Garrett Biblical Institute with that of B.D., in 1882. He then wrought as a Christian minister in Norway two years and studied two in the university of Christiana. He was elected to his present position in 1885, beginning his work in 1886 and receiving from his *alma mater* the degree of M.A., in 1887.

CLARKE T. HINMAN, D.D.,
FIRST PRESIDENT OF OUR UNIVERSITY.

The query is most interesting: When did you first meet a distinguished man or woman, who were they and how were you impressed? I have often thought that upon this query might be founded a "Game of Twenty Questions," full of helpful hints. After about seven years of farm-life isolation, our family saw in the pulpit on a pleasant summer morning the first men of note beheld by us in that long interval, and the first notable Methodists upon whom we had ever laid eyes. My father whispered, "That portly man wearing spectacles is Bishop Morris; next him is Dr. J. V. Watson, the brilliant Englishman, that edits *The Northwestern Christian Advocate;* and the younger man with active form and movement, black hair, standing straight up, pale face and keen, dark eyes, is Dr. Hinman, just elected president of our new university at Evanston."

Microscopic was the scrutiny directed by our country eyes toward that bishop and the lesser lights on either side of him. I have since then seen Queen Victoria, Pius IX and General Grant, but no personages ever struck into my memory like the trio of that morning in the plain little brick church in Janesville, Wis.

Dr. Hinman was especially attractive by reason of his comparatively youthful appearance and his ardent enthusiasm in the cause of education. He was seeking to induce Methodists to purchase scholarships in the new institution, and pictured in glowing terms the future of Chicago and the first college located in its vicinity. Doubtless the words uttered that day helped to determine my future fate, for while my mother eagerly desired to send her children to school in Oberlin, father then and there became a devotee of Evanston.

Clarke Titus Hinman was born in Kortright, Delaware county, N. Y., August 3, 1817, and was the son of parents sufficiently well-to-do to send him to Wesleyan University, from which institution he was graduated in 1840. He was licensed to preach in the M. E. church, and from 1839 to 1846 was principal of Newbury Seminary, Vt. He then removed to Albion, Mich.; became principal of the Wesleyan Seminary, procured an endowment for that institution and left it in 1853 in a prosperous condition. He was elected president of the Northwestern University, June 22, 1853, but the institution was not formally opened until November 1855. So Dr. Hinman, who died in 1854, was never a resident of Evanston. His family, consisting of a wife and three children, lived on the West Side, Chicago, and he traveled in the interest of the university, the breadth of whose original plan was largely due to his foresight and experience. My neighbor, Mrs. John A. Pearsons, tells me that she "stood up" with the bride at Dr. Hinman's marriage in Newbury, Vt., to the daughter of Timothy Morse, a leading business man of that State, resident in Newbury. Mrs. Pearsons says of Dr. Hinman, "He was a man of wonderful energy; nothing ever waited with which he had to do. Dr. Dempster, who was the procuring cause of his coming to Evanston, knew that. He was oratorical and impressive in the pulpit; —was what is known as 'a popular preacher.' Such was his zeal for the infant university that in presenting it to conferences and leading churches, he wore himself out, and when taken acutely ill with something like cholera, while off on a trip, he insisted on traveling, and died in Troy, N. Y., en route to Vermont, where his family awaited him."

Dr. Hinman owned the lot where the Button homestead[86] is now located—just south of the college campus, and had great pleasure in speaking of that beautiful spot as the site of his future home, but this was not to be, and the indomitable "First President" is to Evanstonians little more than a name. His portrait hangs in University Hall; our oldest (open) literary society bears his name, as does one of our most beautiful avenues, and a few faithful hearts still cherish memories of the bright star that rose so fast and set so soon.

BISHOP FOSTER.[87]

Bishop Randolph S. Foster, once a resident of Evanston, and first president of our university, is too important a factor in the history of the village to be omitted from this series of sketches, though I fear many equally prominent names will have to be left unwritten, for lack of space.

Rev. Dr. Boring dictates his early memories of this great man in the following terms:

EARLY LIFE OF BISHOP FOSTER.

"Bishop Foster's parents were Methodists of the old stamp; his father, his mother, and nearly all their relations were of Methodist origin. His parents' home was the home of the preachers. Of course he was brought up in the Methodist church, and did not know anything else. I knew the relatives of his father and mother; his mother was a Sinks; they were all Methodists and highly respectable people.

"The bishop's father was one of the most prosperous men of his day. Very few men in the country had better means of taking care of their families; he was a pushing, driving, business man, and just as intense in his religious life, but in a different way from what his son was. At the time I first knew the bishop, his father lived at Neville, on the Ohio river. I first became acquainted with Bishop Foster in 1833, when he was but a lad thirteen or fourteen years old. I met him for the first time at a camp meeting, in the summer of that year.

I was older than he was in years. We had begun a religious life about the same time, but we lived In different neighborhoods. Neville, where his father was in business, was the birthplace of General Grant. Randolph at that time was a small boy; he still wore the boy's jacket and dressed like a boy, but he was the leader of the young men's tent, as it was called, at the camp meeting. He was a natural leader, and the boy was emphatically the father of the man. He was very religious, and exhorted and prayed. I remember that at that camp meeting the old preacher, George W. Maley, held him up in his arms and let him exhort the people,—he was too small to be seen standing in the congregation,—and he did so with tremendous force and energy. That was my first acquaintance with him. It was not long after that he was licensed as a local preacher, and he exercised his gifts around the neighborhood. Then he went to Augusta college in Kentucky. At that time Joseph S. Tomlinson was president, and Henry B. Bascom, for whom Dr. Ridgaway was named, was the professor of rhetoric and history, and mental and moral science, a famous man, a great pulpit orator; it was doubtless during his stay at the college that the bishop imbibed his habits of study and oratory, and he was more indebted to Dr. Bascom, late Bishop Bascom of the church South, than perhaps to any other man. He was then the great pulpit orator of the Methodist church in the United States; that was his reputation. Bishop Foster never graduated in a regular course. Too full of zeal for souls, before he entered the Senior year he joined a conference, and went to preaching as a mere lad. Although so young he was in very fact a consuming fire. He was specially gifted in exhortation; had a wonderful influence over the people, and wherever he went he conducted great revivals. In western Virginia and southern Ohio; he was a living flame, excessive in labors and wonderfully successful. Of course it was but a short time until he attracted attention, and was sought for by the best pulpits in the Ohio conference, of which he was a member. "He commenced his ministry in the Ohio conference about Cincinnati, Chillicothe, Dayton, Hamilton and places of that grade. He was then transferred to the New York conference, and stationed at Mulberry Street, I think it was, the leading appointment at that time in the city of New York. The habits of the people in the west and in the east were very different. He was asked for to be transferred to that popular church, and it was their custom to have service in the morning, and in the afternoon, and in the evening. The evening service was but lightly attended. Three services a day ;—he had not been accustomed to anything of the kind—only to two services —and he did not know anything about the specialties of New York. Without consulting anybody he announced that they would dispense with the afternoon service and have only two services a day. This greatly astonished his people; the official board had not heard of such a thing; the afternoon was the great time; people came out in the afternoon more than they did in the morning or evening. But they did not know what to do with him. They had invited him there, and he was perfectly innocent about it, and his custom was twice a day. The official board saw him and talked with him about it, but they couldn't chide him because they dared not do it. Finally they compromised the matter by arranging that he should only preach twice a day, and that they should supply the afternoon service in some other way. Well, that went along for a little while, and the people attended a little, till finally they abandoned the afternoon service, and only had two services a day; so that became the dominant practice in that city after he reached there. He said he was perfectly innocent about it. He never thought of violating their usages, but simply did what he had been accustomed to, and what he thought was best. But he entrenched himself with the people, and stayed there, and wrought out that change. I had this story from his own lips, and did not know of it personally.

"Bishop Foster is pre-eminently a preacher. As a student he has always been exceedingly diligent, always a hard worker. He is distinguished for his power of thoroughly mastering any subject he takes up. I know that when geology was thought to be a very dangerous thing for people to study, as antagonizing the Bible, he went into a thorough examination of that science, made a profound study of it, and got as thorough a mastery of it as one could with the opportunities he had. He then preached and delivered lectures on geology and the Bible. The same is true of astronomy. Without any adequate facilities he became quite an astronomer, and he delivered a great many sermons on astronomy, showing how God rules in the heavenly world among the stars. The fact is, that became a specialty with him. He has also made a special study of evolution, but he is not an evolutionist in the modern sense of that word. Every study that is kindred to these subjects, he has gone through with thoroughly. Recently he has written a very extensive work on all the branches of theology, from theism to eschatology, in some eight or ten volumes. As a thinker, writer and preacher, in the estimation of many in the Methodist Episcopal church, he "ranks next to Bishop Simpson.

"Being brought up in the midst of plenty, he was especially cared for by his father; and even after he became a man his father supplemented his small income. The bishop never had any idea of economy; he never knew the value of money; he never saved anything and never made anything. He is one of the most generous men that live, a kind, true, manly man.

"I knew his wife; she was a Miss Sarah Miley, a sister of Rev. John Miley, D. D., professor of systematic theology in Drew seminary. I knew her when she was a girl, one of the best, truest, purest and most unselfish women that ever lived, devoted to her husband, lost and swallowed up in him; she lived for him, planned for him, took care of him, and kept a home that was always open to his friends, with the most generous hospitality."

My own early memories of Evanston (1858 to 1860) reveal a figure standing in the midst, of regal height and symmetry; strong, well-knit and vigorous, the fitting temple of a great soul. The head was nobly carried; its dark hair thrown straight back from a square brow, under which glowed a pair of dark eyes every bit as remarkable as those rendered immortal in the opening sentences of Carlyle's "Frederick the Great." The sculpturesque nose and mobile lips were fit adjuncts of the intense gaze, and few countenances of greater persuasiveness and potency have adorned the annals of our time. Dr. Foster, as we young students used to look upon him, was an ideal character,—worthy of romance, of art, of fame. I never saw a teacher so beloved. Every lecture of his was thronged, and on that Sunday morning when he preached his farewell sermon the whole church was in tears, and he stood before us in the old church pulpit, his face buried in his handkerchief, and thus we cried together.

I remember this sentence: "I have rejoiced in you and been proud of you young gentlemen—I have loved you as a father loves his boys."

Though he had a scintillating intellect and the gift of eloquence in a remarkable degree, he was so simple-hearted that he shared his children's games, and even helped to compose and decorate those absurd little valentines that boys were wont to send out in those days. He would give us a series of sermons on the Christian evidences, such as no one else could approach, then go home and write a chapter in his (unto this day) unprinted novel or shed tears over a passage from "David Copperfield," as read aloud to him in the thrilling tones of his daughter Florence, who strongly resembled him in person and was intellectually his other self when she was but twenty years of age. He was so genial and approachable that we all felt free to go to him with any subject on which we needed counsel, and was the life of every company in which he joined.

His wife was, as Dr. Boring says, a "wholly selfless woman." As Blaine puts it in speaking of James A. Garfield's wife in his famous eulogy, "her life all lay in his." Beautiful, tender, devoted, she had the love of all who knew her. Their eight children were remarkably bright, loving-hearted and well-behaved.

Just where the elegant home of Mr. and Mrs. Hugh Wilson now stands,[88] Bishop Foster's son "Dolphy," as we used to call him, a boy so admirable in every way that his father said he "was the most stubborn argument he ever came across against the doctrine of total depravity," established himself in a rough little box of a store, a veritable diminutive shanty, with Atwood Vane as his partner. Many a time have Evanstonians, sauntering down that pleasant street to the pier, stopped to patronize the two bright-looking fellows, who at that early age had learned "how to keep store."

In my desire to write of the bishop as all who knew him would wish me to do, I sent a note to him in his beautiful home in the suburbs of Boston. It brought a reply that I shall always treasure along with one from Whittier and one from Rev. C. H. Spurgeon. It is full of his own beautiful and generous spirit, that sees only the good in his friends. He must forgive me, should he see this sketch, if I copy a few sentences:

"Elm Hill Avenue, Roxbury, Mass., Aug. 12, 1889.

"My Dear Friend: I know you will excuse me from writing anything about myself. There are no incidents in my poor little life worth mentioning. I can see in it almost nothing but sorrow and failure. My darling is gone. Annie is gone. Randolph is gone. My remaining children, John, Talmadge, Fred and Will, of the boys, and Bessie and Eva, are a great

comfort to me. Bessie lives near me; Will and Eva and Randolph's widow and her children make up my home. Fred and Tal are happily married. John remains a bachelor in Cincinnati. Tal and Will are also lawyers, the former in New York, the latter in Boston.

"I have not mentioned my dear Annie in this note, and yet I dare not close it without saying that I never think of you without thinking of her and the 'two Marys,'—yours of 'nineteen beautiful years,' and little Mary Bannister. Had Annie lived, what a joy she would have had in you. Her going away, and then the loss of her dear mother, has left a cloud that never lifts. Some day maybe we shall understand meanings that now seem so obscure."

That daughter Annie was to me one of life's most complete ideals, and her early death a smiting grief at first, and afterwards a great opening into the heavens, of which she said, as her wonderful spirit made the transit, *"The mountain tops are gleaming from peak to peak!"*

Bishop Foster has always loved Evanston with no ordinary love. Very seldom coming back, he has made us all feel, when he did so, that he always carried the little village of yore in his great heart, even as we who dwelt here have always carried him and his. The sermon on immortality preached almost within this year formed a spiritual epoch to those who heard it. His best beloved theme is immortality, ever since in quick succession the two women passed away, who were heart of his heart. When elected bishop, a few years after their going, he spent a day beside their graves at Greenwood, saying to a friend afterward, "Those for whose sacred sakes I would have been rejoiced to win such honor, I have lost."

One day last summer my sister, Mary B. Willard, sitting on the steps at home, saw a grand figure passing by with a slighter young figure beside it. Instantly she knew him and rushed to the sidewalk, when he turned with the tender look of a father in his eyes, saying, "Why, Mary Bannister! It does my heart good to see you once more; I stole up here between trains to let my boy Will see where he was born."

Evanston has a jewel casket of beautiful beloved names, but none gleams with a heavenlier radiance than that of Randolph S. Foster, the poet-natured, philosophic-minded man—one of the most progressive bishops and most blessed saints in Christendom.

REV. JOSEPH CUMMINGS, D. D.

ERASTUS O. HAVEN, D.D., LL.D., OUR FIFTH PRESIDENT

On a commanding eminence in the suburbs of beautiful Salem, the capital of Oregon, not far from the Pacific sea, lies all that was mortal of that most peaceful and pacific character, Erastus O. Haven. In 1883 I stood beside his lonely and far-distant grave, blessing his memory out of a full heart, for all the great and gracious words and deeds of which his life was full. He was indeed a friend to women, a champion wise and brotherly. When invited to the presidency of our university he said that he would not think of leaving that of the University of Michigan, so much larger and more famous, unless the doors of the Methodist institution were flung wide open to women. This was then done, and thus at one stroke Dr. Haven did more for the higher culture of American homes than many a man of equal powers has achieved in a long life. Dr. Haven was a born diplomat in the best sense; he was always in touch with his environment; his sympathy was so universal that all felt the atmosphere of good will radiating from his hospitable brain and generous heart. He was not afraid of the next thing because it was the next, but that very fact gave it advantage in his estimation. No man of more benignant spirit has lived in Evanston or one who left a memory more fragrant. Under his mild, progressive sway of three years, all too brief, the university made steady progress in all its lines of work, and became better known abroad than in all the years of its previous history. Appleton's new "Cyclopedia of American Biography" has the following fair notice of our fourth president:

Erastus Otis Haven, Bishop of M. E. church, was born in Boston, Mass., Nov. 1,1820, died in Salem, Oregon, Aug. 1881. He was graduated at Wesleyan University in 1842, and afterward had charge of a private academy at Sudbury, Mass., at the same time pursuing a course of theological and general study. He became principal of Amenia Seminary, N. Y., in 1846, and in 1848 entered the Methodist ministry in the New York conference. Five years later he accepted the professorship of Latin in Michigan University, which he exchanged the next year for the chair of English language, literature and history. He resigned in 1856, and returned to Boston, where he was editor of *Zion's Herald* for seven years, during which period he served two terms in the state senate, and a part of the time was an overseer of Harvard University. In 1863 he was called to the presidency of Michigan University, which place he occupied for six years. He then became president of Northwestern University, Evanston, Ill., and in 1872 was chosen secretary of the board of education of the Methodist Episcopal church, which place he resigned in 1874 to become chancellor of Syracuse University, N. Y. In May 1880, he was elected and ordained a bishop. Bishop Haven was a man of great versatility of talent. As a preacher he was able and earnest, didactic and hortatory, rather than oratorical; he was judicious and successful as an administrator, but wearied among the details of preceptoral duties.

His religious convictions were positive and controlling in all his life, and while ardently devoted to his own denomination, he was also broadly and generously catholic toward all other Christian bodies. He was given the degree of D.D. by Union College in 1854, and a few years later that of LL.D. by Ohio Wesleyan University. He served five times in the General Conference, and in 1879 visited Great Britain as delegate of the Methodist Episcopal church to the parent Wesleyan body. He wrote largely for the periodical press, and also published "American Progress" "The Young Man Advised," made up from discourses delivered in the chapel of Michigan University (New York, 1855), "Pillars of Truth," a work on the evidences of Christianity (1866), and a treatise on "Rhetoric."

CHARLES H. FOWLER, D. D., LL.D., OUR SIXTH PRESIDENT.[89]

This remarkable and famous man stood at the head of the university from 1872 until 1876. From *Appleton's Cyclopedia of Biography* I take the following biographical sketch:

> "Charles Henry Fowler was born in Burford, Canada, August 11, 1837. In 1841 he was taken, with his father's family, to Illinois, where he spent his early years on a farm. After studying at Rock River Seminary in Mt. Morris, Illinois, he entered Genesee College, Lima, New York, where he was graduated in 1859. He soon afterward began the study of law at Chicago, but soon after this he was converted and at once changed his purpose, began a course of preparation for the ministry, and in 1861 was graduated at Garrett Biblical Institute, Evanston, Illinois. The same year he was admitted on trial into the Rock River conference of the Methodist Episcopal church, and was appointed successively to the chief Methodist Episcopal churches in Chicago, till in 1872 he was elected president of Northwestern University. He held this office till 1876, when he was elected by the General Conference to the editorship of the New York *Christian Advocate*. Four years later he was elected one of the

corresponding secretaries of the Missionary Society of the Methodist Episcopal church, and in 1884 he was elected and ordained bishop. He received the degree of D. D. from the Northwestern University, and afterward that of LL. D. from Syracuse University, New York. He was a delegate to the General Conferences of 1872, 1876, 1880 and 1884. Since he was made bishop he has traveled through all parts of the country in the performance of his official duties, and has also visited South America and made the tour of the world. His residence is in San Francisco, and he has devoted a large share of his labors to the interests of the Methodist Episcopal church in the Pacific states."

OLIVER MARCY,[90] LL. D.,
OUR SEVENTH PRESIDENT.

This genial and genuine Christian gentleman acted as President from 1876 until the election of Dr. Cummings in 1881. The first picture of him that comes to me shows him entering my little "Grove School" in 1865, a man of medium height, strongly built, with alert figure, fine head, fair complexion and hair, and smiling blue eyes. In his hand he carried a stalk of mullein in full flower, and with this as a text he delighted my young folks as if he had been a magician, wand in hand. This incident illustrates the enthusiasm and "aptness to teach" that have given Dr. Marcy a hold so strong upon our students. His enthusiasm is no less contagious than it is enlivening. In his long years of service Dr. Marcy has become the patriarch of the university, and wherever he appears, his presence is the signal for tokens of reverent affection and good will. His home is one of rare attractiveness by reason of the intellectual powers of Mrs. Marcy and their daughter, Mrs. Anna Marcy Davis. Some of us cherish a memory sacred as it is sweet, of the beautiful girl so early called,—Maude Marcy, the pet and darling of that household, whose death cast a deep shadow over a happy home.

REV. JOSEPH CUMMINGS,[91] D. D., LL. D.

Dr. Cummings was a man of noble presence, dignified but agreeable manners, and tremendous personal force and energy. He was of Scotch descent and Methodist birth and breeding. His father was a Methodist itinerant whose parish stretched out over Maine and extended even to Canada. He was the eldest of six brothers and five sisters, one of whom, Judge Cummings, deceased, was a prominent lawyer in Brownsville, Texas.

His mother was the daughter of a well-to-do citizen, and a woman of remarkably vigorous mind. Her father's house was the Methodist ministers' headquarters in Bucksport, Me. Dr. Cummings made his own way through college, teaching between times, studying while he taught, and even in spite of all these drawbacks, getting ahead of his own class so far that he was promoted to the one above it. Not so robust physically as his large frame would indicate, his will power was such that until his illness of a few weeks, in 1885, he had not missed a college duty or six consecutive recitations in all his period of service, covering over forty years as a college President. So persistent was he in fulfilling his engagements at the college that when a new student would say, "The doctor is sick, let's let up on lessons," the old ones would reply, "Never neglect *his* lessons unless you've heard the bell *toll.*" The motto of his life has always been, "Whatsoever thy hand findeth to do, do it with thy might." He had great strength and pertinacity in the support and defense of every moral and Christian enterprise, but at the same time, great generosity to friends and foes. He always took hold of the special work intrusted to him, whether ministerial or educational, with an energy and grip that steadily increased as the obstacles multiplied. In the self-sacrificing devotion that he gave to the strengthening and enlargement of his work, he never seemed to know either discouragement or weariness. And this was equally true even when the sympathy and assistance to which he was entitled, came to him reluctantly.

In the early days of the anti-slavery movement, when ministers were cautioned by their superiors against bringing into the pulpit a subject so delicate and so difficult, he stood undaunted, while condemning in no measured terms the crime of human slavery. When, after a time, the booming of cannon along the hills of New England was heard calling upon all to join hands in saving the country, and the strains of martial music were wafted upon the breeze, he heard in them the song of deliverance to the bondman and one of distant victory for a freed and united land. From the beginning he saw the greatness of the struggle and at what cost the country would be redeemed. In the darkest day of the abolition movement, when Anthony Burns[92] was carried back into bondage, he stoutly persisted that "in twenty years there wouldn't be a slave in the United States."

To him his college work was a sacred duty that he never neglected; but when the cares of the day were done he was found night after night in successive weeks and months on the platform of the town hall in

Middletown, Conn., pleading the cause of our country before an excited community, and striving to arouse in them a true spirit of patriotism. He was in the midst of Southern sympathizers and a foreign race, who feared for their calling if the slaves were set free. These men were so carried away by passion that the life of Dr. Cummings, as a government champion, was in danger, a deadly missile being hurled at him in the darkness as he crossed the college campus, and his house the first one marked for the torch. But through all these scenes of strife and hatred he stood firmly for the right. No regiment left the county without a farewell address of encouragement and sympathy and good cheer, and a loving handshake and "God bless you," from Dr. Cummings. It was a current saying after the war that Dr. Cummings had made more "war speeches," as they were called, bidden adieu to more regiments, presented more flags, and spoken the last words at the graves of more soldiers slain in battle, than any other man in the state of Connecticut.

This great strength and firmness in the support of whatever he thought to be right would perhaps lead some to think him wanting in the finer qualities of the heart. He was reticent, but his heart was ever tender and sympathetic toward the poor and afflicted. One little incident will illustrate his fatherly regard for the young men under his care. In the middle of the college term one of the students was taken down with small-pox. Without alarming any of his companions, Dr. Cummings had him shut up with an attendant until he could be removed. When that was accomplished he procured a nurse who had had the terrible disease, but who was not very reliable as a nurse, though he was the only one answering to the necessity of the case. To make sure that the young man was well cared for, Dr. Cummings would go to the house at all hours of the night and inspect the condition of things through a window. The young man recovered and is now one of the chief ministers of the New York conference. No struggling student who was free from stain ever went away from him without sympathy and material aid.

The doctor was as clear-headed in finance as he was in the classroom. Every school with which he has been connected has a monument to him in stone and brick crowning its campus, in the form of libraries, chapels, dormitories and halls of recitation, while endowments have always flourished under his fostering care. When he had been in Evanston eight years, debts to the amount of two hundred thousand dollars had been cleared off, three new professors secured and three substantial buildings added to the growing group upon the college campus.

For more than forty years Dr. Cummings was a staunch temperance man, as well as a most earnest speaker and worker in that great cause.

He was always a strong believer in the co-education of the sexes, which was introduced into the oldest Methodist university during his administration, after forty-two years of contrary precedent.

Women have had in him a loyal friend, his name having long been allied with the woman suffrage cause as well as with that of woman's education. He believed that no door should be closed to women, but that all honorable careers should be open to talents capable of entering upon and succeeding in them. His special lines of study have been moral science; above all, mental science and political economy. He was fond of writing, and has contributed to quarterlies, etc., but though he mapped out two or three books, he never found the time to write them. No man was ever more industrious. His only recreation was an hour after tea, when he liked to hear the news and have a bright recess with his family and friends. His accomplished daughter Alice (now Mrs. Dr. Bonbright), was, next to Mrs. Cummings, his greatest solace, his comfort and oftentimes his assistant in correspondence and research. The students of Wesleyan University like to tell how she used to come over to his study in the college, and go home on his shoulders, it being hard to see which most enjoyed the frolic, the stately president or the winsome child. Intent upon personal impressions of this great man, I recently sought my kind friend, Professor Cumnock, in his beautiful home on Hinman Avenue.[93] Genial as ever, he responded to my "say on" about as follows;—at least this is what my flying pencil then and there recorded:

"Did you know that Dr. Cummings graduated Dr. Fisk, Philip Shumway, who is gone, Professor Morse, Professor Carhart and me? What did we think of him? Why, he was almost worshiped by the students. I will not qualify those words, strong as they seem. But he was a stern disciplinarian, and during his administration there was a first-class disturbance. I was there at the time, and nearly all opposed him, but before I left he so won back the love of everybody that they would have kissed the dust under that man's feet. He never gave way; he made no sacrifice of dignity or conscience; his administration was just as firm as ever, but his true manliness and strength were such that nobody could help bowing before them. He didn't form a resolution one day and relinquish it the next, but it was a straight pull all the way through. When a man like that says to a lot of young fellows at class day, after a year in which there had been disturbance, 'I, of all men, am least able to do without the sympathy and love of my pupils,' it brings them to their senses. I can tell you Dr. Cummings is so beloved by the alumni of Wesleyan University, that when he went back a few years ago, every

OLIVER MARCY, LL. D.

DANIEL BONBRIGHT, LL.D.

REV. HERBERT F. FISK, D. D.

PROF. JAMES T. HATFIELD.

other person was forgotten, even the president and Bishop Foss. Dr. Reed, who was toastmaster, said that when Dr. Cummings rose to reply to the toast assigned him, every man was on his feet,—undergraduates who only knew him by his glorious traditions, alumni whose names are household words throughout our church,—and for five minutes they made the welkin ring with such cheering, when you consider quality and quantity, as seldom salutes the ears of anybody on this earth, no matter how successful he may have been. It is not overmuch praise to say that the doctor, by his long and splendid period of service, merits the title of an educational Nestor and *the* college president of Methodism. He impressed all his students with the sternness of his moral character—its absolute rectitude—and his enthusiasm that they should accomplish something for humanity worthy of the age in which they lived. These were the two great features of his work. He was a mighty inspirational force with students; he never granted a favor unless necessary, and never asked one for himself. Duty was evermore his polar star, and he helped them to make it theirs. No body of college men has been more effective than his graduates; they are the kind that cause things to come to pass. Uprightness and energy came as nearly to a climax in him as seems possible to man. Though stern, he has the kindliest human feeling. He was 'a square man,' as the saying is an 'out and outer,' too big to wear list slippers or to peep in key holes; he'd a good deal sooner fight! Indeed a belligerent student would get little quarter should the case ever come to blows— which, by the way, it never could; that towering personality was blow enough for the average collegian. The Doctor grew even better with age. How wisely he conserved this great university of ours! He gained constantly in favor, his administration being at once safe, broad and prosperous. In Middletown, Conn., he was right at the front as a citizen. The townspeople, irrespective of denomination, looked up to him as a great man, a tower of strength.

Dr. Raymond said the following of Dr. Cummings when I interviewed him in 1889:

"In the New England Conference he was at the head of the heap, pastor of Hanover Street church, Boston, when it was the leading M. E. church in Boston and its glory, and he filled the bill. He was in every way a great man in New England; had attained to a mature mind and reputation when he entered our conference. He has repeatedly reminded me that I was on the executive committee when he was admitted. He was always popular in the East, is now. One of the great qualities that has had no small part in his success, is his unconquerable will. He is alive because he wouldn't die when the doctors told him to three years ago. His industry is prodigious and unremitting. I saw him one day leaning on the shoulder of a student going up to University Hall, and I declare I thought he was near the end, but since then he has put in years of most effective work. I think of him as an illustration of the fact that will power can control physical conditions. He is a grand old Roman; long may he wave."

"Throughout his long career he steadily, though I think unconsciously, avoided attracting to himself what is commonly known as popularity. He spurned working for place; his indifference to what is unhappily known as ' church politics ' is the only reason that he has not had the highest place in our beloved church. He would not even use what are legitimate means of advancement, and he taught the students that;—he always had a sneer for men who push themselves toward place and power. We have not had a figure in the church in fifty years more suitable for bishop. He was a great preacher, one of the greatest in our church, strong, logical, inspiring. His present [1889] political affiliations (with the Prohibition party) are not of recent birth. When I was a student in college he was a candidate for governor on the Prohibition ticket in 1866, and a member of their state committee,—a target set up to be fired at. He took up new ideas because he could not help it. First of all he took them up in his own conscience; he never allied himself with any movement unless it had the full support of his great head and heart. Fear of disfavor never seemed to enter into his mind when he had a 'thus saith the Lord.' "

"Above all, let me say this,—he was great as an instructor. The professor's chair was always his throne. In the classroom he played with us boys as a cat would with a ball."

"What can you tell me of Mrs. Cummings?" was my climax question. The professor replied with zest:

"I knew her in the heyday of her power. She is a born diplomat. She knows how to enlist friends for the school. Her life was exhausted in the interest of the college when I was a student. She had just what the doctor lacked. Her receptions were the great social features of the time in the Methodist circles of this country. The beautiful, aristocratic old town at the head of navigation on the Connecticut river, was originally made up of old families that had grown rich in the West India trade. They were Episcopalians of the old school and our college had been an innovation. But Mrs. Cummings won all their *prestige* for the institution of which her husband was the head. She was to Middletown what Mrs. Dr. Kidder was to Evanston in former days. Mrs. Cummings is earnest and public-spirited. She here helps on the noble enterprise of College

Cottage to the extent of her power, and there can not be a better work than to assist young women who are glad to help themselves to the higher education. She is a woman of great tact, energy and intelligence, full of sprightliness and power; a conservative as her husband was a radical; but a descendant of the Puritans, whose watchword still is duty. Of their surviving children, Helen F. married Major S. P. Hatfield, and resides in New York. Alice Cummings was the idol of that old man's heart,—a young lady of rare accomplishments and nobility of character."

HENRY WADE ROGERS,[94] LL.D., EIGHTH PRESIDENT.

The election of Dr. Rogers to the presidency of the Northwestern University at Evanston is an event of more than ordinary significance. The old school of college presidents, as represented by McCosh, Porter and Hopkins, is rapidly passing away. In the evolution of the American college a new type of presiding officer is appearing. The college president of a generation ago united in himself the functions of a legislative, a judicial, and an executive officer. Presiding over an institution with limited resources, or in its very infancy, he was obliged to teach, to preach, to administer discipline, and to solicit funds, to meet the pressing needs of the struggling college.

The last few years have brought large accessions to the endowment of our leading colleges; their resources have increased until they have become great corporations, demanding of the trustees and presiding officer a very high degree of executive skill. The college president of to-day must be pre-eminently a man of great business ability; there is an increasing tendency to limit his functions to those of a purely administrative officer, leaving to others the various subdivisions of labor that have become too numerous for a single person to perform. In nothing is the tendency of the times more strongly marked than in the recent appointments of laymen to the presidency of our more prominent colleges. The election of Mr. Seth Low to Columbia, and the simultaneous call of Dr. Merrill E. Gates to Oberlin and Amherst are significant of the changes that are taking place in the educational world. The election of Dr. Rogers to the presidency of Northwestern is fully in keeping with the tendency to place distinguished laymen at the head of our universities.

Dr. Rogers is, by training and profession, a lawyer. Born in 1853 in the state of New York, he entered Hamilton college in 1869, but graduated from the University of Michigan in 1874, from which institution

HENRY WADE ROGERS, LL. D.,
Prest. Northwestern University.

he received the degree of Master of Arts three years later. He began his study of law in the University of Michigan, and in 1877 he was admitted to the Michigan bar. He spent some time in the law office of Judge Cooley, who was at that time Chief Justice of the state, and Dean of the Law School of the University of Michigan. In 1880 he was appointed to a professorship in the Law School of Michigan University. When Judge Cooley severed his connection with the law school with which he had been connected for twenty-five years it was feared that the school must suffer greatly from this retirement. In 1885 Dr. Rogers was appointed the successor of Judge Cooley. During the five years of his administration the school has so increased in numbers that it is now the largest law school in America. The attendance during the present year is nearly six hundred.

Dr. Rogers has already achieved a national reputation as a writer on legal topics. He was offered the editorship of a leading law journal, but declined the offer. His work on "Expert Testimony" has already reached a second edition. He has also edited the "Illinois Citations." His contributions to legal periodicals have been frequent and important. He was associated with Judges Cooley, Mitchell, Hammond and Wood, in the editorship of the *American Law Register,* of Philadelphia. Among the periodicals of a more popular character to which he has contributed articles on legal subjects, are the *Princeton Review,* the *Forum,* and the *North American Review.* His article in the *North American Review,* in June 1884, under the title "Harboring Conspiracy," excited general attention at the time. He contributes an introduction of twenty-five pages to a work entitled " Constitutional History as Seen in American Law," just published by Messrs. Putnam & Co., in New York.

Dr. Rogers comes to an institution already possessing great resources, and at an interesting stage of its history. Under the administration of the late President Cummings, the attendance became very great; during the present year there were about two thousand students in actual attendance. The number of departments has steadily grown until Northwestern may justly lay claim to that much abused title, "university." The departments now in active operation are, the College of Liberal Arts, the Academic department, the Colleges of Theology, Medicine, Law, Pharmacy, Dentistry, Music and Oratory. The faculty numbers one hundred and ten professors and instructors. The last report of the treasurer showed the total revenues of the university to be about two million five hundred thousand dollars, most of this in city real estate, highly productive.

It is evident that great possibilities lie before the university under a skillful administrator. Dr. Rogers' brilliant record gives every assurance that he will prove equal to the duties of his new position. The city is to be congratulated on this accession to its educational forces of one who may be relied on to develop still further a university which already holds a high place among those great educational institutions which have elevated Chicago to the dignity of a literary and art center.

PROFESSORS OF THE UNIVERSITY.

DANIEL BONBRIGHT, LL. D., Professor of Latin Language and Literature.—Dr. Bonbright is of Pennsylvania birth, rearing, and education until his junior year,—having studied at the most classic old college of Methodism, Dickinson, Carlisle, when Dr. Emory was president. He was graduated at Yale in 1850, during the presidency of Dr. Woolsey, and was afterward a tutor there. Subsequently he went abroad for purposes of study and travel. In the autumn of 1858 he came to Evanston as professor of the Latin Language and Literature, and has now for nearly thirty-three years been an integral part of the university, having held his professorship four years longer than any other member of the present faculty. During this period he has been abroad several times, and in 1870, while in Germany, he purchased for the university the Schultz Library, collected by Johann Schultz, a member of the Prussian ministry. He also accompanied his beloved brother James Bonbright (of the well known firm of Hood and Bonbright, Philadelphia) on his health trips to Europe, the seashore and the South. With all that is highest, purest and best in Evanston Dr. Bonbright has been associated from the day of his arrival until now. Of profound scholarship and proverbial thoroughness as a professor, he has always enjoyed the highest social distinction that Evanston or Chicago had to confer, while his character as a Christian gentleman has been ideal. The phenomenal modesty and reticence of his nature have alone held him away from the larger fame for which his rare natural abilities and great culture combined to prepare him. An incident of his earlier years in Evanston illustrates the heroic side of his character, and will be well remembered by "old timers." At the hotel where Dr. Bonbright boarded, a Chicago gentleman named Kirchoff was stricken with small-pox, whereupon everybody departed in terror, except our professor of Latin, who, with an attendant that (unlike Dr. Bonbright) had had the disease, stayed by the patient until he died.

Dr. Bonbright is said by the students to "exert a pressure to the square inch" by reason of intellectual force and weight of character, that makes him by college tradition and present fact, a king in his classroom, while he is a "brother born for adversity" to all who need special counsel and help.

On the twenty-eighth of August, 1890, Dr. Bonbright married Miss Alice Cummings, daughter of the lamented Rev. Dr. Cummings, upon which happy event in their scholarly annals, both of the contracting parties have been warmly congratulated by the host of friends in Evanston and elsewhere, who hold them dear.

**

J ULIUS F. KELLOGG, A. M., Professor of Mathematics.—Long after Sturm's theorem is forgotten, the kindly twinkle in Professor Kellogg's eye will shine out bright among the dusty memories of all his pupils. Although mathematics and merriment are not usually associated in the student mind, yet in this character, many generations of Northwestern freshmen and sophomores have had the opportunity of "observing the rare combination of a sympathetic, fun-loving spirit with a precise mathematical mind. No member of the faculty is more genuinely loved and venerated. The young men tell him their good stories. The young women remember him with flowers and always have a smile for his genial anecdotes.

Professor Kellogg was born in McGrawville, N. Y., February 4, 1830. He received his education at Brown University, and took an honorary degree at Lawrence, Wis. In 1855, he was married to Miss Elizabeth Quereau, a charming and accomplished lady. Three sons have graced his fireside and then gone out into the world—William, Howard and Albert.

**

H ERBERT F. FISK, D. D., Professor of Pedagogics and Principal of the Preparatory School.—A tower of strength to our educational enterprises was the coming of this thoughtful and serious spirit, so mild but masterful; so gentle yet indomitable. He has built up the preparatory school until, with its twenty-three expert instructors, it rivals Phillips Exeter or Phillips Andover on the intellectual plane and excels them on the moral, as a count relative to the number using tobacco or intoxicants could hardly fail to show. The fact that many of the young men contemplate studying for the ministry and that nearly one-third of the students are young women, helps to explain the high religious status of the school. Two such men as Doctor Fisk, the principal, and Rev. Joseph L. Morse, A. M., assistant principal, have seldom combined their forces of brain and conscience in the instruction, care and oversight of six hundred and seventy-one young people. The outcome is growingly satisfactory to patrons, and the outlook for this noble school has brightened to such an extent that a building worthy of its record and achievement is already planned, and no better monument need be desired by a rich and loyal Methodist or a public-spirited Chicagoan, than to associate his name with this school by furnishing the funds with which our veteran principal can fulfill his heart's most profound desire by saying, "Let us arise and build." The annals of this helpful life are in this wise:

Born in Massachusetts, 1840; prepared for college at Wesleyan Academy, Wilbraham, Mass.; entered the Wesleyan University in 1856; graduated in 1860; teacher of Latin in Delaware Literary Institute, Franklin, New York, one year; two years principal Shelburne Academy, Vermont; for four years, 1863-1867, teacher of ancient languages in Cazenovia Seminary, New York; one year, 1867-1868, teacher of ancient languages Wesleyan Academy, Wilbraham, Mass.; five years, 1868-1873, principal Genesee Wesleyan Seminary, Lima, New York; eighteen years, 1873-1891, principal of Preparatory School, and for two years past Professor of Pedagogics in Northwestern University. Married, July 11, 1866, Miss Anna Green, Portageville, New York.

A happy home with lovely wife and two daughters worthy of their parentage and opportunities has been, in all these arduous years, the hiding place of power to Dr. Fisk, next to that faith in God that shines out from his teaching and his life like a pharos brightening evermore.

***

ROBERT MCLEAN CUMNOCK, Professor of Rhetoric and Elocution in our university, was born in Ayr, Scotland, the home of Robert Burns, May 31, 1844. He came to the United States when only one year old, received his academic education chiefly in Wilbraham Seminary, Mass., and was graduated from Wesleyan University at Middletown, Conn., in 1868. Immediately thereafter he came to Evanston and entered on his present profession and professorship. During the winter term he is engaged in giving public readings, for which his services are in demand throughout the nation, no dramatic reader outranking him upon the platform, while his genial manners make him a universal favorite.

Professor Cumnock's first wife was Miss Charlotte Nye, of Middletown, Conn., who died in 1874. His present wife is Miss Annie C. Webster, of Evanston, an accomplished woman and alumna of the university.

Professor Cumnock is the author of several books relating to his specialty, published by McClurg & Co., Chicago. Poorly as the fact may be illustrated in action, I was the pupil of this accomplished artist in speech, during the winter of 1872, when to help our Woman's College, he taught its president as a freewill offering on the shrine of improved English and ameliorated manner.

Professors Griffith, Robert Kidd, of Cincinnati, Moon, of Philadelphia, Charles A. Roberts, of New York city, and Faverner, of all along shore, have each tried their hand in a similar missionary fashion, upon the same difficult subject, but it is the testimony of an impartial pupil that our own canny Scotsman excelleth them all.

***

Robert Baird, A. M., Professor of Greek.—Three, scholarly men have filled this position since the founding of the university; William D. Godman, Louis Kistler and Robert Baird, who was the latter's most enthusiastic and thorough student. We are fortunate in having two Scotchmen in the faculty,—Professors Cumnock and Baird, the latter being a native of Glasgow, born in 1844. He has the sturdy, solid physique and qualities, mental and ethical, of the fittest survivals of his race, among which stands conspicuous a genius for hard work. He came to this country with his father's family, when five years of age; studied in the public schools of Illinois until he was nineteen, then served as a student for seven years faithfully in our preparatory school and university, acting as tutor a large part of the time until his graduation in 1869. Twelve years of instruction of the most thorough and invaluable kind were then given by him in preparatory school and college, and in 1881 he was made professor of Greek. He has studied abroad, visiting Greece and other continental countries, and is still a student insatiable as at first.

In 1874 Professor Baird married Miss Sarah Heston, of Michigan, a beloved pupil of mine and one of the most promising intellectually, among my galaxy of two thousand or more. They have three children and a quiet home on Sheridan Road, near college campus. [95]

***

Charles W. Pearson, A. M., professor of English Literature.— The poet member of the faculty is Charles William Pearson, A. M., Professor of English Literature. There is no better fit of chair to man than this. In busy after years the alumnus can not hear the names Shakespeare, Milton, Gray, without recalling the vivid picture of this professor with his gentle-voiced but deep-eyed enthusiasm for all things high and exquisite in thought and speech. Born at Silby, England, in August, 1846, he brought from his sturdy home a keenness and resolution of disposition that, united with rare scholarship and taste, have made him an easy victor in life's Olympian games.

Professor Pearson graduated from the Northwestern University in 1871 and received the degree of A. M. in 1872. In 1881 he was made a professor in the institution. His marriage to Sarah Helen French took place in 1875. Five children adorn this happy home, Mowbray, Margaret, Ethel, George and Muriel.[96]

Professor Pearson is a man whom culture has not degenerated into conservatism. He is alert and progressive in his attitude toward the temperance question, the woman question, and other reforms that are founded on that gospel of Christ to which he is loyal and devoted.

***

ROBERT D. SHEPPARD, D. D., Professor of History and Political Economy.—Long ago and long ago it was we had an oratorical prize contest in the old chapel of the university, as a result of which the prize was carried off by a young man of fine presence, sonorous voice, and a marked taste for literature. Subsequently we learned that he was a native of Chicago, born there July 23, 1846, and that he had been prepared for college in the public schools of that electric city. After studying awhile in Evanston he attended and graduated from Chicago University, in 1869, and later on from Garrett Biblical Institute (in 1870). He then joined Rock River conference and was pastor of leading churches within its borders until 1886, when he was elected to the professorship he now holds, after which he spent a year or two in foreign travel and study. In 1872 he married Miss Virginia Loring, and they have four children, of whom the eldest, Coring, is a student in the university.

Dr. Sheppard received his degree from this theological *alma mater* in 1880.

***

ABRAM V. E. YOUNG,[97] PhB., Professor of Chemistry.—It was not an easy matter to follow a scientist so distinguished as Professor Carhart, but this young man has sustained. himself admirably in his department, coming to us well furnished by a course of study in Michigan University (Ph.B. in 1875) and postgraduate work at Johns Hopkins and Harvard Universities. He was elected to his present chair in 1885.

***

CHARLES S. COOK, A. M., Professor of Physics.— Like Dr. Bradley, Professor Cook comes to us from Dartmouth College, where he was graduated in 1879, and was a professor when elected in 1887 to the chair he now fills. Professor Cook is a native of Keene, N. H., and brings the fruits of New England character and culture to his responsible duties in the West.

***

GEORGE WASHINGTON HOUGH,[98] A. M., Professor of Astronomy in Northwestern University, and Director of Dearborn Observatory.— Our new observatory is the gift of James B. Hobbs, Esq., of Chicago, and was completed in July, 1889. It stands upon an open bluff fifty feet above the lake and three hundred feet from the beach. The dome is constructed on a new and improved plan. The principal instruments of the observatory are: The great twenty-two foot equatorial refracting telescope, made by Alvan Clark & Sons, of Cambridge, Mass., in 1861. This instrument was the largest in the world until a few years ago, and now has very few superiors. A meridian circle of the first class, constructed in 1867 by Messrs. A. Repsold & Sons, of Hamburg. This instrument has a telescope of six French inches aperture, and a divided circle of forty inches diameter, reading by four microscopes. Hough's printing and recording chronographs have been added, for making an electrical record of the time of star transits. The observatory has a chronometer, Wm. Bond & Son, No. 279, three mercurial pendulum clocks, and an astronomical library, containing nearly one thousand three hundred volumes and pamphlets.

To man this splendid outfit, we have Professor Hough, the distinguished astronomer, whose numerous original investigations and scientific publications on astronomy, meteorology and physics, given to the world, through the principal European and American journals treating of these subjects, are well known to specialists. His "Annals of the Dudley Observatory," Vol. I "Astronomy," Vol. II "Meteorology" and his "Annual Reports from Chicago 1879-87" should be particularly mentioned. He was director of the Dudley Observatory at Albany, N. Y., from 1860 to 1874, and director of Dearborn Observatory, Chicago, and professor of astronomy in Chicago University from 1879 to 1887, when he came to Evanston.

In 1856 he received the degree of A. M. in course from his *alma mater*, Union College, Schenectady, N. Y. Professor Hough prepared for college at Seneca Falls Academy, N.Y. He married Emma Q. Shear, at Albany, N. Y., in 1870, and three sons have brightened their pleasant home.

***

JAMES TAFT HATFIELD, Ph. D., Professor of German.—"An Israelite indeed," is this accomplished young scholar, whose whole life has been devoted, under the most favorable conditions, to the acquisition of knowledge, and whose mental powers are so subtle that at twenty-two, having graduated with high honor from our university and made a tour to the antipodes, he prepared (in 1884) the " Elements of Sanskrit Grammar," published in Lueknow, and a few years later (1890) issued at Bonn, Germany, "A Study of Juvencus," and in the same year at Baltimore "A Gothic Index to Kenge's Dictionary."

Born in Brooklyn, N. Y., in 1862, graduating from Northwestern University in 1883, taking the degree of A. M. in 1886, and from Johns Hopkins University that of Ph. D. in 1890, a "Hospitant"[99] in Bonn University, Germany, in 1890, and at twenty nine a member of the American Oriental Society, American Society for the Extension of University Teaching, member Auxiliary Council of World's Exposition and frequent contributor to various learned societies and periodicals. Surely the university has done well to call home her gifted son and claim his powers in her own interest. Professor Hatfield is the son of that flaming herald of the gospel, Robert M. Hatfield, all of whose children share the endowment of their father's vigor of mind and their mother's wealth of character.

***

ELIAKIM H. MOORE, Ph. D., Assistant Professor of Mathematics.—At twenty-one[100] this young man had taken his diploma and degree of A.B., Yale College being his *alma mater;* at twenty-three he was a Ph. D. in the same great institution. He then studied mathematics a year at the University of Berlin (1885-6), in the next year taught in our Preparatory School and went in the year following to Yale as tutor, being recalled here as assistant professor of mathematics in 1889. With such a record it is not hard to forecast the future of a Christian young man whose father is Rev. Dr. David H. Moore of brilliant record among the leaders of the M. E. church.

DEANS OF THE WOMAN'S COLLEGE.

The Woman's College has had five deans, each of them thoroughly individualized. The relations of the first dean to "a classic town" have been set forth in a voluminous record entitled, "Glimpses of Fifty Years;"[101] her immediate successor was Mrs. A. E. Sanford, of Bloomington, Ill., then a successful teacher, and now a greatly esteemed white ribboner of that educational center, who lived in Evanston 1874-5 and in troublous times wrought well and valiantly. Mrs. Sanford was succeeded by Dean Ellen Soulé of New York, a lady of high accomplishments and quite exceptional advantages; the daughter of a Methodist minister, and a relative of Bishop Soulé. After making an excellent record as head of the Woman's College and professor of French in the university, Miss Soulé married Professor Henry Carhart, the distinguished scientist, and they removed to Ann Arbor where he is a leading member of the Faculty of Michigan University. Dean [Dr.] Jane M. Bancroft (now Mrs. George Robinson, of Detroit, Mich.,) is a New Yorker by birth, daughter of a Methodist minister, a graduate of Syracuse University, a "fellow" of Bryn Mawr College, a student of foreign languages and literature of long residence abroad, and later a most effective speaker and writer in the interest of the newly adopted order of deaconess in the M. E. Church.

Dean [Dr.] Rena A. Michaels, the present incumbent, is like all the rest, a native of New York state. She is a graduate of Syracuse University and was dean of the Women's Department in Albion College, Mich., and DePauw University, Greencastle, Ind. Dean Michaels is an accomplished scholar, and universally beloved by the students. Her French translations are becoming standards; her skill as a writer and speaker is exceptional, and she has resigned her position as dean (1891) to give her time to literary and philanthropic work, the latter under the auspices of the National Woman's Christian Temperance Union.

Mrs. Dr. Bayliss is a leader among missionary women; Mrs. Dr. Stowe excels as an amateur artist, and Miss Hetty Stowe as a kindergartner.

Mrs. Jane Eggleston Zimmerman, the only sister of Edward Eggleston, should be named among our literary women and successful mothers; also Mrs. E. E. Marcy, Mrs. Caroline F. Corbin (a former resident and cousin of Louise Chandler Moulton, the Boston author).

Among the galaxy of intellectual women that gains steadily in numbers and in brightness, it is not invidious to name Mrs. Minerva Brace Norton, Miss Helen Brace Emerson, whose art classes and lectures were a brilliant success; Misses Harriet A. Kimball, Lelia Crandon and

Ada Townsend of the university, Mrs. Belle Webb Parks, and Misses Lizzie K. Hunt, Mary Henry and Lodilla Ambrose, who are among its most gifted alumnae; Mrs. Orange Judd, always her famous husband's right hand helper; Mrs. George T. Stone and daughter; Mrs. George S. Lord, and Mrs. Mary Raymond Shumway; Misses Mary Ninde and Lilla Potter, the "We Two" of European travel; Mrs. Marie Huse Wilder and Dr. Sarah Brayton; Miss Whittington, that loved and lamented teacher who "built character" into her pupils, and her brilliant successor, Miss Alice Blanchard; Mrs. Dr. Terry, Mrs. Dr. Bennett, Mrs. Dr. Bradley, Mrs. Dr. Fiske, Mrs. Ella Bannister Merwin, Mrs. Bishop Hamline of saintly memory, and Madam Willard, known to white ribboners as "Saint Courageous."[102]

The Women's Club of Evanston, Mrs. E. B. Harbert, president, counts among its leading lights Mrs. T. P. Stanwood, Mrs. General Singleton, Mrs. Van Benschoten, Mrs. Mary H. Hull, Mrs. John E. Miller, Mrs. Moseley, Mrs. Thayer, Mrs. A. L. Butler, Mrs. W. E. Clifford, Mrs. L. D. Norton, Mrs. C. J. Whitely and Miss Kate Jackson. Among philanthropists, Miss Alice Bond takes first rank, also Mrs. Caroline B. Buell, Miss Esther Pugh, Miss Anna Gordon, Mrs. Elizabeth Wheeler Andrew, Dr. Kate Bushnell, Miss Alice Briggs, all of them officers in the World's Woman's Christian Temperance Union; also Miss Helen Hood, corresponding secretary of Illinois Woman's Christian Temperance Union, Mrs. Dr. Hatfield, Miss Mary McDowell, National Organizer of Young Woman's Christian Temperance Unions; Mrs. Allen Vane, president of local Woman's Christian Temperance Union; Miss Irene Fockler, secretary of temperance literature at Rest Cottage. Mrs. Governor Beveridge, for thirty-five years a resident of Evanston, is a lady of remarkable conversational and executive powers; Miss Julia Ames,[103] one of the editors of *The Union Signal*, organ of the World's Woman's Christian Temperance Union; Mrs. Sallie Ravenhill Kidder and Miss Kathryn Kidder, of dramatic gifts and fame; Miss Katharine Willard,[104] one of our sweetest singers; Mrs. Emma Winner Rogers, wife of the president of our university, a woman who has recently taken a diploma at Michigan University and thus set a keynote for married women who have leisure in this and other educational centers. The list is but begun and my pen stops regretfully half way along the lengthening line.

BISHOP EDW. THOMSON.

BISHOP MATTHEW SIMPSON.

BISHOP RANDOLPH S. FOSTER.

BISHOP WM. L. HARRIS.

OTHER UNIVERSITY PEOPLE.

Mrs. Professor Noyes seemed to me more like Margaret Fuller[105] than any one else that I have met. She had unhackneyed views of life; lived at its kernel rather than in its shell; had a wide horizon and an eye that could see far up among the stellar spaces; was quite humorous in conversation, where she was the bright particular star of any galaxy she was liable to enter; she was an insatiable reader of the best in books; she worshiped justice, was a devotee of truth, and had a realizing sense of God. To spend an afternoon with her, for this we sometimes did in those leisurely, old-fashioned days, was an epoch in one's history. To her I owe the reading of Margaret Fuller's life and works, Niebuhr, John Stuart Mill, Emerson's English Traits, Carlyle's Life of John Sterling, and a score of books equally noble and inspiring. My brother Oliver, then a humorsome young theologue, said that when Mrs. Noyes and certain other "thought-graspers," as he termed them, were in converse, they "shook mental nebulae out of their brains as you'd shake feathers from an old pillow."

I have always thought had Mrs. Noyes been less sensitive to the criticisms which all must face who come before the public by voice or pen, she would by this time have achieved a prominent position in the world of letters or reform, or both. But, united to her undoubted individuality of thought and rare freshness of expression, was a nature that would not brook the world's severity. In that grand school of Principal Charles D. Bragdon's at Auburndale,[106] this rarely endowed woman was for years one of the mainsprings of moral power. Her only child, Margaret (born in Evanston, graduated at Boston, and married to Professor Otis, of the Boston Polytechnic school), having recently become a widow, Mrs. Noyes is with her and her children at the Hub.

Another salient personality of that elder day was Dr. James Z. V. Blaney, a graduate of and professor of chemistry in Northwestern University, in person the beau ideal of a man of science, vigorous, alert, almost vehement in his enthusiasm, yet as gentle as a woman, and ofttimes, when off duty, playful as a boy. He had a home up on Ridge Avenue that was elegant for those days, and the "parties" that he and others gave, along that handsome street, were, with the receptions and levees of the university, institute and female college, occasions most enjoyable to those of us who thirty years ago were young.

Doctor Blaney was a universal favorite among the students, with whom he had that rarest faculty of an instructor, the power of making "common cause." The boys delighted in him, were proud of his acknowledged genius and wide reputation, and, with the village people, lamented his untimely death at the noontide of a beautiful career.

In what has for so long a time been known as the "Somers House," opposite the elegant home of Doctor Cummings,[107] lived for five years, Prof. Wm. D. Godman, who had the chair of Greek. A graduate of Delavan College, Ohio, and a man of undoubted culture; the brother-in law of that most polished among Methodist divines of his epoch, Reverend Doctor McClintock, Professor Godman brought unusual *prestige* to his task. Of medium height, slight figure, broad, peaceful brow, mild, gray eyes, and calm, benignant aspect, with the slightly abstracted bearing of a scholar, this gentleman moved along our streets, the incarnation of refinement. We all esteemed him highly; enjoyed the occasional sermons preached, or, to be more accurate, read by him in the old church, by reason of their high moral plane and choiceness of expression. The students liked him, and several of us date from a memorable lecture that he gave, our devotion to the poetry of Wordsworth. Not long after the death of his accomplished wife, Professor Godman left us, as did his handsome mother-in-law (by a previous marriage), Mrs. Porter, an impressive figure in her home and at all social gatherings of the faculty. I had the pleasure of meeting this lady, after a quarter-century interval, at the annual convention of the Massachusetts W. C. T. U. in Cambridge, and of finding that she was a delegate, and, like myself, wore the white ribbon. It also came about that on a recent temperance trip to Louisiana, I received a telegram, inviting me to "come and hold a meeting," from Professor (now Doctor) Godman, who lives in the locality so charmingly described in Longfellow's Evangeline as the refuge of that heroine, and is president of Baldwin University.

I like to think we never really lose a friend, though the waves of life's unresting sea cluster so close between, that dim horizons seem to separate us, and I like still better to believe this will prove true when beyond the last and longest horizon of them all we emerge upon the smiling shore of immortality.

BISHOP THOMSON.

Of the life of this remarkable and saintly man, no adequate outline can be given here. His son, Rev Edward Thomson, has, at my request, furnished the following:

"Los ANGELES, CAL., Sept. 25, 1889—*My Dear Friend:* I have been wanting to find time to write you a real good and valuable letter, but the demands upon my time increase from day to day, so I shall just dash off something, hoping it may be of some little help in the 'Story of Evanston.'

"I had been born on a college campus, and had lived in Delaware, Ohio, a college town, nearly all my life, and when we moved to Evanston it was not much of a change for the Thomson family. We felt at home among college students and college professors, and with that class of people who naturally settle in college towns.

"We moved to Evanston the latter part of November, 1867. We were entertained by two families while we were getting our goods unpacked. My father and mother stayed with Dr. W. C. Dandy, pastor of the Methodist church, and my sister and myself with Dr. D. P. Kidder, the senior professor in Garrett Biblical Institute.

"Dr. Dandy's family were recently from Kentucky, and were of the warm-hearted Southern style. Mrs. Dandy was a quiet, gentle, motherly spirit. Her throne was the home.

"Dr. Dandy was a broad-shouldered, vigorous man in body and mind. He usually read his sermons, but there was so much about them that was bright and inspiring that no one seemed to regret the use of the manuscript.

"Dr. Kidder was the type of the systematic, careful and exact scholar. Every movement of face, body and limb seemed to be studied, and never did he utter an expression, even under the most ordinary circumstances, or about the most trivial affair, which was not rhetorically perfect. His politeness was of the French style—the most cultured kind of warmheartedness. Mrs. Kidder was so much like her husband in manners that they might be supposed to have been raised in the same home. A sweeter spirit I never knew.

"It was cold weather when we reached Evanston. Snow was on the ground and chilly breezes swept in from the lake. But we felt that the warmth of hospitality with which we were received fully balanced the cold atmosphere to which we were not accustomed.

"But that cold lake wind was undoubtedly a cause that hastened my father's death. His lungs never were strong, yet had not been pronounced unsound. The colds he took at Evanston seemed to take a stronger hold on him than those which he often had in Ohio.

"The next spring my father bought a half block of land on Forest Avenue and Greenwood Street, and erected a very good house (now owned and occupied by Hon. Andrew Shuman),[108] in which we lived very comfortably till the spring of 1870.

"March 21, while my father was on his tour of Southern conferences, we received a telegram stating that he was very ill at Wheeling, West Va., and wanted mother to come to him at once. We started on the first train but we only got as far as Columbus, Ohio, when a message passed over the wires stating that he had breathed his last at 10 o'clock A. M. that day, the 22d.

"As our attachments were chiefly in Ohio, and as my first mother and two sisters who died in infancy were buried at Delaware, the seat of the Ohio Wesleyan University, where my father had been president for sixteen years, we made the interment there, and shortly thereafter the family removed to Delaware, and it continued to be the home of my mother till her decease in 1876.

"My father's life in Evanston was a quiet one. There never was any ostentation about him. He never pushed himself into prominence. So modest and retiring in manners was he that it seems almost a wonder that he received so much honor. Fortunately he had friends who lifted him and urged him into the best positions, and he always proved himself equal to any emergency.

"Much of his time was spent in study. He had a large library and he loved to give his entire morning to work at his desk and among his books. The volume known as 'The Evidences of Revelation' was prepared at Evanston, and also the two books on oriental travel, 'Our Oriental Missions.'

"He also had much other work on hand which was stopped forever by his death. His plans were so elaborate, and involved so much that was dear to his heart, that it was a great trial to him to die when he did. His ambition was to leave many volumes, but the work was so incipient that no one could complete his plans.

"He was a natural writer. He knew how to popularize science and philosophy, and it is a matter of profound regret that he could not have lived at least ten years longer. To die in the face of such lands of promise seemed a great loss to the church.

"The sermons which he preached while living at Evanston were, I think, always delivered from manuscript. Yet he always spoke with pathos and unction. The people were moved and blessed and elevated. The truth of God glowed with heavenly power.

"The young men who, like myself, were in attendance in the school of theology, will not forget the pure style and lofty eloquence that characterized his discourses. Many whom I have met since, who have now attained prominence in the church, say that Bishop Thomson was their model preacher.

E. THOMSON."

BISHOP HARRIS IN EVANSTON.

Miss Mary Harris' beautiful tribute to her father is given below. It goes to our hearts, for we, too, knew and loved him:

"EVANSTON, ILL., Oct. 26, 1889—*Dear Miss Willard:* As I look back to review our residence in Evanston I find the two years so quiet and uneventful, as far as public interest is concerned, I fear my letter in reply to your note of Oct. 21 will be unsatisfactory. My father was elected to the Episcopacy at the General Conference of 1872, held in Brooklyn. It was not until this time that the Episcopal residences were fixed by the conference, and I well remember the excitement, and shall I say disappointment? when we found we were to leave our eastern home and move to Chicago. It was, however, two years and a half before this change was made. By virtue of General Conference action, it was father's prerogative to revise our church manual, and for this purpose he remained in New York one year after his election. He then made his missionary tour of the globe, sailing from San Francisco June 16, 1873, and landing in New York Oct. 18, 1874. This time our family spent in Europe, returning with him in 1874. My brother had preceded us from Europe and entered the Northwestern University. This was really the attraction that turned our thoughts to Evanston. In the spring of 1876, when father was East attending conferences, we moved into Mr. Eli Gage's house, there, and had been living in our Evanston home six weeks before he ever knew where he was located. When he returned, he planned to surprise us with his coming, and so when he reached Evanston, was obliged to ask the stage driver if he knew where Bishop Harris lived. At that time one carriage step served for the two houses,—Mrs. Brainard's and Mr. Gage's,—so when he had alighted he had to ask, 'Now, which house?'

"In September, Bishop Janes, of New York, died, and at the bishops' meeting in November father changed his episcopal residence back to New York. You see legally his stay here was less than six months in duration. We, as a family, remained here until the spring of 1878, when my brother finished his college course and entered Columbia Law School; then we joined father in New York. I say 'we,' but my only sister was left in Chicago, permanently located, she having married in the winter of 1876 Dr. M. P. Hatfield, a physician of that city.

"Ever since I was a little girl my father's church duties kept him away from home, I might say the greater part of the time. When he was at home it seemed as if he was an honored guest. This absence from home naturally gave all the direction of family affairs to mother, and right royally did she fulfill her mission.

"As a bishop, to quote from Dr. Buckley, 'his most conspicuous qualities were as parliamentarian and administrator. His judgment was sound, his will firm, his decisions prompt. In church law he was without an equal, its study he loved, and both knew its precedents and understood and reasoned independently upon its principles. His Christianity was of the manly type, not less important than that impersonated in the saintly Thomson, the pathetic Simpson, or the intense and self denying Janes. As clearly marked as any of these, Bishop William Logan Harris will stand forth upon the pages of our history as preeminently a genius in ecclesiastical affairs.'

"Father left little manuscript of any kind. As an author he was not widely known. He wrote and had published in 1860, for private circulation, a little volume called 'The Constitutional Powers of the General Conference.' Recently, with Judge Henry of Ohio, he published a volume—'Ecclesiastical Law.'

"Had he lived until September 14, 1887, he would have celebrated the fiftieth anniversary of his admission into the ministry. But the gates opened, and September 2 he whom we loved passed through. Memory, love and hope are left us, for they that are not ignorant concerning them that are fallen asleep in Christ, 'sorrow not as they that have no hope.'
"Sincerely yours,

Mary Harris."

To those Evanstonians who had the privilege of a personal acquaintance with Bishops Thomson and Harris, the above letters, delineating with filial delicacy the grand characteristics of these two men, so prominent in the M. E. church, will seem scarcely to do them justice. And surely these old-time friends can never forget the sincerity of manner, the cordial hospitality and the exalted purposes that animated these missionary bishops.

EDWARD EGGLESTON.

This undoubted genius of a man made a strong impression upon Evanston. Here he rose to fame and from here went to New York city to enter on the broad life work that the world knows. A more genial, humorsome, brotherly nature never helped to make our village luminous. Absent most of the time of his residence, I learned of him most of all through my mother, who was then a Bible class teacher and a regular attendant upon the delightful Sunday-school teachers' meeting during his superintendency of our school. She thought him worthy of the famous compliment, "His stock are God Almighty's gentlemen."

His leaving was a signal loss to Evanston, which always cherishes his name with loving admiration.

My friend, Mrs. Jane Eggleston Zimmerman, the only sister of the "Hoosier Schoolmaster's" originator, herself the author of a book entitled "Gray Heads on Green Shoulders," has written the following:

"EVANSTON, December 4, 1890.—*My Dear Miss Willard:*

"Your request that I prepare some reminiscences of my brother, sets for me a welcome task. To me he has been father, mother, brother, sister, all in one. No one I have ever known has wider or warmer sympathies, and there is, I believe, but one Evanstonian more famous to-day. Edward Eggleston was born in Vevay, Switzerland county, Indiana, December 12, 1837, and is, therefore, almost exactly fifty-three years of age at the present writing. Always exceedingly delicate in health, he never, I believe, finished one whole term of school in his life. His passion for study was so intense, however, that he was always able to enter the more advanced classes of every school he attended, even after the most prolonged absences. He delighted especially in literature and had searched out for himself the beauties of Wordsworth, Coleridge, Shelley, Keats, as well as whatever was worthy of mention in American literature, before he was sixteen. He was always trying to interest us younger children, who found the world of childhood so much more absorbing, in the world of fancy which so fascinated himself.

"Conscience and the religious faculty were dominant traits in his character, and he was an ideal Puritan, although it so happened that no drop of Puritan blood ran in his veins. His puritanism led him such a race, that at one time he almost starved himself to death. This freak prolonged and increased his ill-health to such an extent that at the age of eighteen my mother sent him to Minnesota to try the restorative effect of that wonderful climate. The trip had to be made at that time, 1856, by boat from St. Louis. On the way up he was so ill that many of the passengers urged him to turn back and go home to his friends. 'You won't live two weeks,' said one. 'You are going to Minnesota to find six feet of ground for yourself and that mighty quick,' was the cheerful remark of another.

"He landed at either Hastings or Red Wing, I have forgotten which, and to everybody's surprise, his own most of all, began to improve immediately. He could do nothing like other people, however, and so hired himself to a man to drive oxen in breaking prairie, acting exactly as if he had never seen a thin, red stream issuing from his lips or felt the awful night-sweats of the consumptive for weeks previous. Becoming tired of the delightful occupation of handling a pair of brilliant and versatile oxen, he joined himself to a peripatetic photographer, taking views of the scenery. His choice of occupations proved fortunate, for they kept him in the open air all day long, which I believe is the only possible salvation of the consumptive seeking the Minnesota summer climate.

"In September, for the sake of seeing the country and proving himself an athlete of the first water, this robust youth set out to walk home. He passed through Iowa, looked in on Kansas, whose historic bloody soil had a great attraction for him, and finally reached Chicago a good deal the worse for wear, especially as regarded shoes. Here his money gave out and he found himself too tired to walk any farther. This redoubtable theorist was not above having the blues, and so he had 'em, then and there, sitting in the depot at Chicago—I do not now recall which one. A young man looking like a Kansas settler, which I think he was, got into conversation with him, and making use of the advantage of his own greater stock of common sense, told Edward he was too nearly worn out to walk any farther, and advised him to take the cars for the rest of the journey. 'But I haven't enough money to pay my fare, and I am bound to surprise the folks at home, and I am determined not to send for any,' said my brother. 'Sho! if that's all' replied the Kansas man, 'I'll lend you all you want.' My brother looked at him in astonishment. Unlimited credit on acquaintance of ten minutes! The matter ended by his borrowing ten dollars, which took him to Lafayette, where his step-brothers, the late Colonel Ferrell and Major Ferrell, now of Omaha, were conducting the Lafayette *Journal*. Here he relieved his mind by forwarding the borrowed money to his trusting friend, whom we shall none of us ever forget for his kindness.

"He reached home on a warm afternoon in the early part of

September, bright-eyed, brown-faced, and actually fat! His hair was so long and so thick as to give him a very startling appearance indeed, and within an hour my mother had discreetly taken him into the back yard and cut off as much as was consistent with the then prevailing fashion in hair.

"That winter he began his chosen work, preaching, being then nineteen. He traveled the Lawrenceburg circuit, as junior preacher, holding revival services with great zeal, and I am told 'made a very good stagger at sermon making.' But his health again failed as it was to do after every attempt at preaching he was to make in years to come.

"The next year, 1857, he again went to Minnesota, joined the conference in the fall, and lived there, trying to preach, and as often failing in health, for a period of nine years. In the spring of 1866 he came to Evanston, having become editor of the *Little Corporal*, published by Alfred L. Sewell.

"Here, feeling the need of a kindergarten for his own children, he built a cottage in his own yard and established the first kindergarten of Evanston, which will be well remembered by many Evanston young people who attended it. Miss Lottie Collins, sister of Judge Collins, of Chicago, was its first principal, and Miss Maria Goodsmith, now Mrs. Braidwood, of Chicago, was the assistant teacher. My brother had studied Froebel's methods profoundly, and lacking trained teachers, was obliged to train these young ladies himself. He also translated and arranged many of the German kindergarten songs, there being at that time no book of kindergarten songs and plays accessible. His love of children has always been a ruling passion. While his own were small, he lived with them, a jolly comrade to whom they told all their secrets. He now has for playmates his six grandchildren, who believe 'Bonpa' to be the most delightful companion in the world.

"While in Evanston, he entered heartily into Sunday school work, was superintendent of the First M. E. Sunday school, and teacher of the Bible class, where I recall seeing you as a member. He also had a boys' class, which met at his own house, and whose religious experiences were interspersed with views of Minnesota scenery through a stereoscope, and such other innocent entertainment of the earth earthy, as his slender purse could furnish. He believed heartily in boys, entering into their enjoyments and winning their confidence to a remarkable degree.

"From Evanston he went to New York, to become managing editor of the *Independent*, whose western correspondent he had been for a year or two previous.

"He was, later, editor-in chief of Mr. Orange Judd's *Hearth and*

Home, while that paper was yet in its glory, before Mr. Judd sold it to the *Graphic* company, who ruined it. It was while editing *Hearth and Home* that he wrote 'The Hoosier Schoolmaster,' which immediately achieved a wide popularity as surprising to my brother as to any one else. The story, as it appeared from week to week, was republished in the Vevay, Ind., paper, about which office my brother had nosed a good deal, while a boy, in his intervals of bad health, setting up type, reading proof, and occasionally writing for its columns. One day the editor said to him, 'Ed, we haven't any good poetry on hand. Haven't you got a sister who writes poetry?' My brother guessed he had, and went home to get one of the many 'poems' which I, a mature girl of eleven years, had written. The 'piece' was published, and I was for once in my life famous on as small a capital as any author who ever dipped pen in ink, not even except Martin Farquhar Tupper.

"The young editor who had published my little screed was still editor and proprietor of the *Reveille* (how the untutored American tongues stumbled and fell over that name!) when 'The Hoosier Schoolmaster,' coming out in its very own diggings, lifted his paper into a circulation never before dreamed of. One of the characters, Jeems Phillips, the champion speller, had been drawn from life to a hair and eyelash, name and all. One day the original Jeems Phillips walked into the printing office and began to lay off his coat, preparatory to thrashing the unlucky editor who had published so faithful a portraiture of himself. Only the most vehement denials on the part of the editor of having any knowledge that there was such a person as Mr. Jeems Phillips, saved him from one of the worst thrashings any editor has ever felt.

"For five years, in the early part of the seventies, my brother was pastor of what is now the Lee Avenue Congregational church, but which was at that time au undenominational church, which my brother called the 'Church of Christian Endeavor,' refining the title of 'Bud Means,' 'Church of the Best Licks.' Of later years he has devoted himself to historical research, going abroad twice in order to collect materials for his 'History of Social Life in the Thirteen Colonies,' to be followed, he hopes, by a similar history of the United States. Time, which has whitened his hair and changed materially his religious beliefs, has not marred the beauty of his character or the depth of his love for humanity.

"Very truly yours,
Jane Eggleston Zimmerman."

My mother writes this little reminiscence concerning her old friend and former neighbor:

"My recollections of Edward Eggleston, as our Sabbath school superintendent, at the teachers' meetings, as a neighbor, as a writer and friend, and as a Christian gentleman, are most pleasant and appreciative.

"Mr. Eggleston once said, I remember, in a teachers' meeting, that we should be careful to commend those who did well. He said his own life, he believed, had (when he was young) been repressed for want of timely praise. He said he once overheard some one say that he 'acquired readily,' and thought it must be something bad, as he had never heard anything good said of himself."

FATHER WHEADON.

This genial old saint, who is a sort of Christian Diogenes in respect of bravery, reminds me of some cherished sayings in the discourses of Epictetus. That great philosopher declared in a passage worthy to be graven in gold:

"Difficulties are things that show what men are. For the future, in case of any difficulty, remember that God, like a gymnastic trainer, has pitted you against a rough antagonist. For what end? That you may be an Olympic conqueror; and this cannot be without toil. No man, in my opinion, has a more profitable difficulty on his hands than you have, provided you will but use it as an athletic champion uses his antagonist.

"Suppose we were to send you as a scout to Rome. But no one ever sends a timorous scout, who, when he only hears a noise or sees a shadow, runs back frightened, and says: 'The enemy is at hand.' So now, if you should come and tell us: 'Things are in a terrible way at Rome; death is terrible, calumny terrible, poverty terrible ; run, good people, the enemy is at hand!' We will answer, 'Get you gone and prophesy for yourself.' Our only fault is that we have sent such a scout. Diogenes was sent a scout before you, but he told us other tidings. He says that death is no evil, for it is nothing base; that calumny is only the noise of madmen. And what account did this spy give us of pain, of pleasure, of poverty? He says that to be naked is better than a purple robe; to sleep upon the bare ground the softest bed; and gives a proof of all he says by his own courage, tranquillity and freedom; and, moreover, by a healthy and robust body. 'There is no enemy near,' he says; 'all is profound peace.' How so, Diogenes? 'Look upon me,' he says. 'Am I hurt? Am I wounded? Have I run away from any one?' This is a scout worth having. But you come and tell us one thing after another. Go back and look more carefully and without fear."

Our cheery old local preacher gives us the same ideas, only he talks the United States language in the Methodist dialect thereof. He has fought a good fight and kept the faith for over eighty-five years, and his beaming countenance, almost boyish in its trustfulness, tells us all that the world is a kind place to this kind of a man. Some of us miss him greatly from the prayer-meeting these days since the good people beyond that separatist called "the track" have named a church for him, and he, who is the father of that church, goes there to worship.

On his eightieth birthday an army of his friends visited him at the pleasant home on Hamline Street, rejoicing in the joy of the smiling saint who lingers in the Beulah land to show how heavenly life's sunset hues may grow.

Rev. Edward D. Wheadon, "class leader on DuPage circuit," in 1873, can tell us some curious things concerning the beginnings of Christian worship hereabouts. It seems that the first Home Missionary work of the Methodists was the appointment of Rev. William Royal as a missionary to "the Fox river region," in 1835. During the year he formed a very extensive circuit of twenty-six appointments. " Du Page circuit" first appears in the plan of work for 1837. Its first quarterly conference was held November 11 of that year, in the schoolhouse "at the head of the big woods," wherever that may be. The members then and there pledged $500 for preachers' support and voted to provide "two stoves for their use." Each of the two preachers was to circulate a subscription to secure said stove, and the presiding elder was armed with a third subscription " for the purpose of obtaining aid to build him a log cabin." Brother Wheadon was one of the class leaders on this circuit;—so was our brother Leander Clifford. Rock River conference was organized in 1840, at Mt. Morris, formerly the literary center of Western Methodism, where ex-Governor and Mrs. Beveridge and other well known men and women were educated. The conference sessions were held in a log cabin about twenty feet square. Straw served as a floor, and in recognizing a member Bishop Waugh would facetiously say, "The brother has the straw." Here Rev. Hooper Crews was present, J. F. Mitchell, John Nason, and other familiar names.

WILLIAM DEERING.

William Deering, born in South Paris, Maine, April 25th, 1826, was converted at the age of twelve and united with the Methodist church of his own village. He was educated in the district school, and in several Methodist academies of Maine. He commenced business with the South Paris Manufacturing Company, owning a small woolen mill, saw-mill, etc. At twenty-three years of age he was appointed agent and put in charge of the entire business. In 1861 he removed to Portland, and executed several contracts for army clothing, to the satisfaction of the government authorities. In 1865, in connection with S. M. Milliken, he established the house of Deering, Milliken & Co., Portland. In 1870 he took an interest in the manufacture and sale of grain and grass harvesting machinery with E. H. Gammon of Chicago. In 1873 he removed to Evanston, on account of the impaired health of his partner in Chicago. The business of the firm increased rapidly, and in 1879 he bought out Mr. Gammon's interest. In 1883 he formed a corporation, and admitted his two sons and a nephew to a share of the business. This is the largest enterprise of its class in the country, the sales amounting to several millions of dollars annually, and giving employment to hundreds of working people. The manufacturing headquarters is Deering, in the suburbs of Chicago. Though quiet and unobtrusive in deportment, Mr. Deering is a man of remarkable business skill and energy. For twenty years past he has paid for charitable purposes an average of $15,000 a year. His largest gifts have been to the Northwestern University, of which he is a trustee, as also of the Garrett Biblical Institute, which has shared his benefactions, and of whose board of trustees he is president, as he is also of the Chicago Home Missionary and Church Extension Society; was a lay delegate from the Maine Conference to the General Conference of 1872, and from the Rock River Conference to the General Conference of 1884. In the midst of his numerous engagements he has often served as a teacher in the Sunday-school, and has faithfully responded to the claims of the church upon his money and time. He is a man of decided convictions and broad views, a courteous, intelligent, Christian gentleman.

The beautiful home of Mr. and Mrs. Deering, near the lake,[109] is the seat of a hospitality ample, refined, and ministering to the good and great Christian movements to which they have been so long devoted.

WILLIAM FREDERICK POOLE.

In the long, low building of red brick at North State and Oak Streets which contains the volumes composing the Newberry Library is a sunny room, with windows looking to the south. Its walls, like every other available portion of the building, are lined with books. This is the office of the librarian, Dr. Poole. Here he transacts the business of the library and imparts information on all sorts of subjects to the people who call to explore the treasures of the shelves and are doubtful how to begin the task.

Dr. Poole has devoted his life to the selection and classification of books; he is acknowledged to be a high authority on libraries, and his writings on the subject are quoted throughout the world. As the chief executive officer of the most lavishly-endowed public library in existence, his opportunities for creating a marvelous collection of books are unsurpasssd. Though young, the library is already great in the character of its volumes. At the beginning of the present year it possessed 60,614 books and 23,872 pamphlets. Among the former are a very large number of rare works, many of them in magnificent bindings. The accession of books during the year was 23,242, and of pamphlets 11,610. The purchase of the famous library of Mr. Henry Probasco, of Cincinnati, added greatly to the value of the collection. The library was represented at all the principal book sales of both continents during the year. Among its most valued possessions are eighty-eight early and rare editions of the Bible; the first, second and fourth folios of Shakespeare; ten early editions of Homer, beginning with that of Aldus, 1517; nine editions of Dante, including that of 1477; eight editions of Horace, beginning with Aldus, 1519; eleven editions of Petrarch; many early and extremely rare works relating to the voyages of Columbus, and the colonization and government of America. But the list must be brought to a close, though the Groliers and the other prizes invite further enumeration.

William Frederick Poole, under whose direction this great library is forming, was born in Salem, Mass., Dec. 24, 1821. He is a descendant in the eighth generation of John Poole, one of the first settlers of Massachusetts colony. Dr. Poole received his early education in Danvers, Mass. In 1838 he entered Leicester Academy, where he fitted for college. In 1842 he entered Yale College, but his studies were interrupted at the end of his freshman year because of lack of money. He engaged in teaching and other employment for three years, and then returned to Yale College, from which he was graduated in 1849. During the last term of his sophomore year he became assistant librarian of the Society

PROF. WM. F. JONES,
N. W. Female College.

L. L. GREENLEAF.

EDWARD EGGLESTON.

REV. R. W. PATTERSON.

of Brothers in Unity, which had a library of 10,000 volumes. Here he received his first taste of library administration.

During his junior year he prepared an index to the bound sets of periodicals in the library, which was received with great satisfaction by the students. It was published in 1848, by George P. Putnam, in an octavo volume of 154 pages, with the title, "Index to Periodicals to Which No Indexes Have Been Published." The first edition was soon exhausted and the author thereupon began the preparation of a more extensive work. This was published in 1853, with the title, "Index to Periodical Literature." A third edition of the work was published in 1882, the references being brought down to January of that year. It made a royal octavo volume of 1,469 pages, and was immediately accepted everywhere as a standard work. A fourth edition was published two or three months ago in two large volumes, the references having been brought down to a very recent date.

During his senior year at college Dr. Poole became librarian of Brothers in Unity. In 1851, after his graduation, he became assistant librarian of the Boston Athenaeum. In the following year he was made librarian of the Boston Mercantile Library. During the four years that he remained there he prepared and printed a catalogue of the books under his care. In May 1856, he became librarian of the Boston Athenaeum, which was then the largest library in that city. He remained in that position for thirteen years. In 1869 he adopted the vocation of library expert, and within a few months he organized a number of libraries and also arranged and catalogued the Naval Academy Library at Annapolis, Md. Late in that year he was invited to organize and take charge of the great Cincinnati Public Library. There he remained for four years.

The Chicago Public Library, which grew out of the sympathy felt for the people of this city by the people of England after the great fire, and to which Queen Victoria and many of her most distinguished subjects contributed volumes, was organized by Dr. Poole, who was chosen its librarian in October 1873. He entered upon his duties Jan. 1, 1874. The library opened May 1 with seventeen thousand three hundred and fifty-five volumes. Under his able management it soon grew to be one of the largest in the country and attracted more readers than any other. In August, 1887, he resigned his position to take charge of the Newberry Library, the creation of which had not then begun. With its splendid fund of more than two million dollars he is now bringing into existence a collection of books which is destined to be one of the greatest in the world.

Since taking up his residence in Chicago, Dr. Poole has organized eight or ten large libraries in other cities, selecting and buying the books and arranging all the details of administration, in more than half the instances without visiting the localities. In the United States Bureau of Education's " Report on Public Libraries," issued in 1876, appears a paper by Dr. Poole on "The Organization and Management of Public Libraries," which is the standard authority on the subject. In the last edition of the Encyclopaedia Britannica his many papers on library construction, printed by the Bureau of Education, in the *Library Journal* and the *American Architect,* are accepted as the highest authority. He has written for many publications during the past thirty-five years. In 1874 and 1875 he edited in Chicago a literary monthly called the *Owl,* and for the past ten years he has been a constant contributor to the *Dial* of this city.

From 1885 to 1887 he was president of the American Library Association. In 1877 ne was vice-president of the international conference of librarians in London. He received the degree of LL.D. from the Northwestern University in 1882. He is a member of the American Antiquarian Society and many historical associations. Among his numerous historical works are "Cotton Mather and Salem Witchcraft," "The Popham Colony," "The Ordinance of 1787," "Anti Slavery Opinions Before 1800," and the chapter on "Witchcraft" in the "Memorial History of Boston."

He has published many papers on library and historical topics, including the construction of buildings and the organization and management of public libraries.

REV. ROBERT W. PATTERSON, D. D.

Was born January 21, 1814, in Blount county, Tenn. His ancestors emigrated to America about the middle of the eighteenth century. Shortly after the birth of Robert, his parents, being very strongly opposed to slavery, left Tennessee and came to Illinois, a free state. Mrs. Patterson exerted a strong influence upon all her children by religious instruction and example.

Robert W. Patterson began to attend school at the age of nine; at nineteen he taught school three terms; entered Illinois College, Jacksonville, in 1833, and graduated in 1837. He became a student in Lane Theological Seminary under Professors Dr. layman Beecher, Calvin E. Stowe, Baxter Dickinson and Thomas J. Biggs. In 1838, when the Presbyterian church was divided into the Old and New Schools, he took sides with the latter.

In 1839 he became tutor in Illinois College,[110] and in 1842 accepted a call to become pastor of the Second Presbyterian church, Chicago, which had just been organized. In 1856, when the great national conflict arose about the extension of slavery into the territories, Dr. Patterson was active as to the moral aspects of the question, and when in 1860 Mr. Lincoln was elected, he took the side of the government, and throughout the war preached and prayed for liberty in no uncertain tones.

About 1867 Dr. Patterson became professor of apologetics in the Presbyterian Seminary of the Northwest, which position he held until 1881, when he resigned, and engaged to lecture for three years in Lane Theological Seminary in the department of apologetics. In June, 1867, the twenty-fifth anniversary of the Second Presbyterian church was held, and immediately afterward a furlough was granted to Dr. Patterson to visit Europe, his salary being continued by the church, and his expenses being paid by a friend.

Upon the seventieth anniversary of his birth a notable reception was given Dr. Patterson and his family, by his old church. He is still vigorous and able to perform ministerial work. His interest in the good of the church and public affairs has not abated. In theology Dr. Patterson has always been of the moderate Calvinistic or new school type. In 1873 when charges were preferred against Professor Swing before the Presbytery of Chicago, Dr. Patterson was against the prosecution. He was married in May, 1843, to Miss Julia A. Quigley, of Alton, Ill. They have had eight children, three sons and four daughters. Robert W., Jr., is managing editor of the Chicago *Tribune*. Dr. Patterson and family came to Evanston to reside in 1885.

ORANGE JUDD.

Orange Judd, the famous agricultural editor, was born near Niagara Falls, N. Y., 26 July 1822. He was graduated at Wesleyan University in 1847, and, after teaching until 1850, spent three years in studying analytical and agricultural chemistry at Yale. He became editor of the *American Agriculturist* in 1853, and in 1856 its owner and publisher, continuing as such until 1881, and also holding the place of agricultural editor of the New York *Times* in 1855-63. He was the principal member of the firm of Orange Judd and Company, which made a specialty of publishing agricultural and scientific books, and also published *Hearth and Home*. During 1863 he served with the United States sanitary commission at Gettysburg, and then with the Army of the Potomac from the Rapidan to Petersburg. In 1868-69 he was president of the New

York, Flushing and North Side railroad, and also president of the New York and Flushing railroad. He has taken an active interest in the affairs of Wesleyan University, and edited the first edition of the *Alumni Record*. The Orange Judd Hall of Natural Science, dedicated in 1871, is the result of his munificence, and he held the office of trustee in 1871-81. Mr. Judd has written for the press, notably in his own journals; and originated in 1862 a series of Sunday school lessons for every Sunday in the year, upon which the later Berean and International lessons have been modeled. His has been the hand upon the rocking stone to many and varied movements for the advance of civilization, his vivid and tireless mind being adventurous along new paths. For seven years Mr. Judd and his family have lived in Evanston,[111] himself and son conducting the leading agricultural paper of the Northwest.

WILLIAM S. LORD.

Was born in Sycamore, Ill., Aug. 24, 1863, the child of Doctor Frederic A. and Emily Bull Lord. Doctor Lord was surgeon in the Union army during the war, at the close of which he practiced in Sycamore successfully for two years, removing in 1867 to Chicago, where, just when he was beginning to reap the rewards of faithful, competent devotion to his profession, he died. He left a widow with four children, of whom William, then nine years of age, was eldest. Doctor Lord had accumulated little of this world's goods, and the necessity of the case called for the oldest son to "get to work" almost at once, so that his regular schooling amounted to but little.

Always fond of books and reading, the culture which Mr. Lord has attained is the result of his own efforts, and has been oftentimes at the expense of his strength, as the greater part of his time has been given since that early age to practical business affairs, in which field he has well established himself as partner and manager of one of Evanston's largest mercantile houses.[112]

Mr. Lord came to Evanston in 1886. The intervening five years have found him so busy at business and private literary work and study that he has not had the time for social and public life, he would have enjoyed otherwise.

In 1890 he was made one of the directors of the Evanston Free Public Library, and this spring was elected a member of the school board.

Mr. Lord has issued two small volumes of poetry. The first, "Verses," appeared in 1883, and the second, "Beads of Morning," in 1888. He contributes frequently to various magazines and newspapers.

The severest critic Mr. Lord has had says of his work, "it is promising," and we believe that the modest desire Mr. Lord expresses on the title page of his first volume, will at least be realized.

* * * * * * * *

I would not ask for fruit from all
The flowers of my rhyme;
But I would be o'erjoyed to find,
When come the harvest days,
That time's rude blasts had once been kind
And spared a few for praise.

* * * * * * * *

THE KIRK FAMILY.

Mr. James S. Kirk was born in the city of Glasgow, Scotland, and at a very early age he came with his father to Montreal, Canada. Here he attended school till he was about nineteen years of age. He married in Canada, and removed to Utica, N. Y., where he established his soap business in 1839. In 1859 he removed to Chicago, and took up his residence in Evanston about twenty-four years ago.[113] He died in June of the year 1886. His family consists of seven sons and one daughter, of whom three are residents of Evanston. The sons, James A., John B., Milton W., Wallace F., Charles S., Arthur S., Edgar W., are all connected with the business formerly conducted by their father. His only daughter, Helen, is the wife of Mr. Charles Haskin, of Evanston. Madam Kirk, mother of the family, is still a resident of Evanston during a part of each year, and endowed the Kirk prize in the university.

Mr. James S. Kirk, founder of the house, was a very successful business man. His fortune lay in his energy and perseverance, and a genius for hard work. By his efforts the enterprise grew till it became the largest of its kind in the country, and it has ranked first for a number of years. Mr. John Kirk is a trustee of the university; Mr. Milton Kirk has been president of the village board of trustees.

JAMES S. KIRK.

JAMES S. KIRK, (DECEASED,) CHICAGO, ILL.

By the death of James S. Kirk, the city of Chicago lost one of its most respected citizens, its business community one of its brightest lights, and the cause of education one of its strongest champions.

His father was a shipbuilder and civil engineer of prominence in Glasgow, Scotland, where James was born in 1818.

When a child only six months old, the family moved to Montreal, where his early childhood and earlier manhood days were passed.

After receiving a thorough academic education (graduating from the Montreal Academic Institute) he engaged in the manufacture of soaps, candles and alkali, in Montreal. He next entered the lumber business, and personally superintended the camp in the woods, and the drive down the Ottawa river.

When scarcely twenty-one years of age, he married Miss Nancy Ann Dunning, at Ottawa (then known as Bytown), and removed to the United States, making Utica, New York, his home. He immediately began the manufacture of soap and perfumes, and thus in 1839 founded the house of James S. Kirk & Co., which has become the largest establishment of its kind not only in the United States, but in the world.

In 1859, James S. Kirk and his family removed to Chicago and continued in the soap manufacturing business. With the exception of the disastrous effects of the fire of 1871, the prosperity of the house has been uninterrupted.

For fifty years the stern old churchman (for all his life he was an earnest and consistent Christian) had striven to perfect the business scheme of his life. Success crowned his efforts and he was enabled to pass his declining years in well earned retirement, in a luxurious home in South Evanston.

An undivided family of seven sons, scarcely less tenacious than their persevering father, have since their earlier boyhood been engaged in the business. The four elder sons, James A., John B., Milton W., and Wallace F., are the active and directing members of the firm.

The ground that the manufacturing plant of James S. Kirk & Co. covers is the historical site of the first house ever erected in Chicago. Less than a century has passed since then, and no more fitting comparison can be drawn than the statement that the spot where a solitary hermit made his abode ninety-odd years ago, is covered by a manufacturing plant, that has an output greater than any of its kind in the entire world.

There is a fraternal feeling between the seven surviving sons of

James S. Kirk that is indeed commendable in them all. This respect and love for one another is doubtless due to the kindly training of their esteemed father, who ever nursed this feeling.

The business is still continued under the same name with which it was organized, an uninterrupted period of fifty-two years, and is now one of the very few establishments (if not the only one) in the United States, that have passed through a half century of existence without change of name. It will ever remain a monument to James S. Kirk, to which every member of the Kirk family can point with pride.

The Northwestern University, located in Evanston, that most beautiful of Chicago's suburbs, always found in James S. Kirk a warm champion and firm friend. His family still follow his desire in regard to assisting this worthy educational- institution, and take great and honest pride in aiding, both financially and personally, any deserving and needy cause that will advance the people to a higher degree of education. Mr. Kirk was esteemed as a scholarly gentleman; he was very highly educated, and took great interest in everything pertaining to' higher cultivation.

In summing up the events of his life, it can most truly be stated that there never was a resident of Chicago who was more highly respected and esteemed than James S. Kirk. During the years of his life he was looked upon as a model of honor, and an example of the truly honest business man. He ever endeavored to instill into the minds of his sons the honorable principles that placed him on such an elevated pedestal. That his descendants have treasured his desires and his good precepts, is proven by the universal respect and esteem in which all members of his family are held.

On the fifteenth day of June, 1886, in the bosom of his family he passed peacefully and quietly away from the earth, like one fully confident of meeting in a more sanctified place, those nearest and dearest to him.

BISHOP WILLIAM XAVIER NINDE, D. D.

Born Cortland, N. Y., June 21, 1832; graduated from Wesleyan University, Middletown, Conn., 1855, and after teaching in Rome, N. Y., entered the Methodist ministry in 1856, serving in various pastorates in Ohio. Visited Europe and Palestine 1868-9, and in '70 was transferred to the Detroit Conference. In 1873 he was appointed professor of practical theology in the Biblical Institute at Evanston, Ill., and became president of that institution in 1879. He also served from 1876 until 1879 as pastor of Central M. E. church in Detroit, Mich. He

HOME OF JOHN KIRK.

HOME OF LATE GOV. SHUMAN
(Former Home of Bishop Fester.)

was a delegate to the Methodist Ecumenical Conference in London, in 1881, and in 1884 was elected bishop; visited India 1885-6, when he reorganized the conferences and inspected missions; attended Denmark Conference in 1887. In 1874 he received the degree of D. D. from Wesleyan University.

JOHN B. FINCH.

Was born in Chenango Co., N. Y., March 17, 1852. He was a student from his youth, and seemed to have prepared, whether consciously or not, for his life work. He studied both medicine and law. In 1876 Mr. Finch married Miss Frances E. Manchester, of Cortland, N. Y., who was truly a " helpmeet" for her husband, a woman of individuality and strength. We now see these two going together out into the temperance harvest of their native commonwealth, where, in Buffalo and many other towns and cities, rapidly grew the reputation of this brilliant young orator. In 1877 they went to Nebraska, where Mr. Finch led the " red ribbon" movement, spoke sixty successive nights in the Opera House at Omaha, and in that state won sixty thousand names to the iron-clad pledge. In 1878 he was elected representative from Nebraska to the Right Worthy Grand Lodge, Good Templars. In 1884 he became a resident of Evanston, and was elected the same year "Right Worthy Grand Templar." This position at the head of the Good Templar organization—and also that as chairman of the National Prohibition committee, he retained until his death, which occurred at Lynn, Mass., October 3, 1887.

LORADO TAFT, SCULPTOR.[114]

Was born in Elmwood, Peoria county, Ill., April 29, 1860. He graduated from Illinois State University at Champaign, in 1879. Studied at the *Ecole des beaux arts,* Paris, during 1880-83, and afterward with Marius Jean Antoine Mercié and others.

Since removing to Chicago in 1886, Mr. Taft has received several important commissions, such as the Colfax statue in Indianapolis, that of Lafayette in Lafayette, Ind., the Grant statue at Fort Leavenworth, besides many smaller busts and medallions. He has just completed four figures for the soldiers' monument at Yonkers, N. Y., which probably represent the best work he has done. Mr. Taft has for some years been in charge of the classes in modeling at the Art Institute, Chicago, and is a pleasing speaker, often in demand on the lecture platform; was married October 4, 1890, to Miss Carrie Louise Scales, of Evanston.

SOME FORMER EVANSTONIANS.

The famous young scientist, Prof. James, sends me this at my request:

"*Dear Miss Willard:*—Inclosed, please find a short sketch of Dr. Patten and his work. Another Evanston boy who is destined to make his mark is Mr. Joseph Johnston, at present on the editorial staff of the Chicago *Tribune*—a rare man in very many ways, whom we hope to draw very shortly to Philadelphia. Also Alfred Cook, who has just been appointed Docent in Philosophy in the New Clark University at Worcester, Mass. They were both at Evanston at same time with me. I would not forget, either, the Rev. Henry Frank, of Jamestown, N. Y., who was my chum at Evanston, who was there converted from Judaism, and has become a very prominent figure in certain religious movements in the State of New York.

"Very truly yours,

EDMUND J. JAMES. *University of Pennsylvania.*"

Professor Simon N. Patten was born May 1, 1852, near Sandwich, Ill. He remained at home taking advantage of such facilities for education as a country district school affords until he went to Jennings' Seminary, in Aurora, Ill., where he prepared for college, graduating from the seminary in 1873. He entered the college department of the Northwestern University in the fall of 1874, where he remained for four terms. Having then decided to devote himself to economic and social studies he determined to go to Germany. He chose the University of Halle, where other Evanston boys had studied before him and where he found two former students of Evanston still prosecuting their studies. He remained in Germany about three and one-half years, taking at the end of his course the degrees of A. M. and Ph. D.

On his return to America he entered the law department of the Northwestern University, but ill health compelled him to leave before the completion of his first year. After a period of forced quiet and rest he took up the work of teaching, and for five years taught in the public schools of Illinois and Iowa. In the spring of 1888 he was chosen professor of political economy in the Wharton School of Finance and Economy, the political science department of the University of Pennsylvania in Philadelphia.

Dr. Patten's writings have been few, but weighty. His Doctor thesis, written in German and published in Germany, was entitled, "Taxation in American States and Cities." His *magnum opus* thus far is a work on the "Premises of Political Economy," a work which attracted much attention in Europe as well as America as one of the most original treatises on the subject which has appeared in the last fifty years. An eminent German professor declared it to be the ablest of all the works on that subject produced on this side of the water. His subsequent writings, which have all attracted wide attention in economic circles, are entitled: "The Stability of Prices," "Publications of the American Economic Association, 1888," "The Consumption of Wealth," "Publications of the University of Pennsylvania, 1889," and numerous articles in economic and educational magazines.

Dr. Patten is an original and powerful thinker also in the field of education, and was selected by the American Economic Association to prepare a paper for it on the much mooted question of " Manual Training." He is one of the few American students who can say they lived in Germany for over three years and yet never touched a drop of alcoholic liquors. He is a strong advocate of prohibition and of the woman suffrage movement. His coming to the University of Pennsylvania was hailed with joy by all those interested in these two questions, and in the short time he has been there he has vindicated his claim to be considered a leader in these movements as well as in all questions concerning education. E. J. J.[115]

SOME WOMEN OF EVANSTON.

Evanston is remarkable in nothing if not in the ability, individuality and enterprise of its women. The keynote was early set in opportunity for higher education and later on in co-education itself—the bright consummate flower of a Christian civilization. The absence of saloons and hotel bars reduced to a minimum the separatist conditions between men and women, with which most places are cursed, while the Eclectic and other social clubs, even to our own day, when an elegant club house adorns our principal thoroughfare, included men and women equally in the scope of their provisions. The reflex results of all these and many other circumstances of similar character are manifest in the fact that no institution of like grade, but not co-educational, can show

MRS. E. E. MARCY.
Cor. Sec. Rock River Conf. Home Miss. Soc'y

EMILY HUNTINGTON MILLER.

MARY BANNISTER WILLARD,
Prin. American Home School for Girls,
Berlin, Germany

MRS. I. R. HITT,
Pres. N. W. Branch Woman's Foreign Miss. Soc'y.

so small a percentage as our university, of students who use neither intoxicating liquors nor tobacco; and no village on the continent illustrates more of mutual respect, generous admiration and helpful good will between the brothers and sisters of the human household, than "our ain familiar town."

The witty Congregational pastor, apologizing for some light remarks on woman's ballot, said "He had not been here long enough to learn that it was an article of faith in Evanston." This is hyperbolical, but all the same the woman question is by no means unpopular among us.

I had intended to characterize some of the leaders among women in my series of sketches but time and space have failed. A few chief names, however, must not be overlooked.

In Mrs. Elizabeth Boynton Harbert we have a social and reformatory force of marked beneficence. When she first came her reputation as a devoted woman-suffragist doubtless caused some to think she would not altogether fit into the mosaic of our village, noted then more than now for holding "a calm view" of subjects pending in the congress of public opinion. But Mrs. Harbert had been born and reared in Crawfordsville, Indiana, a most cultivated college town (the home of General Lew Wallace, Maurice Thompson and other literary lights), and proved herself one "to the manner born." She founded the "Pro and Con club," for discussing all phases of the woman movement. I remember that though my mother was averse to having me join, she was herself among the leading members, going alone, after her sturdy, individual manner, and bringing me back most piquant accounts of the good talk they had, in which General and Mrs. Beveridge, Judge and Mrs. Bradwell and other bright people bore a part. A member of the Woman's Congress and of almost every other national movement for the emancipation of women, Mrs. Harbert is at the front in every good word and work, within the church and outside in the beautiful courts of philanthropy. Her attractive home[116] is the center of a hospitality that is intellectual as well as of the heart. For seven years she edited that department in the Chicago *Inter Ocean* known as the "Woman's Kingdom," and by pen and voice she illustrates on a large scale the fact that public spirit, patriotism and reform work are altogether compatible with the utmost success as a wife, a mother and home-maker. Captain Harbert, her husband, is a successful lawyer and one of those brotherly men who rejoice in the higher opportunity and development of woman even more than she does herself,—which is saying a vast deal,—while their children are among the choicest illustrations I have known in proof that to have a strong-minded mother is to begin life on a vantage-ground.

Mrs. Emily Huntington Miller, now happily returned to us from St. Paul, Minn., where her name has become fragrant, is a graduate of Oberlin College and a literary woman in the best sense which includes the rarest home and household qualities. Her stories for the *Little Corporal* laid the foundation of a fame that has grown "like the swell of some sweet tune." For years she and her noble husband, John Miller of blessed memory, conducted that choicest among the pioneer papers for children. Meanwhile she was helping to found the Woman's college and he was superintendent of the M. E. Sunday-school, and one of the best presiding officers it ever had. Then they left us for "the land of the sky-tinted waters," and a few years ago he died. Mrs. Miller kept right on with her Sunday-school and literary work, bringing up her three boys in the nurture and admonition of the Lord. She was secretary of the committee on organizing the National W. C. T. U. in 1874, and has been from that time a prominent Chautauquan, having had charge for years of the women's interests at that great summer camp, as we hope she may continue to do, for under the gentlest womanly exterior she has an intellect of far-reaching liberality and a heart as brave as that of a commodore.

Mrs. Kate Queal, the devoted friend and comrade of Mrs. Miller, is fittingly referred to here. A woman of splendid physique — tall, strong, commanding, and yet gracious; with a face full of blended dignity and sweetness; her presence was a benediction to those whom most people forgot, a solace to the bereft, and carried with it always the warm, vivid sense of a friend in deed as well as word. To the children of Evanston she was a pastor-at-large, and in her own church the ideal worker. Her strong sense of humor and good fellowship added the final charm to a large nature and most unique individuality. Rarely have two been so well mated as Kate and Robert Queal, the loss of whom in the plenitude of their benignant powers is one of the greatest losses that Evanston has suffered.[117]

Mrs. Mary H. B. Hitt, for many years the chief foreign missionary leader among northwestern Methodists, had rare inheritance in a father's and mother's memory that is as ointment poured forth. A chapter of striking interest would that be which recounted the blessed life and work of Rev. and Mrs. Arza Brown Among the remarkable old ladies that have here foreshown the joys of Beulah land, Mrs. Brown, at eighty-two years of age, with her versatile and cultured mind and her old-fashioned Methodist piety, stands conspicuous. Dying in her daughter's home, she left along the mountain tops of death a light that made them lovely. Her gracious daughter, graduating from Cincinnati

Wesleyan college as valedictorian in 1850 (having been a classmate of Mrs. Lucy Webb Hayes),[118] has been the mother of philanthropies as well as of two noble sons, and her husband's large comprehension of woman's work in the world has greatly enlarged her sphere of usefulness. I well remember my first acquaintance with this family—dating from the winter of 1871, when, soon after my return from Europe, I began to make missionary addresses in Chicago and was repeatedly a guest of Mrs. Hitt while we together filled appointments in various M. E. churches of the city. I recall also a Sunday evening in Robert Collyer's church, where, at the time of the Woman's Crusade, we addressed a temperance mass meeting in which the famous Unitarian, and Rev. L. T. Chamberlain of the New England Congregational church united. Mrs. Hitt had just returned from the inspiring scene —her early home having been Ohio—and gave graphic accounts of what she had personally witnessed. I read what Mr. Chamberlain mischievously characterized to a friend as "a school-girl essay," and Robert Collyer passed the hat with many a droll remark as the coin went rattling in. We white ribboners knew that Mrs. Hitt would have made a W. C. T. U. leader, as would Mrs. Queal, to whom I used often to speak about it, and who said she hoped "to help us sometime," but they found their favorite field in the foreign missionary work, and there is no better one.

Mrs. Frank P. Crandon always stands out in clear relief as one of this remarkable trio of "missionary women," and to her business tact and faithfulness the "Northwestern Branch" owes as much as to any other one, for the splendid achievements that have in nineteen years placed four hundred and twenty-five thousand dollars in the treasury and sent out thirty missionaries to the foreign field.

Mrs. Dr. Ridgaway is another of our missionary chiefs, also Mrs. Francis Bradley, for many years treasurer of the Woman's Congregational Board.

Miss Nina G. Lunt[119] is a friend admired and studied by me with ever increasing pleasure since 1862, when, by her invitation and that of Mrs. John L. Scripps, I helped serve at the latter's booth in the great sanitary fair and first saw Generals Grant and Sherman. Miss Lunt's beautiful home on Michigan Avenue was one of the first to which I was ever welcomed in Chicago. There I first met Rev. John H. Vincent, then pastor of what was popularly know as the "pepper box," i.e., the wooden structure named Trinity M. E. church. There in her artistic room called "Penetralia," a "Den" that seemed to me an Eden at the top of the house, a room reflecting her own mental hospitality and rare taste. I met her friend Lizzie Clark (Underhill) one of the most

HOME OF DR. M. C. BRAGDON.

HOME OF L. D. NORTON.
(Site of Former Home of Dr. Evans.)

intellectual of Chicagoans, and later, Mrs. Mary Lowe Dickinson, that regnant woman, so well proportioned in endowments of person, mind and heart, of tongue and pen, who became to me a prized possession of sisterly regard. A brilliant conversationalist, remarkably gifted as a musician, and with literary abilities that would have brought her fame and money, Nina G. Lunt specifically chose as her role in life what may be called aesthetic philanthropy. If the record could be made of her helpfulness in "bringing people out" who had either gift or appreciation of art; of the societies, clubs and movements she has originated in music and literature, of the struggling artists she has befriended, the financial distress she has removed, the friendless ones to whom she has extended that hand so delicate and yet so steadfast, it would be found that "Lady Bountiful" is a name none too gracious to be given this genial lady whose kind deeds have been done "all in silence and with a smile."

SILHOUETTES.

C. G. Ayars is a resident of Evanston, of twenty years' standing. During his earlier life he was engaged in farming, and later held several different county and town offices. Since 1881 he has given his entire attention to the fire insurance business, being now special agent of the Phoenix Insurance Company, of Hartford, Conn.

Harry L. Belden, is a native of Pawtucket, R. I., where he was born twenty-seven years ago. After spending a few years in Philadelphia and other places, Mr. Belden's parents selected Evanston as their home, and here he has received the greater part of his education, graduating from the Evanston high school in 1881. Mr. Belden has been elected township clerk several times, and is at present the youngest person on the village board of trustees.

General John L. Beveridge, was born at Greenwich, N. Y., July 4, 1824; came to Evanston in 1854 and began the practice of law. At the beginning of the Civil War General Beveridge organized a company and in September, 1861, this regiment was mustered into service with him as major; in this capacity he served two years with the army of the Potomac; he then organized the Seventeenth Illinois Cavalry. As colonel of this regiment he entered the department of the Missouri, where for gallant conduct he was brevetted brigadier-general, and served the remainder of the war, after which he resumed the practice of law, but did not long remain in private life, as he was successively chosen sheriff of Cook county, state senator, senator-at-large, lieutenant-governor, and governor of the state of Illinois. In November, 1881, he was appointed assistant treasurer of the United States at Chicago. General Beveridge was married January 20, 1848, to Miss Helen M. Judson, daughter of Rev. Philo Judson, of Chicago.

Professor H. L. Boltwood,[120] principal of Evanston Township high school, is a native of Massachusetts, and graduated from Amherst College in 1853. After teaching eight years, and engaging in business in New York city for a short time, he entered the service of the sanitary commission, being ordained chaplain, but did not serve with the regiment. Later he was superintendent of schools in Griggsville, Ill., and became principal of the high schools at Princeton, Ottawa, and Evanston, Ill., successively, all three of which schools he organized, the one at Princeton, Ill., being the first township high school started in the state. He has risen to prominence in his profession, and is the author of three text-books, an English grammar, a reader, and a history.

L. H. Boutell, was born in Boston, Massachusetts, in 1826. Graduated from Brown University 1844, and from Cambridge Law School 1847. Admitted to the bar 1848, and practiced law in Boston and vicinity until 1863, when he removed to Chicago. Mr. Boutell and his estimable wife (who is a niece of Hon. William M. Evarts) have resided in Evanston since 1865.

M. C. Bragdon, M. D., one of Evanston's popular physicians, was born in Auburn, N. Y., 1850, and removed with his parents to Evanston in 1858.

Dr. Bragdon graduated from Northwestern University in 1870, and from Hahnemann Medical College, Philadelphia, 1873. After studying a short time abroad, he returned to Evanston, since which time he has been most successful in the practice of his chosen profession. Dr. and Mrs. Bragdon have just completed a tour around the world.

A. J. Brown, was born in 1820 in Otsego county, New York; was admitted to the bar in 1842; came to Evanston in 1867; has been a member of the Methodist church nearly fifty years, and was one of the chartered incorporators of the Northwestern University.

D. H. Burnham,[121] who is one of the most prominent architects in this country, was born September 14, 1846, at Henderson, Jefferson county, N. Y. His father, who was a wholesale merchant, moved here in 1855, and died in Chicago fifteen years ago. Mr. Burnham was educated at public and high schools of Chicago, and studied three years in Massachusetts with private tutors entirely. After several years spent in various architects' offices he formed a partnership with Mr. J. H. Root in the spring of 1873 which continued till the death of the latter in January 1891. He was elected chief of construction of the World's Columbian Exposition in October 1890, and at the same time Mr. Root was made consulting architect. Since Mr. Root's death Mr. Burnham has been both architect in chief and chief of construction.

Alonzo Burroughs[122] is one of Evanston's oldest residents, having come to the place in 1844. Most of his life has been spent in farming. He was born in 1820 in Ohio.

H. W. Chester, of the firm of Redington & Chester, Chicago, was born in Bainbridge, Ohio, Dec. 25, 1840. Has been prominently connected with various railroads, and was secretary of the Chicago & Western Indiana railroad until 1882. The present firm of Redington & Chester was organized in 1881, and controls a number of lumber yards in the southwest. Mr. Chester has been a resident of Evanston since 1881.

E. H. Clapp, M.D., was born in 1810 in Martinsburg, N. Y. Graduated from Cincinnati Medical College in 1844 and removed to Evanston in 1874. He was well known in agricultural circles, having held the position of vice-president of the Illinois State Agricultural Society, and also served two terms on the State Board of Equalization.

E. P. Clapp, M. D., one of Evanston's prominent young physicians, was born in Rome, N. Y., 1859; graduated from Northwestern University 1881, and from Hahnemann Medical College, Chicago, in 1882, after which he spent some time in Europe, pursuing special studies at Vienna.

W. P. Cragin, one of Evanston's leading business men, is a native of Rhode Island; is connected with the Cragin Manufacturing Co., Cragin, Ill., and has resided in Evanston since May 1877.

F. P. Crandon, was born in New England, of Puritan parentage. He engaged in teaching for some time after leaving college, and coming to Illinois he held the position of principal of a public school in Kane county, till 1862, in which year he enlisted as a lieutenant of cavalry. He served during the war under Generals Burnside, Hooker, Meade, Butler, and Ord, and was present at the opening of the doors of Libby prison after the evacuation of Richmond. Shortly after, he held the position of superintendent of the bureau of refugees, freedmen, and abandoned lands, for the Fourth district of Virginia. After leaving military service he was elected county clerk of Kane county, Illinois, and in 1873 became tax commissioner of the Chicago & Northwestern Railway company, which position he still occupies. He became a resident of Evanston in 1878, has served several terms as a trustee of the village, is a member of the village board of education, and prominent in Methodist circles.

James Currey, has been a resident of Evanston since 1868; was born near Peekskill, N. Y., in 1814, and spent his boyhood days on a farm.

Mr. Currey has been engaged in the lumber business for many years, and has held various offices of trust in the village of Evanston.

Dr. N. S. Davis, who was for some years a resident of Evanston, and for whom our principal business street is named, is one of the most distinguished physicians in the United States. He was one of the originators of the American Medical Association, and has been twice chosen its president. In consideration of his eminent services a medallion of him was struck a few years ago by this association. He was also elected president of the Ninth International Medical Congress, held in Washington, D. C, in 1887. It was chiefly owing to his efforts that the courses of study in medical colleges were lengthened. Dr. Davis is dean of the Chicago Medical College, and besides many papers, reports, and addresses, he is the author of ten works of importance. He is known throughout Christendom as a physician who for over forty years has not used alcoholics in his far-reaching practice in Chicago, the largest of western cities. As such, Dr. Davis is probably more honored by the temperance people of this country than any other physician, and holds a place analogous to that occupied by Dr. Benjamin Ward Richardson, of London, England.

Simeon L. Farwell, was born in the State of New York, March 22, 1831, and has resided in Evanston since 1876. Mr. Farwell was for many years connected with the firm of John V. Farwell & Company, Chicago. He is well known as a successful business man, and as a generous giver to every good enterprise.

Julian R. Fitch, born September 17, 1837, at Gambier, Knox county, Ohio. He was educated by his father, after which he studied engineering and surveying under A. G. Conover, of the state board of public works; went to Kansas in the summer of 1854, where he was employed in the government surveys until 1856, when he was appointed to West Point by Jefferson Davis, secretary of war under President Pierce. His father not approving of a military career, he again entered the service as a government surveyor. In 1861, on the first call for troops, he enlisted in the Sixth Ohio, and re-enlisted in the Thirty-fifth Ohio; was promoted to lieutenancy, and was present at the battles of Mill Spring, Shiloh, Perryville, Stone River, Chickamauga, Lookout Mountain, and many others; he was brevetted for gallant service in time of battle. After the close of the war, he was sub-assistant commissioner of the Freedman's Bureau in Texas. From 1869 to 1873 was stationed in the Indian country in New Mexico. Located permanently in Evanston in 1873.

Volney W. Foster,[123] is the son of a pioneer settler in Jefferson county, Wisconsin. After leaving school he taught for some time, and then engaged in business in Chicago. Later on he followed the occupation of a lumberman in Canada, and finally went into partnership in Chicago in the firm, Hitchcock & Foster, dealers in railroad ties, etc.

Mr. Foster is a public-spirited man, and has evinced his interest in public affairs in many ways. He is known as the "father of the Sheridan road," as it is chiefly through his efforts that that splendid highway has come to be a fact.

When in school he showed himself to be a very apt student, and has in later years supplemented his mental acquisitions by extensive reading. He is a generous-hearted man, and specially interested in the welfare of young people, as evinced by the organization of the "Back Lot Studies Society," of which he was the originator. This society, which meets in "The Shelter," a pleasant little retreat attached to his tennis court, is composed of about seventy intelligent and industrious boys who listen to lectures from business and professional men and educators on subjects of all kinds. This society was formed last November for the purpose of helping boys who earnestly seek self-improvement, and bids fair to be of immense value to worthy youth of Evanston.

General William Gamble, a resident of Evanston in its early days, was connected with the office of public works in Chicago, previous to the late civil war. On September 18, 1861, he was mustered into service as lieutenant colonel of the Eighth Illinois Cavalry. December 5, 1862, he was promoted as colonel, and commanded this regiment until June, 1863, when he was assigned to the command of First brigade of First division of cavalry corps of the Army of the Potomac, and continued in that command until December, 1863, when the regiment veteranized, and Colonel Gamble returned to Illinois. About February 1, 1864, he returned to Washington with the regiment, its ranks filled with new enlistments, and served in the department of Washington until the close of the war. July 11, 1865, he was brevetted brigadier-general, and on July 17, 1865, was mustered out of service. Later he was appointed major in the regular army, and was assigned to duty in Eighth United States Cavalry, and served in that capacity until his death in 1867.

C. J. Gilbert, one of Evanston's most public spirited citizens, was born at Lima, N. Y., in 1829, and became a resident of Evanston

REST COTTAGE—FRONT VIEW.

REST COTTAGE—REAR VIEW.

REST COTTAGE—THE DEN.

in 1867. Was connected with Chicago board of trade previous to five years ago, since which time he has been engaged in real estate business. Mr. Gilbert was the first president of the village of Evanston, and has served on the village board of trustees thirteen years. He is always active in every public enterprise, and was instrumental in introducing the waterworks in Evanston.

Mark Watroo Harrington was born August 18, 1848, at Sycamore, Ill., prepared for college and passed through the freshman year at Evanston, 1864-65 ; graduated B. A. at Ann Arbor, 1868 ; was assistant in museum and mathematics at Ann Arbor, 1868-70; on the coast survey in Alaska, 1870-71; instructor in the natural sciences at Ann Arbor, 1872-76. He married Miss Rose M. Smith, of Sycamore, and studied in Leipsic with his wife during 1876-77. In China he was professor of astronomy in the cadet school of the Chinese Foreign Office, 1877-78; was driven away by illness. He next became professor in Louisiana State University at Baton Rouge, 1878-79; returned to Ann Arbor as professor of astronomy, in 1879. In May, 1884, he started the American Meteorological Journal, a scientific monthly of which he is still an editor.

C. G. Haskins, was born in Syracuse, N. Y., in 1851. In 1857 the family removed to Evanston, and Mr. Haskins attended the public schools, and the preparatory department of the university. He graduated from Reed's Institute, Geneva, N. Y., in 1868. After engaging in lumber and salt business in Michigan he spent thirteen months abroad visiting Europe, Egypt, and the Holy Land. In 1872 he started a dry goods store in Evanston, and in 1875 became connected with the firm of J. S. Kirk & Co., Chicago. Mr. Haskins is a prominent member of Emmanuel M. E. Church.

Henry B. Hemenway, M. D., born in Montpelier, Vt., December 20, 1856. Graduated from Northwestern University, 1879, and from Chicago Medical College, 1881, after which time he removed to Kalamazoo, Mich., and held various positions of trust in that city. In 1887 he was appointed secretary of the Kalamazoo Board of United States Examining Surgeons, and in 1884 Division Surgeon of Michigan Central Railway, also of the Grand Rapids and Indiana Railway in 1890. In 1886 Dr. Hemenway was elected vice-president, and in 188 7-1890, treasurer of the Michigan State Medical Society, and in 1890 removed to Evanston. He is a frequent contributor to the *Medical News* of Philadelphia, and other medical journals. In 1882 Dr. Hemenway received the degree of A. M. from his *alma mater.*

Alexander Hesler, the veteran photographer of the northwest, became a resident of Evanston in 1871. In 1879 he removed to Chicago where he has since been actively engaged in the practice of his profession. Mr. Hesler was born in Montreal, Canada, July, 1823.

Isaac R. Hitt, was born at Boonsboro, Md., June 2, 1828. He and his gifted wife have been among Evanston's most prominent citizens since 1871. Immediately after their removal to Evanston, Mr. and Mrs. Hitt became actively connected with the work of the Woman's College. Mr. Hitt's services in superintending the erection of the Woman's College building, entitle him to the lasting gratitude of all who had that project at heart: His sacrifices of time, advances of large sums of money from his Own purse when the funds ran low, are among the unwritten sacrifices which go to make up the history of every such enterprise. Mr. Hitt has been actively engaged in real estate business in Chicago since 1860. He was married November, 1857, to Mary Hyde Brown, the only child of Rev. Arza Brown, of Cincinnati, Ohio. Mrs. Hitt is prominently connected with the Woman's Foreign Missionary Society of the M. E. church.

Thomas C. Hoag, was born at Concord, New Hampshire, September 7, 1825, of Quaker parentage, his father being a book publisher in the New Hampshire capital for a number of years. In 1840 Mr. Hoag removed with his parents to Illinois, and in 1845 settled permanently in Chicago, where he engaged in the wholesale and retail grocery business. In 1862 he was elected trustee of the Northwestern University. In 1864 was also made treasurer of the same institution at Evanston, and has been elected to that position each successive year to the present time. In 1870 he was made president of the Lumbermen's Insurance Company of Chicago, and in 1874 Mr. Hoag established a private bank known as the Evanston Bank, in which business he is at present interested. Mr. Hoag was a member of the old Clark Street Methodist Church until he came to Evanston, when he became identified with the first M. E. Church of Evanston as a steward and also its treasurer. In 1851 he was married to Maria L. Bryant, at Canterbury, N. H., and in 1857 Mr. and Mrs. Hoag removed with their family to Evanston, where they still live on the old homestead.[124]

Holmes Hoge, son of Mrs. Jane C. Hoge, who was a prominent resident of Evanston in other days, was born in Allegheny City, Pa. When quite young he removed to Chicago, where he received his education. When the war broke out he enlisted in the Mercantile Battery of Chicago, and served under General Grant and later under General Sherman. After the war he was connected with the Third National Bank of Chicago, then engaged in real estate business for a short time, and finally entered the service of the First National Bank.

George W. Hotchkiss, was born of revolutionary stock at New Haven, Conn., in 1831. From 1851 to 1886 he was a practical lumberman. He was one of the originators of lumber journalism in 1870, and was connected with the principal lumber journals from that time till 1881, when he was secretary of the Lumbermen's Exchange until 1888. He was known generally as the lumber statistician of the country for a number of years. In 1886 he established the *Lumber Trade Journal* of Chicago. Mr. Hotchkiss is the author of a book on lumber inspections, etc., and also of an article in the Encyclopedia Britannica on lumber matters. In February 1891, he assumed charge of the *Evanston Press*.

Hon. Harvey B. Hurd was born in Huntington, Conn., Feb. 14, 1828. After learning type-setting in Bridgeport, Conn., he came west and attended Jubilee College at Robin's Nest, Ill., for a few years, after which he removed to Chicago in 1846 and was admitted to the bar in 1848. Mr. Hurd came to Evanston in 1855. Was a strong abolitionist, and had thrilling experiences in connection with the underground railroad. In 1856-7 he took a prominent part in the Kansas conflict, being secretary of the National Kansas Committee. From 1869 to 1874 Mr. Hurd was occupied in revising and rewriting the statutes of Illinois, which passed the legislature in 1874. Since that time, with one exception, he has edited, after each biennial session of the legislature, an edition of the statutes; he served a term as county commissioner, and has been prominent in promoting the drainage scheme lately adopted for Chicago. Mr. Hurd has been a professor in the law department of Northwestern University since 1862. He was one of the half dozen persons who organized the first Methodist church in Evanston, and is actively connected with the Emmanual Church enterprise.

Lewis Iott was born in the Province of Quebec, Canada, in 1822, and soon after the family removed to New York state. In 1869 Mr. Iott came to Evanston. He was first engaged in the iron trade, then was connected with a large grocery business for about eleven years, and finally became supervisor of agencies and adjuster for the Phoenix Insurance Co. of Hartford, Conn. After serving this company sixteen years he took the same position with the London Assurance Corporation for five years, and for the past six years has been engaged with his son, M. Bates Iott, in local insurance in Evanston and Chicago.

M. Bates Iott, son of Mr. Lewis Iott, was born in Bouquet, N. Y., in 1848. Removed to Evanston in the year 1869. For some years he was engaged in the furniture business in Evanston, and later he was connected with a mercantile house in Chicago for a short time. About five years ago he engaged in insurance business in Chicago and Evanston, which is his occupation at the present time.

S. A. Kean, banker, is a native of Crawford county, Pa., and has resided in Evanston since 1877. He and his wife, daughter of the late Dr. R. M. Hatfield, are well known and honored citizens.

J. H. Kedzie, is a native of Delaware, where he was born in 1815. After pursuing preparatory studies at several institutions he graduated from Oberlin, Ohio, in 1841. After teaching several years and studying law in the meantime, he was admitted to the bar in New York in 1847, and came immediately to Chicago. He has been a resident of Evanston for about thirty years. In 1877 he was a member of the Thirtieth Illinois Legislature. Mr. Kedzie is the author of a book on "Solar Heat, Gravitation, and Sun Spots," which presents a new and striking theory, and has received very favorable comment throughout the country.

Mather D. Kimball, a nephew of Dr. and Mrs. Bannister, is a graduate of the university, and was for many years a resident of Evanston. He is a skilled writer, and his friends believe that as a composer of humorous verse he has few equals. His contributions have appeared in *The Century* and other magazines. Mr. Kimball is genial, versatile, and one of the best men imaginable in his own home as well as out of it. He married Miss Anna Lewis, one of Evanston's favorite vocalists of other years. They now live in Ravenswood, but are most welcome visitors whenever they return to their old home here.

Prof. H. H. Kingsley, has just completed his fifth year as superintendent of the Evanston public schools. He graduated from the University of Michigan in the class of 1881. Taught two years in East

Saginaw, Mich.; one year at Alexandria, Minn., and two years in his *alma mater* before removing to Evanston.

John B. Kirk, is the second son of James S. Kirk, and was born Nov. 8, 1842, in Utica, N. Y. He received his education in his native city, and began mercantile life in his father's business, with which he has since been connected. No little part of the success of the firm of James S. Kirk and Co. is due to the valuable and practical assistance rendered by Mr. J. B. Kirk. In 1859 Mr. Kirk removed to Chicago with the firm, where their business has grown to be the largest of its kind in the world.

Mr. Kirk has held the position of vice-president of the American Exchange National Bank since 1889. He is a member of the executive committee of the Northwestern University, and a trustee of that institution, and is the donor of the prize of one hundred dollars awarded to the successful competitor in the annual oratorical contest held by the senior class.

Marshall M. Kirkman, was born July 10, 1842, on the prairies of central Illinois, far from any town or school; his education was wholly a private one, save three terms at a public school. Mr. Kirkman has been connected with the Chicago & Northwestern Railway since 1856, and his experience as a railroad man has been varied; it has, however, not been so exacting as to prevent him continuing his studies, which he still pursues. He is the author of many books on railway economy. Mr. Kirkman became a resident of Evanston in 1881. He organized the Country Club, and also the Evanston Club.

Oren E. Locke, has been director of the conservatory of music of the Northwestern University since 1877. He was born in Chester, Vt., in 1842, obtained his musical education in Germany, served as director of the department of music of Genesee College, New York, and taught in the Boston Conservatory of Music nearly nine years.

Thomas Lord, was born at Newark, N. J., in 1824. When he was quite young his parents moved to Bridgeport, Conn., where he resided till he came to Chicago in 1857. Mr. Lord has followed the drug business for fifty-two years, and is senior member of the firm of Lord, Owen & Co., of Chicago. He has lived in Evanston for sixteen years, served on the board of trustees two years, and has been an elder in the Presbyterian church for some ten years.

Dr. O. H. Mann, was born in Providence, R. I., in the year 1838. He is a graduate of the University Medical College (allopathic), of New York city, and also of the Chicago Medical College (homoeopathic). For seven years he practiced in La Salle and De Kalb counties, Illinois, and removed to Evanston twenty-four years ago. About fifteen years ago he was on the board of trustees, and served steadily for ten years on the board of health. At the last election he was made president of the village.

David S. McMullen was born in Prince Edward county, Ontario, August 11, 1846. Was educated in the public schools of Picton, and at Victoria College, Cobourg, Ontario. His father, Rev. Daniel McMullen, was one of the pioneers of Methodism in Canada. In 1866, after learning the printer's trade, Mr. McMullen, with several brothers, came to Chicago and engaged in newspaper business, and at one time he was jointly associated with my brother Oliver A. Willard in management and control of the Chicago *Evening Post.* After disposing of his interest in the *Post* he became engaged in banking in southern Illinois; removed to Canada in 1882 with his brothers, and built the Central Ontario railroad. In 1886 they returned to Chicago, and organized the McMullen Woven Wire Fence Co., in which business Mr. McMullen is still engaged. He has resided in Evanston since 1886.

O. H. Merwin was born in 1842; came to Evanston in 1869, and married, in 1871, one of Evanston's most charming daughters, Miss Ella Bannister, daughter of Rev. Henry Bannister, D. D. As leader for many years of the choir of the First M. E. Church, and as a musician generally, he was one of our most helpful citizens. In 1877 he was appointed postmaster, a position he filled most acceptably until 1885. In 1886 Mr. Merwin removed with his family to Detroit, Mich., and returned to Evanston, in 1890.

George W. Muir was born in 1847, in the city of New York; came to Chicago in 1865, and was for seven years cashier and bookkeeper for Samuel S. White. He has been a resident of Evanston since 1871, and opened his present bookstore in 1872.[125]

C. R. Paul was an Evanston boy who had a bent toward journalism, and who is now president of the Illinois State Journal Company, at Springfield, and at the head of the oldest newspaper of continuous publication in the state, having been established in 1831. After his graduation here in 1872, Mr. Paul was engaged as reporter, correspondent and associate editor in Chicago and Springfield; then he was private secretary to Senator Cullom,[126] at Washington, for six years, before coming into his present prominent position.

William B. Phillips, of the firm of Goss & Phillips, Chicago, manufacturers of sash, doors and blinds, has been one of Evanston's prominent business men since 1872. He was born in 1830, in Massachusetts.

Professor Charles Raymond was born November 12, 1833; educated at Wilbraham, Mass., under the instruction of Dr. Raymond, Dr. Marcy and Bishop Warren, and at Wesleyan University under the presidency of Dr. W. A. Smith, and Dr. Joseph Cummings. In 1859 he married Carrie Chamberlin of Pittsfield, Mass., and together they established the Myrtle Bank Young Ladies' Institute at Natchez, Miss. In 1863 they returned north and took the principalship of the Magnolia Hall Institute at Gloucester, Mass. In 1869 he was called to Evanston to take charge of the public school. During this year plans were formed and the foundation laid for the growth and improvement of our school system: The Benson Avenue building was enlarged; school site bought at Dempster Street and also at Noyes Street, and buildings for primary instruction erected thereon; the course of instruction enlarged, and preliminaries for a township high school commenced. At the beginning of the school year 1870, Professor Raymond was made the first superintendent of schools for Evanston, and during the four years under his supervision the school increased from two hundred to six hundred and fifty enrolled pupils, and from four to nine assistants. The plan formed for a township high school was necessarily deferred by the Chicago fire, but this fact has since been gloriously realized. For several years Professor Raymond was principal of the public schools at Wilmette, and for four years principal of the township high school at Princeton, Ill. The Northwestern University recognizing his services to the cause of education, in 1883 conferred on him the honorary degree of Master of Arts.

C. H. Remy is a graduate of the Law College at Indianapolis, also the Louisville Law College; admitted to the bar in 1870. He has resided in Evanston since 1876; has served as trustee of the village and in other responsible positions.

George F. Stone, secretary Chicago board of trade, was born at Newbury, Mass., in 1836. Previous to Mr. Stone's residence in Evanston, he was president of the corn exchange in Boston; he also held various positions of trust in Boston and vicinity. Mr. Stone has been secretary of Chicago board of trade since 1884, and has resided in Evanston fourteen years.

Allen Vane, one of the pioneers of Evanston, was born in Dorchester county, Md., Sept. 25, 1813; came to Evanston in 1855, and was connected with the paint manufacturing business in St. Louis and Chicago for many years, in company with his sons. Mr. and Mrs. Vane are both prominent members of the First M. E. Church, and Mrs. Vane is president of the Woman's Christian Temperance Union in Evanston; she was also corresponding secretary of the Woman's Foreign Missionary Society of the M. E. Church (western branch) for nearly fifteen years.

E. H. Webster, M. D., one of Evanston's leading physicians, was born in Vermont in 1852. Graduated from Chicago Medical College 1877, and became a resident of Evanston in 1879.

Mr. T. K. Webster, was born in Ithaca, N. Y., in 1849. His father was a physician and used his influence against the use of alcoholics in medicine. After completing his education and spending some time in business in his native town, Mr. Webster made a preliminary visit to Chicago in 1859, and finally settled here in 1867. Later he entered the firm of Goebel & Webster, of Evanston, dealers in groceries and drugs, and in 1875 he engaged in manufacturing specialties for flour mills and grain elevators in the city of Chicago. Mr. Webster is president of the township board of trustees, and an active member of the Presbyterian church.

Col. E. S. Weeden was born near Quincy, Ill., July 10th, 1843; served during the late civil war from 1861 to 1866, after which he studied law, but did not long continue in the practice of that profession, owing to injuries sustained while in the service of his country. In April, 1867, Colonel Weeden was married to Miss Almira Wakeman, of Harvard, Ill.

THE NATURAL HISTORY OF EVANSTON. [127]

GEOLOGY.

Evanston lies wholly within the basin of Lake Michigan. It is therefore within the valley of the St. Lawrence river and not in the valley of the Mississippi. The low divide between the two valleys runs a few miles west of the township line.

The solid rock underneath the lake and town is the Niagara limestone. This limestone does not come to the surface within the limits of the town. Above the limestone lies the bowlder clay. The thickness of this clay varies greatly for different places, but beneath the lake it is considerable, for in this clay the tunnels for supplying Chicago with lake water have been excavated. The surface of the clay under the campus of the university is about two feet above the surface of the lake, but it rises both to the west and to the north. On this clay are three ridges of sand and gravel parallel to the shore of the lake. The outer and older ridge lies in the woods beyond the wet prairie. The second lies east of the prairie and is the one on which Ridge Avenue is situated. The third ridge is the one on which are Hinman Avenue and the university campus. The wet prairie is the surface of the bowlder clay covered by a thin deposit of organic matter. Between the second and third ridges there was, when Evanston became a town, a slough, or peat swamp. Also on Judson Avenue, near Greenwood Street, there was a peat bog impassable for a horse until it was drained.

It was the opinion of Mr. Judson that for twenty years previous to the building of the breakwaters, the lake had worn away the shore at the rate of two rods each year. He referred especially to the shore from the institute northward. In 1882 an old Indian cemetery, north of the institute, was washed away. Dr. Axtell, then a student at the institute, secured a skull and presented it to the museum of the university; it is the only relic we have of the people of Ouilmette.[128]

The action of the waters in those days made nice sections of the eastern ridge. A diagram of a section opposite Heck Hall was made in 1883 and is still preserved. On the surface of the clay is a slight soil on which the white cedar arbor vitae had grown. It does not grow in this vicinity. Above this is a layer of gravel, and on this a layer of peat. The peat contains the remains of many plants which now grow in shallow water. The layer contains also the shells of several kinds of fresh-water mollusks which are now common in our small ponds.

Lying on the peat is a layer of sand in which are numerous trunks of oak trees. These are decayed on the outside, but not at the center. This layer exists under the whole village east of the railroad. In 1863, Professor Mark Harrington, of Michigan University, then a student here, took from the bluff opposite the Swedish institute the pelvis of a deer. It was in gravel eight feet below the surface of the ground. A part of it is now in the museum. A fragment of a tusk of a mastodon was found, when the gravel was excavated at the place where the pond now is, near the tank. It was preserved by James R. Milner, then living in Evanston. Is is now in the museum.

The inference from these facts is, that at sometime, perhaps at the close of the glacial epoch, the arbor vitae grew upon the surface of the bowlder clay. Subsequently, the waters flowed over the whole area of the town. They then gradually subsided to their present level. Bars were formed beneath the waters, and shore ridges were formed by blown sand and the action of the waves during the subsidence. The western ridge was first formed, then the middle ridge, and, last of all, the eastern ridge. The formation of this ridge was, geologically, not very long ago. It was in the human period, perhaps in the time of Caesar. The oaks now under Evanston grew upon the bluff north of the village of Winnetka, which was then the shore of the lake. The waves undermined them and they were washed on the bar, in the position in which we now find them, under the village.

BOTANY.

The botany of Evanston is interesting from the presence of several plants which naturally belong on the shore of the ocean. Among these are the beach pea, the little seaside crowfoot—*Ranunculus cymbularia,*— and that pest which "the old inhabitant" will remember, the "bur grass." Before the roads were made the burs were sure to adhere to and penetrate the stockings of any one who went through the sand fields. Its botanic name will be suggestive of early experiences. It is *Cenchrus tribuloides.* The beautiful trefoil—*Ptelea trifoliata*—with its glossy leaf and winged fruit, and the *Rhus aromatica,* or "fragrant sumach," adhere closely to our shore.

ZOOLOGY.

The animals of Evanston are those common to northern Illinois. As late as 1863 the gray and fox squirrels were common upon the college campus. At that time flocks of quails and sometimes a few stray prairie chickens would alight in what are now the thickly settled parts of the village.

The lake shore seems to be a sort of highway for many birds of passage. In the spring and autumn a multitude of small but beautifully marked birds which go under the general name of "warblers," pass through Evanston. Some are in the tops of the tallest trees uttering their pleasant notes. Others seek the low, sunny copses of shrubs. They do not tarry with us. We see them for a few days, and they pass on. Sometimes a storm overtakes them in the spring on heir northward passage, and they come to our houses; they fly against our windows; they seek shelter with desperate earnestness. Many die. When the sun shines again they pass on to the spruce and hemlock forests of the north, where they lay their eggs and rear their young undisturbed by man. The gray fox and the opossum are still sometimes taken. The last wildcat—*Lynx rufus*—which we have heard of being in town was shot in the "big woods" by Addison DeCoudres sometime in the sixties.

UNIVERSITY.

The following is a copy of Section 1, of the act to incorporate the University:

"Be it enacted by the people of the State of Illinois, represented in General Assembly, that Rev. Richard Haney, Rev. Philo Judson, Rev. S. B. Keyes, Rev. A. E. Phelps, and such persons as shall be appointed by the Rock River Annual Conference of the Methodist Episcopal church to succeed them in said office; Revs. Henry Summers, Elihu Springer, David Brooks, Elmore Yocum, and such persons as shall be appointed by the Wisconsin Annual Conference of said church to succeed them; Revs. H. W. Reed, J. J. Stewart, D. N. Smith, and George M. Teas, of Iowa Conference; (Provision was made for four persons, if chosen, from the Michigan Conference, and Northern Indiana and Illinois Conferences of said Church;) the following laymen: Andrew S. Sherman, Grant Goodrich, Andrew J. Brown, John Evans, Orrington Lunt, J. K. Botsford, Joseph Kettlestrings, George F. Foster, Eri Reynolds, John M. Arnold, Absalom Funk, and E. B. Kingsley ; and such persons, citizens of Chicago or its vicinity, as shall be appointed by the board of trustees hereby constituted, to succeed; be and they are hereby created and constituted a body politic, incorporated under the name and style of 'The Trustees of Northwestern University.' "

COPY OF FIRST SUBSCRIPTIONS MADE AND NOW SHOWN IN UNIVERSITY LEDGER.

Orrington Lunt[129]	$5,000
John Evans	$5,000
George F. Foster	$1,000
Clark T. Hinman	$1,000
A.S. Sherman	$1,000
J.K. Botsford	$1,000
Brown & Hurd	$1,000
J.W. Waughop	$600
Forest Brothers & CO.	$500
Grant Goodrich	$500
N.S. Davis	$400
George W. Remy	$400
Abraham Wigglesworth	$400
E.H. Mulford	$400
John Haywood	$400
George W. Reynolds	$400
Eli Gaffield	$200
George C. Cook	$200
George W. Bliss	$200
E. De Wolf	$100
Joseph Kettlestrings	$100
H. Whitbeck	$100
Jeremiah Price	$100
A. Frisbee	$100
William Justice, M. D	$100
J. V. Farwell	$200
E. S. Wadsworth	$200
Total	$20,600

(Amounts payable in one, two, and three years.)

The University Library contains twenty-four thousand one hundred and sixteen volumes, the Institute Library about six thousand, and the Public Library, nine thousand six hundred and seventy-seven.

The gymnasium of the university, when first built, was owned by a stock company composed of students, but was bought by the university about ten years ago and considerably improved. Professor Philip

Greiner, the present instructor, who came here in 1883, has succeeded in reducing the work to a system, and has made the gymnasium a popular resort for the students. Two years ago a prize was offered by Professor Rena A. Michaels, dean of the Woman's College, to the lady student who should make the best record in attendance and proficiency at the gymnasium, and this has increased the interest of the young ladies of the college in athletic exercise.

THE COLLEGE COTTAGE.

Is a home furnished by the Woman's Educational Aid Association for the accommodation of young ladies while pursuing their studies at the university. It has recently been enlarged and supplied with all modern conveniences at a cost of ten thousand dollars. The young ladies are under the immediate care of the dean of the Woman's College, and the matron of the Cottage, Mrs. E. J. Hudson. Board, including all incidentals, is furnished at the rate of $2.75 per week for the whole term, but in addition the young women are required to do the ordinary work of the cottage, which does not usually exceed one hour a day for each. The officers of the Association are Mrs. J. A. Pearsons, president; Mrs. Dr. Cummings, vice-president; Mrs. W. E. Clifford, recording secretary; Mrs. L. D. Norton, corresponding secretary, and Mrs. J. L. Morse, treasurer.

INSTITUTE.

Mr. Orrington Lunt says that others besides Dr. Dempster were influential in securing Mrs. Garrett's money for the Institute. She made her will December 2, 1853, and in that document wanted her money to go for "a theological institute for the Methodist Episcopal church, to be called the Garrett Biblical Institute, and located somewhere in Cook county," she did not say where. Mr. Lunt and his coadjutors here, knowing about the will, decided they would run the risk of a change in the lady's mind, of her possible second marriage, and of any and all possible human events, and build an institute here in Evanston. This they did, and it was a Biblical institute before it received Mrs. Garrett's money. Dr. Dempster came here on his way to Bloomington, where he expected to start his institute, but learning of this will he assisted the men with this one. Then Mrs. Garrett added a codicil the day before her death, confirming her will giving her property to the Garrett Biblical

Institute, chartered by the legislature. Mr. Lunt has an autograph letter of Mrs. Garrett's. She never visited Evanston but once, that was in January 1855, when Garrett Biblical Institute was opened.

THE WITHINGTON SCHOOL.

The very name of Evanston is synonymous with education, but none of its many schools are more popular, and deservedly so, than that established on Maple Avenue, in 1886, by Miss Withington, a most accomplished eastern lady. Two years later Fraulein Neuschaffer became associated with Miss Withington, and together these ladies labored to build up a school of high order, until Miss Withington's death in 1890.

Fraulein Neuschaffer is ably assisted by Mademoiselle Villeré, Miss Margaret West and Miss Sarah Dickenson. Miss Alice Blanchard, one of Evanston's favorite daughters and a graduate of Vassar College, has been added to the corps of teachers for the coming year. The Withington School designs to prepare students for college; it also has a flourishing kindergarten department.[130]

MARY B. WILLARD KINDERGARTEN.[131]

Six years have passed since Mrs. Mary B. Willard brought before the people of Evanston her project for a free Kindergarten. It was generally looked upon as a kindly thought, but thoroughly impracticable. With her accustomed energy, however, she pushed this, as she has many other enterprises, until sufficient means were secured to warrant at least a trial. The ladies of the Woman's Christian Temperance Union assumed the responsibility of its support, in which they have always been generously aided by the residents of our village. February 1, 1889, it became connected with the Chicago Free Kindergarten Association. During the year 1890 the average membership was thirty-five, and the average attendance thirty-two children, which included Germans, Swedes, Norwegians, Danes, Irish, Africans and Americans.

Mrs. Hester E. Walker has ably conducted this work since its beginning, and is peculiarly adapted to the care and culture of children.

***

There are one thousand three hundred and twelve pupils in the public schools of Evanston, and one thousand two hundred and seventy-two connected with the university and preparatory school.

There are twelve buildings used for educational purposes in Evanston.

The lady principals of the public schools are: Haven School, Lulu C. Robertson; Wesley Avenue School, Jessie I. Luther; Hinman Avenue School, Nannie M. Hines.

The lady teachers of the high school are: Eva S. Edwards, Mary L. Barrie, Jane H. White, Mary T. Culver and Mary L. Childs.

The board of education is composed of the following gentlemen: H. H. C. Miller, president; F. P. Crandon, W. S. Lord, George S. Baker. George S. Lord, Robert Hill and A. C. Buell.

There are eighty-four teachers and professors resident in Evanston.

OUR NEWSPAPERS.

Our first paper was *The Suburban Idea*, edited by that brilliant journalist and lecturer, Professor Nathan Sheppard, author of "Before an Audience." Professor Sheppard supplied the Baptist pulpit for a few months; he was also professor of English Literature in the Chicago University. He died instantly as he was entering the New York post office in the year 1888.

The *Index*, our oldest paper that survived, was founded by Mr. Alfred Sewell about twenty years ago. A number of years since Mr. Sewell sold the paper to its present editor and proprietor, Mr. John A. Childs, who is also postmaster of Evanston.

The *Herald* was the name of a paper published for a few months in the year 1874.

The Evanston *Citizen* was founded by Mr. William Duffell, Jr., the first issue being November 3, 1882, but the paper was discontinued at the beginning of 1891.

The Evanston *Press*, one of the two leading papers of the village, was founded in 1889 by two university students, Mr. R. L. Shuman, and Mr. R. C. Vandercook.

The university papers are the *Northwestern*, which is now completing its eleventh year, and the *Northwestern World*, which was started last fall. The high school boys publish a sheet called the *Boys' Herald*, which was started on its career a few months ago. A paper called the *Lyceum* is edited by Mr. J. D. Corrothers, a preparatory student.

AUTHORS AND JOURNALISTS.

The following is a list of the authors and journalists of Evanston and their works:

Dr. Francis D. Hemenway, author of a Commentary on Isaiah.

Dr. Henry Bannister, author of a Commentary on Jeremiah. Dr. Jewell wrote many magazine and newspaper articles.

Rev. Dr. D. P. Kidder was official editor of Sunday school publications for the Methodist church, edited the Sunday-School Advocate and compiled and edited over eight hundred books for Sunday-school libraries. He is the author of a translation from the Portuguese, entitled, "The Demonstration of the Necessity of Abolishing a Constrained Clerical Celibacy," " Mormonism and the Mormons," "Brazil and the Brazilians," "Sketches of Residence and Travel in Brazil," "Helps to Prayer," and his " Homiletics" has a national reputation.

Dr. Miner Raymond is the author of "Systematic Theology."

Dr. H. B. Ridgaway has written the "Life of Alfred Cookman," "Life of Bishop Janes," and "The Lord's Land."

Dr. Milton S. Terry's great work is "Biblical Hermeneutics," and he has written numerous articles for the *Methodist Review*. He is also the author of "Swedenborgianism," "Man's Antiquity and Language," besides a number of commentaries.

Dr. C. W. Bennett is the author of "Christian Archaeology."

Dr. Chas. F. Bradley has written, "The Life and Letters of Francis D. Hemenway."

Dr. Joseph Cummings edited an edition of "Butler's Analogy."

Dr. H. F. Fisk is part author of "Rhetoric made Racy."

Prof. Rob't L. Cumnock's chief work is "Cumnock's Choice Readings."

Prof. Rena A. Michaels has published French translations, and is a frequent contributor to leading magazines and newspapers.

Mrs. S. M. I. Henry is the author of numerous articles and poems, and the following books: "After the Truth," "Voice of the Home," "Mabel's Work," "One More Chain," and "Beforehand."

Mrs. Emaline L,. Harvey has written several serial stories: "My Sister Nina," "Pen Pictures in the Glow of the Wine Glass," "A True Story," and "Ingleside."

Prof. William Jones wrote "The Myth of Stone Idol."

Mrs. Emily Huntington Miller has written numerous stories for children, among which are, "What Tommy did," "Royal Road to Fortune," "Thorn Apples," "Summer Days at Kirkwood," "The Bear's Den," "A Year at

Riverside Farm," "Uncle Dick's Legacy," and " Fighting the Enemy."[132]
Mr. M. M. Kirkman has issued several works on topics of interest to railroad men, among which are "Baggage, Parcel, and Mail Traffic of Railroads," "Handbook of Railway Expenditures," "How to Collect Railway Revenues," and "Railway Expenditure, " in two volumes.
Prof. W. S. B. Matthews is the author of a book on " How to Understand Music."
Mr. W. S. Lord has issued a volume of poems entitled " Beads of Morning."
Mr. F. M. Elliott has written the history of the local chapter of the Sigma Chi fraternity, under the title of " Omega."
Judge Harvey B. Hurd is the author of "Hurd's Revised Statutes of Illinois."
Mr. J. H. Kedzie has written a book on "Solar Heat, Gravitation, and Sun Spots."
Miss Mary Ninde wrote "We Two Alone in Europe."
Mr. Francis Gellatly is the author of plays entitled "Love Made to Order," and "Necklace of Liberty."
Rev. Arthur W. Little is the author of "Reasons for being a Churchman."
Mr. Walter Lee Brown has written a "Manual of Assaying."
Prof. James T. Hatfield is the author of "Elements of Sanskrit Grammar."
Mrs. Jane Eggleston Zimmerman wrote a serial entitled "Gray Heads on Green Shoulders."
Mr. Albertson made a collection of extracts from great preachers, entitled "Gems of Truth and Beauty."
Prof. Nathan Sheppard was the author of " Before an Audience," and for some time edited a paper entitled *The Suburban Idea*.
Mr. Alfred Sewell was founder and editor for years of the *Index*.
Rev. Edward Eggleston's most famous book is "The Hoosier Schoolmaster." He is the author of several other well known works. Mr. Eggleston was at one time editor in chief of Orange Judd's *Hearth and Home*, after which he became connected with the New York *Independent*.
Hon. Andrew Shuman was for three years editor of the Syracuse, N. Y., *Daily Journal*, and was afterwards for many years connected with the Chicago *Evening Journal*. He is also the author of a story entitled "The Loves of a Lawyer."
Mr. Andre Matteson has been for over thirty years connected with the Chicago *Times*. He is also publisher of a monthly magazine, called *The Law*.
Miss Anna Gordon is author of "Marching Songs," "Questions Answered," "White Ribbon Birthday Book," and "Colloquies for

Children's Evening Entertainments."

Mr. John B. Finch issued a volume of temperance lectures entitled " The People vs. the Liquor Traffic."

Mrs. John B. Finch is chief author of "The Life and Works of John B. Finch."

Dr. E. O. Haven wrote "Haven's Rhetoric," and "Haven's Mental Philosophy."

Prof. C. W. Pearson is the author of numerous essays and poems.

Dr. William Poole's great work is "Poole's Index to Periodical Literature." He also wrote an extended introduction to "Wonder-Working Providence of Sion's Saviour in New England," which was originally printed in 1654. Among his other works are "The Popham Colony," "Cotton Mather and Salem Witchcraft," "Gov. Hutchinson on Salem Witchcraft," "Anti-Slavery Opinions before 1800," "The Ordinance of 1787, its Origin and History." He is a constant contributor to the *Dial*, and has written several articles for the *North American Review*.

Professor H. L. Boltwood is the author of "Boltwood's Topical Outlines of General History," "English Grammar," "Institute, Grammar, and High School Reader."

Mr. Colin Shackelford is a writer for the Chicago *News*.

Mrs. Elizabeth Boynton Harbert was for many years editor of the "Woman's Kingdom" in the Chicago *Inter Ocean*, and is a frequent contributor to leading papers.

Mr. Orange Judd edited the *Prairie Farmer*, and is now editor of the *Orange Judd Farmer*.

Mrs. Mary B. Willard at one time edited the *Union Signal*.

Miss Mary McDowell is the author of a book entitled "A Young Woman's Notion."

Mrs. C. B. Buell is the author of "A Helping Hand," a W. C. T. U. manual.

Mr. James C. Ambrose was long connected with the Chicago *Post*, and at present contributes to the New York *Independent, Our Day*, and the *Northwestern Christian Advocate*.

Miss Mary Henry formerly issued the W. C. T. U. *Bulletin*, and afterward became assistant editor of the *Chautauquan*.

Rev. C. H. Zimmerman is a well known writer for the religious press.

Rev. Henry Laurens Hammond is the author of "New Stories from an Old Book," "The Valley of Pearls," "Memoir of Deacon Philo Carpenter," and other books.

Miss Julia A. Ames is one of the editors of *The Union Signal*, national organ of the Woman's Christian Temperance Union.

Mr. Alanson Appleton is editor of *In The Swim*, Chicago.

Mr. H. Ten Eycke White is managing editor of the Chicago *Evening News*. John M. Dandy, a graduate of the university and son of Rev. Dr. Dandy, once pastor of the M. E. church, is editor of the *Saturday Evening Herald*, Chicago.

Mr. Arthur Henry is author of a book entitled "Nicholas Blood."

Dr. George C. Noyes was for a long time the western correspondent for the New York *Evangelist*.

Mrs. Mary C. Van Benschoten has written for the Chicago *Tribune*, *Inter Ocean*, and *Times*, and was correspondent for the Brooklyn *Argus*. She is also editor of the *Record and Appeal*, organ of the Illinois Industrial School for Girls.

Bishops Foster, Simpson, Thompson, Harris and Fowler, have all lived in Evanston, and have written books.

THE POST OFFICE.

Mr. John A. Childs is postmaster, Mr. George A. Bogart, chief clerk, Miss Bessie Stewart, money-order clerk, Miss Katharine Schaefer, general delivery clerk, and Mr. Nathan Branch, special delivery messenger. The following are letter carriers: W. C. Dorband, James Cunningham, J. A. McDonough, A. H. Hallstrom, J. J. Lutz, H. R. Gibbard, and Asa Carson, substitute. Free delivery service was established in 1887, and in 1890 the post office at North Evanston was discontinued, being now supplied by this service. Five authorized stamp agencies have been established in various parts of the village. The following is a statement of the free delivery operations for the year ending June 30, 1891, and these figures represent about five-sixths of the entire mail received, and one-half the mail dispatched, the remainder being delivered and deposited at the office:

Registered letters delivered, 190
Letters delivered, 649,572
Postal cards delivered, 103,609
Second, third, and fourth-class matter delivered, 475,742
Local letters collected, 26,840
Mail letters collected, 187,263
Local postal cards collected, 12,262
Mail postal cards collected, 22,980
Second, third, and fourth-class matter collected, 18,159
Total number of pieces handled, 1,497,617

Total postage on all local matter collected by carriers, and on all local matter deposited in the office, including second, third, and fourth-class matter, $3,159.96

The following is a statement of the finances of the post office for a year: Receipts, $20,658.29; Expenditures, $11,141,53; Deposits, $9,516.76.

THE BUSINESS MEN'S ASSOCIATION.

This corporation was founded in the summer of the year 1889. "Mutual interest and social intercourse" are declared to be the objects of the association. There is no question about the good results already accomplished. Competition of trade has a narrowing influence. It begets, especially in small towns, rivalries and jealousies which are overcome by a better acquaintance among business men. The fact is often lost sight of that all business men in any town have mutual interests as well as individual interests. Through the able management of Mr. Wm. Stacy, the Business Men's Association has been a power for good. The free kindergarten and other institutions which depend largely upon voluntary contributions for support, can testify to the liberality of the association.

The present officers are: President, William Stacy, vice-president, William E. Suhr, secretary, George Kearney, treasurer, Isaac Wilson.

The board of directors is composed of D. F. Reed, George Iredale, Theodore Price, T. T. Hallinger, Charles Roberts.

The standing committees on Railroads and Transportation, Arbitration, Business Interests, Amusements, Grievances, By-laws, Public Improvements, will show how much ground the work of the association covers. A pleasant feature of the regular monthly meetings during the winter is the series of papers. Such subjects as Education, The Credit System, Business, etc., were discussed during the last year in an able manner by the members of the association.

THE CITIZENS' LEAGUE.[133]

The Citizens' League was organized in Evanston nearly ten years ago for the purpose of enforcing the law regarding sale of intoxicants within four miles of Northwestern University. Dr. D. R. Dyche has been its efficient president, to whom the citizens of Evanston owe a lasting debt of gratitude.

Y. M. C. A.

The Y. M. C. A. of Evanston was organized in 1885, with Mr. M. P. Aiken as president. Mr. C. B. Congdon is now president, and Mr. F. D. Fagg general secretary. Successful work is carried on in Bible classes, religious meetings, and sociables for the members. The Junior Department is very strong, numbering one hundred and thirty-seven boys. The total present membership, including this department, is four hundred and fifty-seven. A movement is on foot to secure a lot for a suitable building. The regular annual membership fee is five dollars fee for students three dollars and for juniors three dollars.

G. A. R.[134]

The G. A. R. Post of Evanston, which is number five hundred and forty, was organized October 1885, by Commander E. R. Lewis. It received its charter as Gamble Post, October 23, 1885, and its first officers were: Commander, E. R. Lewis; Senior Vice-Commander, Thos. Bladder; Junior Vice-Commander, N. Morper; Officer of the Day, W. H. Langton; Officer of the Guard, E. H. Blush; Quartermaster, F. P. Kappleman; Surgeon, Dr. Isaac Poole; Adjutant, Thos. J. Noyes; Chaplain, James Huse. Upon the death of General John A. Logan, the Evanston Pest changed its name to the John A. Logan Post. The present Commander is H. W. Chester. The Post has a membership at the present time of one hundred and twelve, and is in a flourishing condition. It has Building Loan Association stock amounting to two thousand dollars, and property amounting to about five hundred dollars, and a fund is also being raised for the erection of a soldiers' monument in this town.

THE LIGHTHOUSE

Is situated at Grosse Point, which, on account of shallow water, is one of the most dangerous places on the lakes. The light is the largest in the district, and is a fixed white light varied by red flashes every three minutes. It is one hundred and nineteen and one-half feet above the sea level, and the tower is ninety feet high from base of structure to the lantern. It was built in 1873. In connection there are two first-class steam sirens, giving a blast seven seconds long every minute and a half. Mrs. E. J. Moore has been keeper for the past three years.

THE LIFE SAVING STATION.

In 1876 the University donated a piece of ground for the founding of the Life Saving Station, this being a particularly dangerous coast. The crew has always been composed of students, but the station is under control of the government. Since 1880, Captain L. O. Lawson has been at the head, and he has now a force of six men. During the past eleven years there have been thirty-seven vessels assisted and two hundred and two lives saved. Last fall, according to a general provision made by act of Congress, each of the crew was awarded a gold medal for heroic service rendered October 23, 1889, by which twenty-seven lives were saved. For some years prior to this, however, a lifeboat, duly manned, was kept in readiness for service. It was obtained from government officials through the efforts of the class of '72, and the following members of that class constituted the original crew: L. C. Collins, Jr., George Lunt, George Bragdon, Eltinge Elmore, Edward Harrison and Mather D. Kimball. The need of life-saving appliances was. felt long before this, notably when the ill-fated Lady Elgin was wrecked off the Evanston coast. The following, furnished by Mr. John Pearsons, is not out of place here, as matter of history:

> "On the morning of September 8, 1860, the Lady Elgin, a large lake steamer, took the Highland Guards on au excursion from Milwaukee to Chicago, going home that night. There was dancing, and they were carrying on in high glee. Along between two and three o'clock in the morning a vessel ran into them—I believe they never knew what vessel it was—and the Lady Elgin went to pieces about ten miles north of us. The bodies that floated were washed ashore near Grosse Point, about two miles above here. People were up there watching them come ashore. One of the students, Edward Spencer, a brother of Dr. Spencer of the Church Extension Board, had a rope tied around him, and going into the water he helped people ashore, and rescued a great many. They had a lot of cattle on board, and they were drowned, and lay on the shore for days. There were said to have been between three and four hundred people lost. I know I helped to pick up the bodies on the beach for a number of weeks afterwards. George N. Huntoon was justice of the peace, and he acted as coronor. The next Sunday a train came from Milwaukee with friends of the people that were lost, who took what they could home, and as the bodies were found and identified, they were

sent to Milwaukee. I have a fragment of the Lady Elgin in my house— a piece of mahogany — used as a threshold. Most of the older settlers have some such memento of that great catastrophe.

"Another vessel went ashore, by the name of Johnson, opposite the university building. The crew were saved, but the boat went to pieces. That was several years after the wreck of the Lady Elgin. The vessel came ashore about a mile below here, opposite South Evanston, in the fall of the year. The masts were gone, and the five men on board the vessels were nearly frozen. Rev. J. C. Hartzell, now a noted man in our church, took a rope to the vessel and helped the men off. The inhabitants built up fires on the shore, took blankets down to warm them, gave them provisions, and saved the lives of all but one. This J. C. Hartzell was then a student here; he is now a D. D., and secretary of the Freedman's Aid Society."

THE FIRST GRAVE AT ROSEHILL CEMETERY.

Madam Bragdon contributes this paragraph of sad interest: "I recall that Sabbath morning, July 10, 1859, when Dr. Bannister was preaching for my husband, and word came, 'Dr. Ludlam is dying.' That night he entered into his rest. We were all in tears. His grave was the first in Rosehill; he was laid in the cemetery only a few weeks before its dedication— alone. Now how full it is! More are there than remain, of our dear ones."

***

The oldest person in Evanston, Mrs. Judith W. Burroughs, was born February 14, 1799, at Ackworth, N. H. Her maiden name was Judith W. Stevens.

The first charter for a railroad through Evanston was issued to the company to be known as the Illinois Parallel Railroad Company, in 1851, and it was amended in 1853, when the name was changed to the Chicago & Milwaukee Railway Company. In 1855 the road was built to the State line, where it was met by the Green Bay, Milwaukee & Chicago Railroad, which was chartered by the State of Wisconsin. These two roads united and formed the Chicago & Northwestern Railway in 1855, with the following officers: W. S. Gurney, President; A. S. Downs, Secretary; H. A. Tucker, Treasurer; H. W. Blodgett, Attorney.

There are thirty-five passenger trains daily each way on the Chicago & Northwestern Railway between Evanston and Chicago, and eighteen trains daily each way on the Chicago, Milwaukee & St. Paul Railway.

The value of the real estate in the village of Evanston at the present time, as given by Mr. Joseph Lyons, is in round numbers ten million dollars.

Mrs. Beveridge tells this anecdote of early days:

"A young student who boarded at our house as a member of our family, was passing down to Chicago on one of the first trains that ran after the railroad was built, and near him sat an Englishman and a returned Californian,—the Englishman a very pompous personage, and the Californian seeming to have known something of this country before. The foreigner noticed a large building out towards the lake, and turning to the student, said:

"'What town is that?'

" 'Heavingstown.'

"'What building is that?'

"'A lunatic asylum. It has been furnished by Dr. Heavings, a very benevolent physician of Chicago, for his own private patients.'

"After that the students, instead of being called 'bibs,' as they are now, to distinguish them from college students, became 'lunatics,' and continued to be known by that appellation for a long time."

SOUTH EVANSTON.

South Evanston is a beautiful little town about one mile south of Evanston. It was founded by Gen. Julius White, who bought the Muno farm in 1866, and Mr. Colin Shackelford, who removed from Evanston, was the first settler. General White was financial agent of the Travelers' Insurance Company for many years, and but a few hours before his death last year the news came to him that he had been elected as commander of the Illinois Legion of Honor.

South Evanston has about three thousand inhabitants. Waterworks have been established, the village is lighted by electricity, and nearly two hundred thousand dollars worth of street improvements are being carried on at the present time.

There are four churches: the Presbyterian, of which Rev. William Smith is pastor; the Methodist, pastor, Rev. W. H. Holmes; Episcopalian, pastor, Rev. Daniel Smith, and the Roman Catholic, pastor, Rev. Father Greenebaum. There are two public schools, at the head of which is Professor Scudder.

The Illinois Industrial School for Girls at South Evanston[135] was organized in 1877, as the outgrowth of the Women's Centennial Association of Illinois, the surplus funds of the latter organization being used for the benefit of destitute girls. Mrs. General Beveridge, who was one of its most active promoters, was the first president, holding that office about ten years in all. Mrs. Gen. R. M. Wallace is now chief officer. In 1879 a bill passed the Illinois legislature securing legal protection for the institution. Though girls are received on recommendation from all parts of the State, the school is not a State organization, being maintained by private charity. Each county, however, pays ten dollars a month toward the support of each girl it sends to the school. There are about one hundred and fifteen girls at present in the school. Permanent buildings are to be erected at Park Ridge on property that has been secured for the purpose.

BOOKS
BY
MISS FRANCES E. WILLARD.

Glimpses of Fifty Years,
AN AUTOBIOGRAPHY.
INDIVIDUALITY IS IMPRESSED UPON EVERY PAGE.
EXCELLENT PAPER. FINE WORKMANSHIP. ELEGANT BINDING.
PRICE: Cloth, $2.75; Half Morocco, Gilt Edge on Top, $3.50; Full Morocco, Full Gilt, $4.25; Presentation Edition, $10.00.

Woman and Temperance,
An account of the temperance reform and some of its leading spirits.
REDUCED PRICE, - - $1.50.

Nineteen Beautiful Years,
A biography of her sister, Mary. Very touching and beautiful, with extracts from her diary.
PRICE, CLOTH, - - - 75 Cents.

How to Win,
An excellent book for young people, showing conditions upon which success is based.
PRICE, MUSLIN, - - - - $1.00.

Woman in the Pulpit,
A strong argument in favor of the ordination of women.
PRICE, CLOTH, - - - - $1.00.

SEND ALL ORDERS TO
WOMAN'S TEMPERANCE PUBLISHING ASSOCIATION
161 LA SALLE STREET, CHICAGO, ILL.

NOTES

1   After merging with two other institutions, the Chicago Training School and the Evangelical Theological Seminary, the Garrett Biblical Institute is now known as the Garrett–Evangelical Theological Seminary.

2   Reed lived on Ridge Avenue at Lee Street in South Evanston. *The Evanston and Wilmette Directory, 1890.* Evanston: University Press Publishers, 1890, 256.

3   South Evanston would not merge with Evanston until 1892, the year after the publication of this book. At one point, another "Evanston" existed; the village of North Evanston, which merged with Evanston in 1874.

4   In 1892, Woman's College was renamed "Woman's Hall," following the college's complete merger into the university proper. Ironically, in 1901, the name was changed again to "Willard Hall," in honor of Frances Willard.

5   Daniel Fayerweather, of Brooklyn, N. Y. [F.E.W.]

6   Augustus Garrett served as the seventh mayor of Chicago, elected in 1843. After he passed away in 1848, his widow, Elizabeth Garrett bequeathed much of his large estate to the Garrett Biblical Institute. *Politics and Politicians of Chicago, Cook Country and Illinois: A Complete Record of Municipal, County, State and National Politics From the Earliest Period to the Present Time.* Compiled by Fremont O. Bennett. Chicago: The Blakely Printing Co., 1886: 56.

7   Barbara Heck (1734 – 1804) was an early Methodist and an immigrant from Ireland. She settled in New York State and played a central role in the development of the religion in the United States.

8   Known for his support of the arts and culture, Gaius Maecenas was an advisor to Caesar Augustus, the first Roman Emperor.

9   Ridge Avenue and Greenleaf Street.

10   Benjamin F. Hill (1830-1905) was six years old when he arrived in Grosse Point with his father, Arunah Hill, mother, and seven brothers and sisters. The Hill family settled on Ridge Avenue, in a cabin built by Major Mulford. *Transactions of the Illinois State Historical Society for the Year 1908,* Springfield, IL: Illinois State Journal Co. State Printers, 1908.

11   Lake and Sheridan.

12   Judson's home was on Ridge Avenue and Davis Street. The 1890 directory lists Hill's residence at 35 Forest Ave. His business address was 410 Davis Street.

13   Northeast corner of Chicago Avenue and Davis Street.
14   209 Church Street.
15   806 Sheridan Road.
16   The first building of the Garrett Biblical Institute, completed in 1855, and later named "Dempster Hall." Robert Dickenson Sheppard and Harvey Bostwick Hurd, eds. *History of Northwestern University and Evanston*. Chicago: Munsell Publishing, 1906, 342.
17   Northeast corner of Davis Street and Orrington.
18   The following are the sums of $100 and over. Orrington Lunt, $300. Grant Goodrich, $100. Geo. H. Bliss, $100. John Evans, $300. Philo Judson, $100. A. S. Sherman, $100. Daniel P. Kidder, $300. J. K. Botsford, $100. L. L. Hamline, $100. A. J. Brown, $100. F. H. Benson, $100. [F.E.W.]
19   Now adjunct professor. [F.E.W.]
20   Frances Willard's brother Oliver Willard (1834-1878) married Mary Bannister Willard in 1862.
21   For the foregoing I am Indebted to Rev. C. F. Bradley. [F.E.W.]
22   The same property was bought by Mr. Lunt and Dr. Evans about five years afterward for thirty-two thousand dollars. [F.E.W.]
23   At Clark, Quincy, LaSalle, and Jackson. The hotel was built in 1873. William R. Host and Brooke Ahne Portmann, *Early Chicago Hotels*. Charleston, SC: Arcadia Publishing, 2006, 46.
24   Northwestern University's Preparatory School (renamed the Evanston Academy in 1892) was a pre-secondary and secondary school designed to prepare students for college work. The Preparatory School closed in 1917.
25   In 1871, the university's first building, "Old College" (built in 1855 at Hinman and Davis) was moved to the current location of Fisk Hall, 1845 Sheridan Road, and turned over to the Preparatory School. After Fisk Hall was built in 1899, it housed the Preparatory School; the Old College building was moved again to the future site of the McCormick-Tribune Center. Records of the Evanston Academy, 1857-1967, Northwestern University Archives.
26   Willard is mistaken about the year 1873. The cornerstone for University Hall was laid in 1866 and dedicated on September 8, 1869. *The Northwestern Song Book*. Evanston: George W. Muir, 1879, 123.
27   The Snyder Farm was a sixty acre site, located south of Dempster and north of Greenleaf, extending from Chicago Avenue to the lake front. Northwestern University purchased it for $24,623.12 in 1867. Sheppard and Hurd, 77, 297, 515. On the site, in 1848, Abraham Snyder built his farmhouse at 1225 Chicago Ave. Viola Crouch Reeling, *Evanston: Its Land*

and Its People. Hammond, ID: Fort Dearborn Chapter, the Daughters of the American Revolution, 1928; 137, 240.

28   Designed by Holabird and Roche, Science Hall was located on Hinman Avenue. Its construction was funded by a gift from Daniel B. Fayerweather. Arthur Herbert Wilde, ed. *Northwestern University: A History, 1855-1905*. Volume 1. New York: The University Publishing Society, 1905; 314.

29   Sherburne Wesley Burnham (1838-1921).

30   The Harvard Annex was founded in 1879 as an institution of higher education for women, with courses taught by Harvard faculty. It had no official affiliation to Harvard University, which resisted coeducation and remained closed to women until 1943. No Harvard degrees were issued to the women students of the Annex. Radcliffe College, Harvard's "sister school," was founded in 1894 as the successor to the Annex.

31   Viz.: A financial excess in the treasury of the Biblical Institute. [F.E.W.]

32   Also known as "semi-lunar fardels." Here Willard is referring to the "D.D." (Doctor of Divinity) after a name.

33   The original section of this building has disappeared, but the "addition," as we called it, now stands on Church Street, one door west of the home of Mrs. Marie Huse Wilder. [F.E.W.] [Ed. note, according to the 1890 Evanston directory, Mrs. Wilder lived at 418 Church Street.]

34   The original board of trustees consisted of Melinda Hamline, Mary F. Haskin, Caroline Bishop, Elizabeth M. Greenleaf, Harriet S. Kidder, Mary Thompson Hill Willard, Harriet N. Noyes, Cornelia Lunt, Maria Cook, Margaret P. Evans, Sarah J. Hurd, Annie H. Thompson, Mary J. K. Huse, Abby L. Brown and Virginia S. Kent. [F.E.W.]

35   Mesdames Willing, Mary Bannister Willard, Queal and Miller. [F.E.W.]

36   Located at 803 Orrington Avenue, the College Cottage was a residence for female students, run by a group called the Woman's Educational Aid Association. It was later renamed Pearsons Hall. For many years, the College Cottage and the Woman's College Building (later named Willard Hall) were the only residences for female students.

37   At the corner of Davis Street and Chicago. Sheppard and Hurd, 19.

38   The Willard family's first home in Evanston stood at the southwest corner of Judson Avenue and Church Street.

39   Garwood's was located at the northeast corner of Davis Street and Orrington Avenue.

40   616 Church Street.

41   At Noyes and Maple.
42   This building, of more historic interest than any other school edifice we have, now stands at the corner of Maple Avenue and Foster Street. [F.E.W.]
43   Willard's sister, Mary, died at age 19. Willard's book about her sister was titled, *Nineteen Beautiful Years*.
44   Literally meaning, "Troy no longer exists." A saying applied to anything that belongs to the past and is gone.
45   Professor Kingsley has kindly contributed the foregoing article, except the allusion to himself, which is my own. [F.E.W.]
46   513 Hinman Avenue.
47   418 Davis Street.
48   Myra Amanda Hitchcock Fowler.
49   To burn the midnight oil while engaged in writing and studying.
50   This building is now removed to 311 Ashland Avenue. [F.E.W.]
51   Norwegian-Danish church.
52   Short for " Biblical Student." [F.E.W.]
53   Susan B. Anthony published a three-volume history of Woman's suffrage in 1887. Elizabeth Cady Stanton, Susan Brownell Anthony, Matilda Joslyn Gage, Ida Husted Harper, eds. *History of Woman Suffrage: 1876-1885*. Rochester, NY: Susan B. Anthony, 1887.
54   This sketch was contributed by S. B. Peeney, Chief Engineer and Superintendent. [F.E.W.]
55   The devotion of Evanstonians to no-license was forcibly illustrated in 1869 when they refused the substantial benefits of an admirable city charter lest it might at some time involve the danger of local legislation favorable to the saloon. [F.E.W.]
56   Mrs. Russell was Deputy Grand Chief Templar in 1875. [F.E.W.]
57   Peking, now known as Beijing.
58   Hon. Geo. S. Baker is still representing us at Springfield, May 1891. [F.E.W.]
59   John Shillito & Co. was Cincinnati's first department store, founded by John Shillito and William McLaughlin in 1832. It was first known as McLaughlin & Shillito.
60   Now Mrs. George Robinson, of Detroit, Mich. [F.E.W.]
61   In 1878, the U.S. Supreme Court ruled that the tax exemption established by Northwestern University it its charter and later in an 1865 statute passed in Illinois would be upheld.
62   Furnished by Miss Lodilla Ambrose, assistant librarian. [F.E.W.]
63   Now known as the Historic Methodist Camp Ground of Des Plaines, this property still exists. The 35-acre site was added to the

National Register of Historic Places in 2005.

64 The Lunt home, known as "Anchorfast," was located at 1742 Judson Avenue. It had been built in 1864 and purchased by Lunt in 1874. After his death, Cornelia Lunt lived in the house until her death in 1934. It was razed in 1949.

65 In recent years, John Evans' role in what is now called the "Sand Creek Massacre" has come under scrutiny. On November 29, 1864, seven hundred armed members of the Colorado militia, led by John C. Chivington, attacked Cheyenne and Arapaho villages, murdering and mutilating 150 to 200 individuals, many of whom were women and children. Their acts were so egregious that the country was shocked to learn what had happened. At the time, it was known as the "Chivington Massacre." Two U.S. Congressional committees and one military committee were formed to investigate the massacre. Eventually, in 1865, guilt on the part of the U.S. Government was admitted. John Evans was implicated in creating the conditions for the massacre to occur. In August 1864, Evans had issued a proclamation authorizing "all citizens of Colorado . . . to go in pursuit of all hostile Indians [and] kill and destroy all enemies of the country." Evans ordered that so-called "friendly" "Indians" should present themselves to various forts for their "safety and protection," and those who did not were "hostile" and should be "pursued and destroyed." (Proclamation by Colorado Territory Governor John Evans, August 11, 1864, reprinted in Nancy Gentile Ford, *Issues of War and Peace*. Westport, CT: Greenwood Press, 2002, 138-139.) Evans testified before the committees and was accused of lying to cover up his involvement. Frances Willard's brother, Oliver, who served as pastor at the M.E. Church in Denver from 1862-1866, was friends with and supporters of both John Evans and John Chivington, who led the attack. Evans and Chivington, who himself had been a pastor in the M.E. Church, were members of the Denver church. In 1865, President Andrew Johnson requested Evans' resignation. He subsequently resigned as governor. See also "Sand Creek Massacre National Historic Site Study Act of 1998." U.S. Public Law 105–243, 105th Congress, October 6, 1998.

 In May 2014, Northwestern University published a study of Evans' role in the massacre. Evans was a founder of the university and a member of the board of trustees for 40 years. In its report, the committee, which had been formed in order to address the demand by some students and faculty that Evans' role be thoroughly examined, concluded: "No known evidence indicates that John Evans helped plan the Sand Creek Massacre or had any knowledge of it in advance. The extant evidence suggests that he did not consider the Indians at Sand Creek to be a threat and that he would have opposed the attack that took place." Report of the John Evans Study Committee, Northwestern University, May 2014, 85.

Despite the committee's conclusions, it is likely that the issue is not entirely resolved and that John Evans' role in the massacre will continue to be examined and debated.

66   Photographer Alexander Hesler (1823–1895) is best known for his portraits of Abraham Lincoln. Born in Montreal, Hesler was most active as a photographer in Chicago, where he operated several studios over the course of his career. In 1871, after the Chicago fire, Hesler moved to Evanston; he operated a photographic studio in Evanston from 1871 to 1880. In 1887, he published *Photographic Views of Picturesque Evanston*. Peter E. Palmquist, Pioneer *Photographers from the Mississippi to the Continental Divide: A Biographical Dictionary, 1839-1865*. Stanford: Stanford University Press, 2005; 319-320.

67   Quote from Queen Gertrude in Shakespeare's *Hamlet*.
68   The refuge.
69   From the hymn, "Behold the Lamb of God," *The Congregational Hymn Book: Psalms and Hymns for Divine Worship*. London: Unwin Printers, 1881, 73.
70   Southeast corner Chicago Avenue and Church Street. [F.E.W.]
71   Charles Dudley Warner (1829-1900) was a writer and close friend of Mark Twain. Warner and Twain co-wrote, *The Gilded Age: A Tale of Today* (1873).
72   A Brigadier General in the Union Army during the American Civil War, Joseph Roswell Hawley (1826-1905) served as governor of Connecticut from 1866-1867 and senator from 1881-1905.
73   Leland Stanford (1824-1893), founder of Stanford University, served as senator from California from 1885-1893. He was governor of California from 1862-1863.
74   Eliphalet Remington (1793 –1861) was the designer of the Remington rifle and founder of Remington Arms.
75   Beirut, at the time part of the Ottoman Empire.
76   NOTE.—Born November 12, 1830, in Chelsea, Vt.; died April 19, 1884; graduated from General Biblical Institute, Concord, N. H., in 1853; taught in Newbury Seminary, Vt., 1853; pastor at Montpelier, Vt., 1855; came to Evanston, 1857, as principal of preparatory department of the Institute. Became professor in the Institute, 1S57; temporarily resumed pastoral office, 1861-'64, at Clark St. M. E. church, Chicago, and Kalamazoo, Mich.; received degree of Master of Arts, Ohio Wesleyan University, 1859; Doctor of Divinity, Northwestern University, 1870;

was twice a member of the General Conference; traveled in Europe with his son, Dr. Henry Hemenway, in 1882. [F.E.W.]

77 The Hemenway United Methodist Church is extant today at 933 Chicago Avenue. The current structure was dedicated in 1887. Prior to that building's construction, two previous churches had been destroyed: the first, located at the northwest corner of Main Street and Benson, was destroyed in a "cyclone" in May 1883. The second was destroyed in a fire in January 1886. Sheppard and Hurd, 348.

78 Matthew Simpson (1811-1884) came to Evanston from Pittsburgh to serve as president of the Garrett Biblical Institute. He was a trusted friend and advisor to President Lincoln. Simpson delivered a eulogy at the President's burial in Springfield, Illinois, and, in 1868, he officiated at the wedding of Robert Todd Lincoln and Mary Harlan. Simpson Street in Evanston is named after him.

79 The original quote: "Duncan Hath borne his faculties so meek, hath been so clear in his great office. . . " from Shakespeare's *MacBeth*.

80 From the poem, "Haste Not, Rest Not," by Johan Wolfgang von Goethe.

81 Pére Hyacinthe Loyson (Charles Jean Marie Loyson) (1827–1912).

82 An accordion.

83 From the song, "Home Again." Compiled by Laura C. Holloway, *The Home in Poetry*. New York: Funk and Wagnalls, 1884, 17.

84 Most likely on the northeast corner of Hinman and Davis.

85 Born in Talbot county, eastern shore of Maryland, September 7, 1830; preparatory studies in Baltimore high school; graduated from Dickinson College, Carlisle, Pa., 1849. Began to preach before he was twenty years old, on Summerfield circuit, Baltimore county, Md. [F.E.W.]

86 832 Hinman Avenue.

87 Randolph Sinks Foster was born in Williamsburg, Ohio, February 22, 1820. He was educated at Augusta college, Kentucky, and in 1837 entered the itinerant ministry of the M. E. church in the Kentucky conference, was transferred soon afterward to the Ohio conference, and in 1850 to New York. From 1837 till 1850 he was pastor of churches in Hillsboro, Portsmouth, Lancaster, Springfield and Cincinnati, and from 1850 to 1857 in New York and Brooklyn. In 1856 he was elected president of Northwestern University, Evanston, Illinois, but three years later he resumed the pastorate and was stationed in New York and Sing Sing. The General Conference of 1868 appointed him delegate to the British Wesleyan conference, and in the same year he was elected professor of systematic theology in Drew Theological Seminary, Madison, N. J. In 1870 he was appointed president of this institution, retaining the chair

of theology. He was a delegate to the General Conferences of 1864, 1868 and 1872. In May 1872, he was elected bishop of the Methodist Episcopal church, and soon afterwards was chosen to make episcopal visitations in Norway, Sweden, Denmark, Germany, Switzerland, Italy, India and South America. He subsequently resided in Cincinnati, Ohio, and Boston, Massachusetts. He has published "Objections to Calvinism as It Is," a polemical work which grew out of a controversy (Cincinnati, 1849,); "Christian Purity" (New York, 1851; revised edition, 1869); "Ministry for the Times" (1852), and "Theism," in the "Ingham Lectures" (1872). He is also the author of "Beyond the Grave," in which he discusses with force and freedom profound questions in Christian eschatology (1879); "Centenary Thoughts for the Pulpit and Pew of Methodism" (1884), and "Studies in Theology" (1886).—*Cyclopedia of American Biography*. [F.E.W.]

88   Southwest corner of Forest and Davis.

89   In 1861, Frances Willard was briefly engaged to Charles Fowler (1837-1908). That same year, Fowler and Willard's brother, Oliver, graduated in the same class from the Garret Biblical Institute. The engagement lasted only a few months before Willard made the choice to break it off. She had been unsure about marrying him from the start. Carolyn DeSwarte Gifford, ed., *Writing Out My Heart: Selections from the Journal of Frances E. Willard, 1855-1896*. Board of Trustees of the University of Illinois, 1995, 114-115. In 1873, while Willard was president of the Evanston Ladies College, the college merged with Northwestern University. Willard was appointed professor and dean of the new Woman's College at Northwestern. Fowler had been appointed president of Northwestern in 1872. Reportedly, Fowler did not support Willard's work and "engaged in a campaign of petty harassment against her." As a result, she resigned her position at Northwestern in 1874. Fowler served as Northwestern University president until 1876. Isobel V. Morin, *Women Who Reformed Politics*. Minneapolis: The Oliver Press, 1994, 35. See also, Deborah G. Felder, *The 100 Most Influential Women of All Time: A Ranking Past and Present*. Revised. New York: Citadel Press, 2001.

Note on the numbering of Northwestern University presidents: in the original volume of *A Classic Town*, both Erastus O. Havens and Charles H. Fowler are listed as the fifth president of the university. I have changed the numbering to reflect the correct numbers.

90   Born in Coleraine, Mass., February 13, 1820. Graduated at Wesleyan University 1846, and taught natural science in various academies. In 1862 became professor of Natural History in

Northwestern University, has since held that chair, also acting as President five years. During 1866 he was geologist on the government road from Lewiston, Idaho, to Virginia City, Montana. He is a member of various scientific societies, and in 1876 received the degree of LL.D. from the University of Chicago. Dr. Marcy has published scientific articles and addresses and also a "Record of the Marcy Family" in the "New England Historical and Genealogical Register" for July 1875. [F.E.W.]

91 Born at Falmouth, near Portland, Me., March 3, 1817. Prepared for college at Maine Wesleyan seminary, Readfield. Graduated from Wesleyan university in 1840. Professor and principal of Amenia seminary. 1846-54—Pastor in New England conference of M. E. church. 1853—Chair of theology in Methodist General Biblical institute. Concord, N.H. 1854- 57—President Genesee college, Lima, N. Y. 1857-75—President Wesleyan university. 1875—Resigned presidency, but retained chair of mental and moral philosophy and political economy till 1878. 1873—Returned to pastoral work in Massachusetts. 1881—Called to the presidency of Northwestern university. 1890—Died at Evanston, May 7. [F.E.W.]

92 Anthony Burns (1834-1862) was enslaved upon his birth in Virginia. In 1853, he escaped. He was captured in Boston and brought to trial under the Fugitive Slave Act of 1850. His trial prompted widespread protests, demonstrations, and brought national attention to his case. Despite outcry among abolitionists, Burns was not freed during his trial, but was convicted and returned to Virginia, where he was enslaved again. After other attempts to purchase his freedom failed, he was eventually freed through the payment of $1,300 to his "owner." Burns returned to Boston, and eventually graduated from Oberlin College. He later moved to Canada.

93 804 Hinman Avenue. The house is no longer extant.
94 This sketch is from *The Chicago Graphic*. [F.E.W.]
95 1506 Sheridan Road.
96 A sixth child, Josephine Charlotte, was born in 1894. Charles B. Atwell, ed. *Alumni Record of the College of Liberal Arts*. Evanston, IL: Northwestern University, 1903; 82.
97 Born in Sheboygan, Wis., in 1853. [F.E.W.]
98 Born Oct. 24, 1836, in Montgomery County, N. Y. [F.E.W.]
99 Guest student.
100 Born Jan. 26,1862, in Marietta, Ohio. [F.E.W.]
101 The first dean being Frances Willard herself.
102 Frances Willard's mother, Mary Thompson Hill Willard

(1805-1892). In 1894, Willard and Minerva Brace Norton would publish *A Great Mother: Sketches of Madam Willard*. Chicago: Woman's Temperance Publishing Association.

103   Julia Ames passed away the same year this book was first published in 1891. Willard wrote and compiled a lovely tribute to her friend and colleague. Frances Elizabeth Willard, *A Young Woman Journalist: A Memorial Tribute to Julia A. Ames*. Chicago: Woman's Temperance Publishing Association, 1892.

104   Frances Willard's niece.

105   Margaret Fuller (1810-1850) was a widely influential writer, journalist, and advocate for various social reforms. She was author of *Woman in the Nineteenth Century* (1845), a seminal work advocating equal rights and education for women.

106   Lasell College, founded in 1851 as the Auburndale Female Seminary (later known as Lasell Seminary for Young Women) is located in Massachussetts. In 1874, Bragdon became principal and his work to expand the curriculum (offering law courses for women, for example) earned Lasell a reputation as one of the most progressive institutions of education for women at the time.

107   836 Chicago Avenue.

108   24 Lake Street. Shuman (1830-1890) was editor of the *Chicago Evening Journal* and served as Lieutentant Governor of Illinois from 1877-1881. Sheppard and Hurd, 563.

109   408 Church Street.

110   Founded in 1829 in Jacksonville, Illinois, the second college in Illinois. It was made co-educational in 1903.

111   At 511 Ridge Avenue.

112   William Sinclair Lord started his career in the dry goods business working as a clerk in Haskins Store, located at the southwest corner of Davis Street and Sherman Avenue. After purchasing the store, he renamed it "The Enterprise," and eventually moved the business into the Rood Building at 701-703 Davis Street. Lord sold the store in 1914. Clyde D. Foster, *Evanston's Yesterdays: Stories of Early Evanston and Sketches of Some of Its Pioneers*. Evanston, IL: 1956, 87.

113   The Kirks lived at Ridge and Mulford.

114   In Evanston, Lorado Taft (1860-1936) lived at 224 Chicago Avenue. In the years following the publication of this book, he would enjoy a highly successful career. In 1893, he created many sculptures for the Columbian Exposition. Along with teaching at the Art Institute of Chicago, he also taught at the University of Chicago and the University to Illinois. In 1903, he published *The History of American Sculpture,* which

was the first full-length treatment of the subject. His many works include the Fountain of Time, located on the Midway Plaisance in Chicago, and the Columbus Fountain, Washington D.C. (1912).

115   Edmund J. James.

116   316 Judson.

117   Robert Queal died in Evanston in 1883 after contracting malaria on a visit Florida. In 1889, his wife, Kate Gillespie Queal died. Mary Elizabeth Queal Beyer, *A Genealogical History of the French and Allied Families*. Cedar Rapids, IA: The Torch Press,1912, 315.

118   The First Lady from 1877-1881.

119   Cornelia Nina Gray Lunt, daughter of Orrington Lunt and Cornelia Augusta Gray.

120   Henry Leonidas Boltwood (1831-1906) worked as an educator for more than half a century, including 22 years as principal of Evanston Township High School. When he retired in 1904, several hundred people attended a reception where he was given fifty ten dollar gold pieces. Over the course of his distinguished career, he would serve roughly 6,000 students. Sheppard and Hurd, 541-542.

121   Daniel Hudson Burnham (1846-1912) moved with his family from Chicago to Evanston in 1886. The Burnham property encompassed two city blocks, bordered by Forest, Dempster, and what was then called Lincoln Place (now Burnham Place). Their Italianate house (no longer extant) was located at 232 Dempster Street.

122   Burroughs was a farmer who settled in Evanston after working as a sailor on Lake Eerie. In 1850, he left Evanston for a brief time to venture to California at the time of the Gold Rush. Upon returning to Evanston, he married Anna Crain, and the couple had six children. Alfred Theodore Andreas, *History of Cook County, Illinois: From the Earliest Period to the Present Time*. Chicago: A.T. Andreas Publishing, 1884, 441. In 1890, they were listed as living at 1513 Ridge Avenue.

123   Volney Foster (1848-1904) lived at 709 Greenwood. In 1887, Foster organized the Sheridan Road Association, "its purpose being to promote the construction of a free pleasure driveway on and near the Shore of Lake Michigan between Chicago and Milwaukee." In 1891 he founded the Back-Lot Studies Society, and built a building on his property for its use. The society offered education for boys who were selected by the principals of ETHS and the Preparatory Department of Northwestern University. He was president of the Union League Club of Chicago, a charter member of the Evanston Club, and a founder of the Evanston Ethical Club. He was also a member of the International Peace Society. Sheppard and Hurd, 505.

124   301 Davis Street.
125   Muir's bookstore was called "University Bookstore," located at 436 Davis.
126   Shelby Moore Cullom (1829-1914) also served as Governor of Illinois from 1877-1883.
127   Furnished by Dr. Oliver Marcy. [F.E.W.]
128   Willard is referring to the Oulimette Reservation. The 1,280 acre tract of land extended south from the border of Kenilworth, north from Central Street in Evanston, east to the lake, and west to the railroad line. Josiah Seymour Currey, *Chicago: Its History and Its Builders.* Volume II. Chicago: The S.J. Clark Publishing Co., 1918, 313-314. The tract was "given" to Archange Chevalier Ouilmette (1764-1840) following her husband's, Antoine Ouilmette's (1760-1841), successful work getting various Native American tribes to sign the second Treaty of Prairie du Chien in 1829. The treaty essentially granted land occupied by Chippewa, Ottawa, and Potawatomi in northwestern Illinois and southwestern Wisconsin to the U.S. government. The land was given to Archange with the stipulation that it could not be sold without permission of the U.S. government. In 1844-1845, after Archange and Antoine's deaths, their children petitioned the government and were allowed to sell the land to "real estate speculators." The entire section of the southern part of the reservation, which included 640 acres in Evanston, was sold for $1,000. The northern section was sold in smaller portions for a larger sum. Frank R. Grover, *Antoine Ouilmette: A Resident of Chicago.* Evanston: Evanston Historical Society, 1908, 22. See also, Sheppard and Hurd, 33-36.
129   The first subscription was Mr. O. Lunt's, and the shrinkage was such that of the first sixteen thousand dollars given to found the university, Messrs. Lunt and Evans gave ten thousand dollars. [F.E.W.]
130   The 1890 Evanston directory lists the Withington School at 627 Chicago Avenue.
131   At 512 Davis Street. Mary Bannister Willard was Frances Willard's sister-in-law.
132   In 1891, Miller (1833-1913) was appointed Dean of Women at Northwestern University, a position she held for a decade. She was also appointed as trustee of the university. Miller was also an associate editor of the *Ladies' Home Journal. The Chautauquan* (December 20, 1913), 313.
133   The Citizens' League operated from 1882-1892. In 1894 it was succeeded by the Four-Mile League. Sheppard and Hurd, p. 319.
134   The Grand Army of the Republic was an organization of

American Civil War veterans who served in the Union Army. It was founded in 1866 in Decatur, Illinois.

135   The school was located at "the foot of Main Street," (Sheppard and Hurd, 305), at the corner of Sheridan Road (Evanston Directory, 191). It was housed in the former Old Soldiers' Home, built in 1871 and operating until 1877 when financial difficulties caused the home to close. The building was then rented to the Industrial School for Girls beginning in 1877. (Andreas, 313.) The school operated in Evanston until 1908 when it moved to a 40-acre farm in Park Ridge, Illinois. Among the first board members of this new facility was Jane Addams. In 1913, the school was re-named, The Park Ridge School for Girls. In 1980, the facility began to admit boys and was renamed the "Youth Farm." It closed in 2012. Jennifer Delgado, "Child-Care Charity Shutting Historic Campus," *Chicago Tribune,* April 30, 2012.

About the Editor

Jenny Thompson is Director of Education at the Evanston History Center and a consultant on public history projects. Her publications include *War Games: Inside the World of 20th-Century War Reenactors* (Smithsonian Books, 2004), *My Hut: A Memoir of a YMCA Volunteer in World War One* (editor, 2006), and *Evanston: A Tour Through the City's History* (editor, 2013). Her essays and reviews have appeared in various anthologies and publications, including *The New York Times*. She has an MA in American Studies from the George Washington University and a Ph.D. in American Studies from the University of Maryland.

www.ingramcontent.com/pod-product-compliance
Lightning Source LLC
Chambersburg PA
CBHW022050160426
43198CB00008B/183